PREVENTING ADDICTION:

What Parents Must Know to Immunize Their Kids Against Drug and Alcohol Addiction

JOHN C. FLEMING MD

To order more copies
of *Preventing Addiction*
See page 303

Or contact:
CrossHouse Publishing
P.O. Box 461592
Garland, TX 75046

CALL: 1-800-747-0738
Fax: 1-888-252-3022
Email: crosshousepublishing@earthlink.net
Visit: www.crosshousebooks.com
www.crosshousepublishing.org

Unless otherwise noted, all Scripture quotations are taken from the
Holy Bible, New International Version, copyright 1973, 1978, 1984
by International Bible Society
Library of Congress Control Number: 2006936797
ISBN 0-929292-45-6

Acknowledgments

Any worthwhile accomplishment in life cannot be achieved without the assistance of others. This book is no exception. Many people have made this book possible, some of whom are unaware of their contributions.

First, I would like to offer acknowledgement and appreciation to addicted individuals, as well as their families and friends. It is from your struggle and experiences that we all have learned a great deal. I hope we can use what we have learned to prevent others from going through the challenges you continue to face.

I also thank my colleagues in research, especially those involved in brain neurotransmitter research, who have made such tremendous breakthroughs in our understanding of addiction and depressive disorders. Keep up the good work. I pray that you will someday find a cure for addiction.

In addition, I extend my appreciation to my colleagues in the treatment side of addiction. Though your success rates are low, among those who have responded, your 100% efforts have made an equal difference in the lives of your patients, and just as important, in the lives of their families and friends.

I am quite pleased with the clarity and readability of this book, which addresses some new and hard to understand concepts. This would not be possible without the contribution of my editor, Virginia McCullough. She has demonstrated a real gift in making this information understandable to the average lay reader. She has further contributed greatly by giving me a fresh perspective on many aspects of this subject, so as to present to you a very balanced approach.

My thanks go out to each member of my immediate family, Breck, Brook-lyn, JC and Barrett, along with my loving wife, Cindy. For my kids, you have filled my life with such joy that you will never be able to know. Your mother and I worked very hard to raise you to be productive, happy, sober, and loving citizens. Our work has been successful and worth every moment of effort. Cindy, your love and support across twenty-eight years of marriage is an incomparable treasure in my life.

Finally, I want to acknowledge God through his son, Jesus Christ. Without God there would be no life. Without His Son there would be no life after life.

I hope that you will enjoy reading this book. At times what you read may make you uncomfortable, but it does something that most books on addiction don't do—it offers solutions.

John C. Fleming, M.D.

Foreword

Dr. John Fleming, an experienced physician and an exemplary father of four, is extremely qualified to have written this book. In *Preventing Addiction* he has focused his towering intellectual powers, his amazing energies, and his immense moral drive on the grave social problem of drug and alcohol addiction.

In laymen's terms, the author explains new scientific information about the disease of addiction. He contends that nothing is more complex than the human brain and that it is imperative for everyone, but especially parents, to understand how addicting substances affect the pleasure center of the brain. Dr. Fleming clearly provides this knowledge and then offers a "blueprint" to rearing non-addicted people.

As a minister and counselor, my horizons of understanding of chemical and non-chemical addictions have been greatly expanded by reading this volume. Many addiction myths that have brainwashed generations are exposed here.

In my opinion, Dr. Fleming has composed a masterpiece of helpful information, and I'm grateful for his extensive analysis of this issue. It is my hope that this book will awaken caring parents nationwide to the enormous danger of "early use" of alcohol and drugs by our children. Best of all, this book will reveal strategies that will help reduce the chances that our kids will become addicted to drugs.

Preventing Addiction deserves to be widely read, carefully studied, and faithfully utilized.

Wayne L. DuBose, B.A. ThM.

Table of Contents

1

What You Don't Know
Can Hurt Your Children

Drug addiction* in the U.S., and all the problems that go with it, worsens every day. Unless we make drastic changes, I see no end in sight. You're no doubt aware that "society" has this problem, but you may be under the impression that it doesn't affect you, at least not directly. Although I understand that thinking, it is the *first misconception* that I ask you to put aside.

I recall that while growing up in the 1950s, our society had an entirely different impression of alcohol abuse and alcohol addiction, as well as non-alcohol drug addiction, than exists today. Alcohol abuse (getting drunk) and alcoholism (addiction to alcohol) were thought of as common and somewhat benign. Almost everyone had a relative or friend who was an alcoholic, although they might not have used that term. More likely, they said that Uncle Joe was a "hard drinker" or Aunt Jodi "liked her martinis." Television programs and movies often depicted alcohol abuse as humorous, perhaps noble at times. Alcoholics were portrayed as comical caricatures. Even drunk drivers were sent home to "sleep it off," rather than put in jail.

Conversely, when we discussed drug addicts, we typically thought of big cities with crime run rampant and abject poverty. These undesirable drug addict types lived in those places far away from us. Today we know better. Alcoholics *are* drug addicts, in that they are addicted to the drug of alcohol. We also know today that there is nothing funny or benign about alcoholism, alcohol abuse, or drunk driving. And further, alcoholics have problems similar to those of non-alcohol drug addicts. Finally, like alcoholics, drug addicts live near us and among us.

During the 1960s, when non-alcohol drug addiction began to receive wider attention, we in the middle class felt shielded by an invisible wall of protection from drug addicts and their problems. Our stereotype of an addict was that of an unkempt, homeless tramp walking city streets looking for dope, or perhaps a saxophone player who would inject heroin into his veins prior to playing all night in some smoky nightclub. If you grew up during the so-called "baby boom" years, as I did, you may have formed a similar mental picture. Or, if you're a younger person, your impression of addicts and addiction might include college campuses or glamorous settings where celebrities congregate. Regardless of your image in your mind, today, drugs addicts may appear quite normal, just like everyone else. It is only after years of addiction that the addict's life may begin to more closely match the down and out image of years past. Unfortunately, too many people, particularly parents, assume a stark difference between the normal "us" versus the abnormal "them." But today, they are "us."

Of course, both of these older, stereotypical images of the typical drug addict (non-alcohol) and addiction are outdated. Today, if we look only at superficial appearances, drug addicts look much like you and I. For far too long, many of us have remained unaware that the tentacles of drug use and addiction have reached into every segment of American society, rich, poor, and middle class. The problem continues to soar to unprecedented rates—up to as much as 9% of the general population if you include all forms of (non-tobacco) drug addiction and alcoholism. That is about 25 million Americans.

Unfortunately, studies show clearly that drug addiction is a chronic, progressive, and incurable disease. Though treatable, recovery rates (the rate at which addicts are able to remain drug free for extended periods of time) are very low, even after treatment. Some authorities have put the recovery rate *below 10%.*. Or, put another way, the rate of relapse stands at about 90%. As you can see, the prognosis is poor.

The Problem Hits Home

One evening in the late 1980s, my wife and I saw a long, detailed article on the front page of *The Wall Street Journal* explaining the disappointing fact that drugs had reached into middle and rural America. Even more distressing, the paper used our own town, Minden, Louisiana (pop. 13,000), as an example of the new wave of illegal drug distribution extending deep into small-town America. Sadly, as I write this in 2006 the problem has only become worse in our town and I would conclude, in your town, too.

I won't bore you by quoting extensive statistics about drug problems in this country, because these numbers often serve only to make the problem seem abstract. However, if you want detailed statistics on the incidence of drug addiction and its impact, I refer you to the National Institute on Drug Abuse *www.nida.nih.gov* (Other resources are listed in the back of this book.) This information is well documented and detailed in many books and periodicals, and for most people, the magnitude of the problem is so great that it's difficult to comprehend.

Why You Should Care

What is important to you and me is the fact that drug abuse and addiction affect our lives daily, even if we don't personally use illegal substances or are not addicted to alcohol. Furthermore, the problem of drug addiction in this country is growing in severity and magnitude. Even sadder, although it is a preventable problem, our current prevention methods continue to fail...and fail...and fail.

How does drug addiction affect you? To begin with, every day you unconsciously adjust your life around society's addiction crisis. Do you avoid encounters with strangers? Have you observed the way children are kept in virtual castles of protection? You may be among the many Americans who arm their homes with security systems and steer away from certain neighborhoods, especially at night.

Based on my own experience, a mere generation ago we often left our doors unlocked when going to bed at night. As a youngster, my parents let me roam freely in the neighborhood to do what I wanted with whomever I chose as long as I was home by dark. Most parents consider that level of freedom far too risky today.

As citizens, we see our public funds poured into appropriations for new prison construction. Then we fill them as fast as they are built. But did you know that virtually every inmate is a product of drug addiction, directly or indirectly? Murder, burglary, theft, child and spousal abuse, sex crimes, and other criminal offenses are often related to drug addiction, either because the offender is an addict or was parented by addicts, who themselves may have been imprisoned, too. In addition, those doing the work of parenting often are not the child's parents. Because of the severe disruption caused by drug addiction, the stand-in parents may be extended family members, a parent's live-in partner, or even casual caretakers.

A complex illegal drug industry exists that includes gangs and less visible criminal organizations. We are awash in violence that has its roots in drug addiction and the intense competition within the very lucrative drug market. It's no exaggeration to say that if we suddenly "cured" drug addiction and took away the market to sell drugs, prisons across America would begin to close as current offenders die or finish their time. In the absence of drugs and the illegal "machinery" and elaborate networks to import, process, and distribute drugs, we'd see a drastic drop in number of new criminals.

Of course, some skeptics will question my claims; not everyone believes in the link between drug use, crime, and the huge numbers of incarcerated individuals. If you need more than the statistically well documented link between drugs and crime, you need only talk to the social workers who daily work with the families of convicted felons, or those whose lives have been devastated by abuse at the hands of drug addicts, some of whom go on to continue the cycle and become addicts themselves.

Social workers will describe many *comorbidities* that typically exist in these homes. "Comorbidity" (also known as co-occurring diseases) is an apt medical term we can use in this context. It means a person or entity (such as a home), which has two or more different medical-social problems or diseases. Social workers will support my contention that for every prison inmate you will likely find a drug-addicted person in his or her family who either caused or suffered from abuse, poor educational performance, more than the average number of medical problems, and less than average income. All of these factors and others are considered comorbidities and contribute to the crime/addiction cycle in the home. This isn't just an example or even fairly typical; the co-morbidity phenomenon is a recurring theme.

Someone inclined to argue with me could point to a particular person and claim that even though he or she is an addict,
all the other problems I mentioned don't exist in the home.
Sure, that could be true in certain cases, but the very nature of
addiction, including its tendency to become a chronic progressive condition, leads to these problems sooner or later. In addition, many of the family problems caused by addiction remain
hidden. Indeed, families may make great efforts to cover up
the problem—the co-morbidities—from employers, other
family members, neighbors, schools, places of worship, and
their doctors.

A Case in Point

In high school, Paul** was an affable, popular athlete and
a very good student. He came from an affluent family that
experienced no lack of material things. Superficially, this
family sounds as if it certainly could be healthy and happy.
However, as a boy, Paul brought friends home after school
while his parents were at work, and by age twelve or so he and
his buddies periodically helped themselves to alcohol from the
well-stocked liquor cabinet in the family room.

Right on schedule, Paul got his driver's license at age
sixteen, followed by owning his first car, a gift from his
parents. Two wrecks later, his parents bought still another
replacement, despite the fact that the crashes were due to
drinking while driving. Paul's car afforded him great independence, but his parents didn't demand an accounting of his
time spent away from home, although he kept very late hours.

Paul made a habit of getting drunk on beer with his friends
during the weekends. By the time he was a senior in high
school, however, beer drinking had become boring. When
some friends offered Paul marijuana, he tried it and liked it
even more than beer. Before long, his senior-year grades

started to slide from mostly As to mostly Cs. Still, despite this obvious change, his unalarmed parents dismissed it as "sowing wild oats."

After Paul went off to a state university about two hundred miles away, he quickly found the other "party" people and his alcohol and marijuana intake intensified. Since Paul no longer had parents nearby to make sure that he studied during the week, let alone show up for classes, college life quickly became party life, and that meant several episodes a week of binge drinking and pot smoking.

Eventually, the school put pressure on Paul to improve his participation and performance, and he began to dread disappointing his parents, who were hard working and loving. He knew they would suffer if he was forced to reveal the truth about his poor academic performance—and he had no reasonable explanation for it. Paul began using marijuana daily in an attempt to manage this anxiety. Simultaneously, he faced mounting legal problems related to his DUIs. By the end of his freshman year, Paul flunked out altogether, and as you've seen, he coped with mounting problems and anxiety over them by sinking deeper into substance abuse.

Paul was adept at offering persuasive arguments to his parents, who were relieved when Paul reported that his professors were so unfair, which explained his grades, and since "everybody" flunked out, he was off the hook. Paul's parents believed that Paul should live in his own apartment and go to a local community college, a plan they agreed to fund. Predictably, this plan failed because binge drinking and daily pot smoking continued to replace all productive activities. After more discussions, Paul and his parents agreed that he needed to "find himself" by getting a job and returning to college later.

Although Paul worked odd jobs, he never kept one long

enough to make enough money to fully support himself. He was fired from some jobs, or not hired at better-paying jobs because he couldn't pass the drug testing required. But even his low-paying jobs (those that didn't require a drug test) didn't last long because of his inability to get along with supervisors and co-workers. He was stuck in a cycle of asking his parents for money to pay for car repairs or more legal bills, and expensive alcohol and drug purchases they were unknowingly subsidizing. (This became increasingly more expensive and a higher and higher priority in his budget).

What happened to Paul next is not an unusual development. His parents reached a breaking point, which meant that at long last they were fed up and insisted he make his own way in the world. Paul quickly became desperate for money to pay bills and to buy the marijuana he used every day. One of the dealers from whom he bought the drug suggested that Paul could make "real" money by selling it, along with other popular drugs like cocaine and methamphetamines. So, Paul found the "answer" to his problem, and slipped into the role of dealer.

Over time, Paul found marijuana calming, in that it temporarily erased his anxiety, but he had stopped feeling a good "high" from it. But, with plenty of powdered cocaine in his inventory, he had another option, although he vowed he'd never use the purified "crack" form of cocaine. Paul had heard crack cocaine was very addictive, unlike pot or powdered cocaine. At least that's what his drug-using friends claimed, and Paul often passed this "wisdom" on to others as well. After all, Paul just wanted to "feel good" at the end of a hard day.

Paul had fallen in love with a young woman who also liked to get high on drugs. She had smoked crack cocaine any number of times and she reassured Paul that she could stop any time she wanted. What's more, she said it was a great drug because it would give him a much better high than any he had ever experienced. Before long, Paul forgot his vow and began using highly addictive crack.

As you can see, nothing about Paul's story is particularly unusual, and in fact, the rest of his story reads like a script, too, although a chaotic one. Paul and his girlfriend had several children over the years, though they never married and sometimes lived with other sexual partners. Based on the way they existed, they were perpetually short of money to buy the essentials of life and keep up their steady supply of drugs, too.

What about the children? Different combinations of adults raised the children, which resulted in an unstable environment. One of the live-in boyfriends sexually abused two of the children over an extended period of time, usually after their mom slipped into a stupor from taking a concoction of drugs. Ultimately Paul and his girlfriend, after several drug busts for which they were given probation, ended up in state prison with long sentences for drug distribution. At that point, the sexual abuse came to light and the boyfriend ended up in prison, too.

Along the way, Paul began to steal in order to increase his cash flow. Initially he stole cash and electronic appliances to exchange for cash from his parents. But eventually he was forbidden to come to their home. He stole from other homes and businesses. These former arrests became relevant when his drug sentence was determined.

Although the children went to live with extended family, their emotional and disciplinary problems were so severe that the state had to intervene and they were placed in foster homes. Not surprisingly, some of these children then recreated the same cycle as Paul with only the details varying. Drug and alcohol use started early, addiction developed, followed by dropping out of school. The destructive effects of this use led to chaotic, failed relationships and then prison time. The chances are good that some family not far from you is deep into one or another stage of this cycle.

Why Paul's Story is Important

It may be easy to dismiss Paul's story as "extreme," because he and his girlfriend ended up in jail. After all, you say, some people start the cycle and get treatment, or they live with some addictions and function quite well. They have careers and attend church and are part of the community. True, some people do manage to function, at least for a period of time. Specifically, alcoholics sometimes function at fairly high levels, especially at their jobs. However, this does not mean that their families don't suffer. Families of alcoholics may experience chaotic home lives, often hidden from public view.

In addition, with the easy availability of illegal drugs today, most people who start with alcohol abuse as young people truly do move on to other substances sooner or later. The strict taboos about drugs and their relative lack of avail-ability is no longer a barrier for young people. It is a rare teenage drinker who does not try marijuana or cocaine, or a host of other drugs, *especially after experiencing alcohol intoxication at a young age.* (The reasons for this are explained in a later chapter.) This has been the trend for a couple of decades now and is not turning around.

And What about Linda?

It's possible that you read Paul's story and concluded that such horrendous problems could never happen to your family. Perhaps your teen's addiction disease would never have progressed that far, or you believe you have responded earlier and more robustly. But would your response be early or strong enough? Let's look at Linda's story.

Linda was the "perfect" child growing up. She rarely required discipline, made straight As, and during high school, she even volunteered for MADD (Mothers Against Drunk Drivers). As the older of two children in the family, she was always thought of as a responsible big sister. Beginning at age nine, she arrived home before her parents and occupied herself by fixing an after-school snack and watching TV until her mother arrived home. At age 11, Linda was given the additional responsibility of supervising her little sister at home during this after-school hiatus. Everything worked quite well, at least at first.

When Linda was 12, a new family moved next door. Their only child, Amy, was 13 and both of her parents worked outside the home, too. Though Linda's parents did not drink alcohol, Amy's parents maintained a well-stocked bar at home for social occasions. Linda and Amy became fast friends. Because Amy was older, Linda quickly got up to speed on life as a teenager.

One of the "fast lane" lessons Linda learned was Amy's daily ritual of tapping into dad's vodka. Within a few weeks of becoming friends with Amy, Linda devised and carried out a good plan to have her little sister situated with a snack in front of the TV while she paid a daily visit to Amy to "get help with her homework."

I'm sure you know where this story is headed. As Linda moved forward into adolescence she regularly consumed alcohol during her daily visits at Amy's house. Next, she began to drink with friends at weekend parties and by age 15 she was smoking marijuana. All of this drug use went on behind the backs of her unsuspecting parents.

True, there were a few warning signs that her parents missed, including a slight change in personality. Linda seemed to vacillate between being quiet and withdrawn to being argumentative. Then her grades seemed to flounder somewhat as well. But it was easy to write off this behavior as typical teenage confusion and acting out.

It came as quite a shock to Linda's parents when at age 16, she was arrested for a DUI (driving under the influence), not long after getting her driver's license. In fact they were in total disbelief. How could our "perfect" child get a DUI when she didn't drink and she was a student member of the local MADD organization? They were even more surprised when they learned the results of her blood tests. Not only was her blood alcohol level above legal limit, but she tested positive for marijuana.

As a condition of Linda's probation she was required to get alcohol and drug treatment at a local rehab center. Her parents were required to participate, too. There, the "dirty little secrets" were revealed. For the first time Linda's parents learned that she had been drinking almost daily since she age 12 and smoking marijuana on most weekends. She had to be detoxified due to her dependence on both alcohol and marijuana.

Finally and worst of all, Linda and her parents learned from the medical director that Linda's life had changed forever. She had developed a chronic disease, addiction, which was incurable. In order to maintain her sobriety and prevent her disease from progressing, she would have to attend AA meetings regularly for the rest of her life. Furthermore, she would never be able to drink socially, or even be in situations where she might be tempted to drink without risking the progression of her addiction. This left open many questions regarding Linda's future, including the assumption that she'd be able to go to college and have a complete range of life choices available to her. So, indeed, Linda's life was changed forever.

Why Linda's Story is so Important

As you probably saw, Linda's parents did everything good parents should do, at least according to current, conventional thinking. But times are changing. The threats of addiction against our children are insidious, occur very early, and are more and more challenging. Linda's parents were, indeed, well-meaning. But well-meaning is not good enough when you consider how willing kids are to experiment, how accessible drugs are, and how quickly addiction can take hold in young people.

Granted, Linda's life didn't sink to the low state of addiction that occurred with Paul. Nonetheless, the discovery of her pre-addiction activities came too late. We certainly hope Linda will never develop the same kinds of problems that consumed Paul's life. The thing is, once addiction is established, there is no return to a non-addicted state. (I discuss the reasons for this in a later chapter.)

Though you haven't read this entire book yet, does it make sense that your top priority should be to prevent your children from becoming Paul or Linda? Doesn't it make sense to prevent our kids from becoming addicts? As a parent and a physician, I believe strongly that for several reasons we should prevent addiction in our children.

First, as you will see in future chapters in this book, it is *preventable*. Second, it can only be prevented in children. Once drug use patterns in adults have been established, there is little or nothing that you as a parent can do to alter this behavior. Third, failure to prevent addiction unleashes the scourge of addiction and possibly touches multiple generations of your offspring and their families.

What's Your Experience?

How many people do you know who currently struggle, or

have in the past, directly or indirectly, with drug addiction? Are you, any of your children, your parents, siblings, or your spouse addicted? If you cannot name at least five people who currently have or have had drug-addiction problems, you're either very lucky or very naïve. For a moment, take the issue out of the family arena. If you're an employer or supervisor, do you have trouble finding employees who can pass a drug test?

In my professional experience as a family physician and employer, I have personally witnessed the sadness and pain associated with drug addiction. I also have friends, neighbors, family members, and colleagues, among others, who have, directly or indirectly, suffered the devastation of broken lives, destroyed homes, deteriorating health, and loss of occupation because of drug addiction. Watching this process occur and then seeing the cycle continue has been so painful for me personally that I recently told my college-student son the only thing worse than learning that he'd become addicted to drugs would be finding out that he'd contracted a fatal disease!

But Why this Book, and Why Now?

I want you to develop an understanding of how you as parents and guardians are critical in the quest to prevent drug addiction in the lives of young people. In addition, teachers, coaches, youth workers, ministers, and so forth also play key roles in the lives of our children. I hope they, too, will take seriously the information presented here. As dismal as the current outlook appears, *excellent science exists that shows us not only how addiction occurs, but gives us the knowledge to prevent it.* You are justified in wondering why so little has been written to date about ways to effectively prevent drug addiction. It's an unfortunate situation, especially because we have new scientific breakthroughs that shed light on brain chemicals and the way a variety of drugs interact with them.

In addition, very recent research strongly suggests the following: *a critical timeframe exists in the life of a young person in which exposure to certain substances (that we don't necessarily consider to be drugs in a traditional sense) can trigger addiction.* This information is powerful, and most certainly empowering to the millions of men and women involved in shaping the lives of future adults. If that concept isn't clear to you now, you will have full understanding of it by the time you have finished reading this book.

I wrote this book because I want you to understand the science that has helped us provide parents and others the tools they need to stop the tragic cycle of substance abuse that has taken such a toll on our society. I've also included a guide to raising your child to be an *NAP (non-addicted person).* As you will see, while this is actually quite simple, it's not always easy.

What You can Bring to this Book

As you read this book, I ask that you temporarily suspend what you know or think you know about the cause(s) of drug addiction and its prevention and treatment. Within this field, great myths abound, and only after careful consideration of all the facts will you find yourself able to effectively change lives, and by extension, create a better society.

In addition to challenging your beliefs about addiction, you may find that I also challenge some of your current beliefs about child rearing, discipline, and parental love. But keep an open mind. If you embrace the information and techniques I present here, you will greatly diminish or remove altogether the chance that your children will end up addicted to drugs, with all the related problems that follow.

Points to Remember

- Drug addiction is the common thread that connects most of society's problems.
- The rate of drug addiction is getting worse and unless we change its course, we will see increasing levels of crime and family destruction.
- Drug addiction is insidious and is discovered only after great harm has been done.
- Drug addiction is incurable. Though treatable, recovery rates remain very low.
- Drug addiction is *preventable*!
- Addiction to drugs depends heavily on when and how a young person is exposed to certain substances.
- This book will teach you how to raise a NAP (non-addicted person).
- What you will learn in this book is backed by—and based on—science.
- To effectively learn and implement the information and techniques in this book, you must keep an open mind.

---

*Although this chapter uses the terms drug abuse and drug addiction, alcohol, tobacco and other substances are usually included in this category unless otherwise specified. Later in this book I discuss alcohol and alcohol abuse and other addictive substances and non-chemical addictions.

**All the names used in this book that involve specific examples of addiction are fictitious and the case studies are compilations of individuals and are not to be confused with specific men, women, or families.

2

Experience is the First Teacher

This discussion about alcohol and drug abuse wouldn't be complete if I didn't talk about the experiences that led me to a special interest in both the causes and results of addiction. Of course, my medical training has been critical in accumulating the information provided here. However, my broad experience in life and as a parent, combined with my training, clinical experience, and reading have allowed me to have a unique multi-sided view of this problem. This is why I want to discuss what I've learned with anyone and everyone who may be in a position to prevent addiction.

In 1978, I found myself sitting in a group therapy session with a group of alcoholics in an alcohol treatment program. Unlike the other individuals in the room, I actually had looked forward to being there. At the time, I was a young Navy physician doing a three-year residency program in Family Medicine. The residents were required to spend two weeks in the VD (visiting doctor) program of the alcohol and drug rehabilitation program at Naval Regional Medical Center (NRMC), in Long Beach, California. Though I was there as part of my training, I also was curious. Why would so many people drink alcohol to the point of destroying their health and losing their jobs and families? Of course, I also wanted to learn how this unexplainable behavior could be treated.

This program, one of the first of its type in this country,

was based on the 12-steps of Alcoholics Anonymous (AA), originally created in the 1930s. Because of its pioneer, Captain Joseph Pursch, "Long Beach" developed the model on which most current residential/hospital treatment programs are based. Dr. Pursch, a unique, charismatic man and an articulate psychiatrist, lectured several times during my two-week stint at the Long Beach center. These lectures, delivered in his thick, Eastern European accent, stand out in my mind even today. While under Dr. Pursch's supervision, the center has treated a number of well-known individuals, including Betty Ford, Billy Carter, and Buzz Aldrin.

At the time, the late 1970s, patients were either active duty military personnel or high-level government employees. As a condition to retain their employment or to remain in the military, all patients were required to be there for six weeks of treatment for already diagnosed alcoholism, which, in most cases, had affected their jobs. The VDs were present in a training capacity for only two weeks, and most of us were either doctors or in some type of administrative capacity in the military, such as supervisors and department heads. The US Navy gauged appropriately that healthcare providers, supervisors and department heads would be in the best position to observe and later refer problem drinkers in the workplace for therapy. I didn't know it at the time, but the VDs also were examined closely for possible alcoholism as well. In fact, some in my group, unlike me, had been ordered there under the guise of training, but were actually sent there because it was suspected, but not confirmed, that they also had drinking problems. In short, everybody ordered to Long Beach for the alcoholism program regardless of the reason, was "fair game" for mandatory treatment if they were determined to be an alcoholic.

You see, nobody can detect an alcoholic/addict like

another. Once in the program, group therapy and other intimate contacts will quickly uncover chemical dependency problems. On the other hand, requiring individuals to undergo alcoholism treatment when they are really not alcoholics could be needlessly damaging to their careers. This was a good way for the Navy to have it both ways. I realize the contradiction, but it seemed to work for the Long Beach program.

One of the doctors in my group was an ophthalmologist, whom I thought was there like me, for training. However, the counselors knew that he recently had a DUI accident and was suspected of being an alcoholic. Since I hadn't known about his situation, I was quite surprised when I learned he wasn't leaving after two weeks like the rest of us.

As I listened to various lecturers, most of whom were recovering alcoholics, I began to think back about my life, particularly my attitudes about and experiences with alcohol and drugs. I had heard about group therapy, but before coming to this program, I had never seen or participated in anything like it. I was required to participate, but I was the only person in my group not there for treatment, though I am not sure the other group members knew that. With every session each of us discussed our personal struggles in life. Quite often, addiction itself wasn't discussed, but rather, the topics revolved around broken lives, broken relationships, and broken health. A new appreciation for the lives of these individuals began to emerge in my soul. But gradually, a louder and louder voice inside of me shouted, "Why can't this be prevented?"

I look upon these two weeks spent at NRMC Long Beach as a time of growth for me. The experience coaxed me to reflect on my own life, and on those of family and friends as well, as I examined the impact alcohol and drugs had on us. I recommend that every adult, especially parents, teachers, and others who supervise children go through a life-assessment process related to the addicting chemicals to which adults and children come in contact.

Early Impressions can be Long-lasting

My first memory involving alcohol occurred at age four, when I recall watching my grandfather take periodic trips to the refrigerator where he kept a bottle of whiskey. He'd grab it, and then turn it up and take a big swig. Naturally I wanted some, too. But my grandmother, who detested his drinking, rebuffed me by saying that "people don't drink for the taste, they do it for the effect," implying, of course, its well-known euphoric effect, which I did not understand. But even as a small child I noticed a few "effects," such as the terrible odor of his breath after he drank. It also seemed that as my grandfather took more trips to the refrigerator he had trouble walking and he argued a lot with my grandmother.

Later, after I'd turned five, my grandmother briefly looked after me while my mother was in the hospital after giving birth to my sister. One day during that time, my dad and I visited a neighbor. While there, we heard my grandmother's screams—screams so loud we could hear them from next door. I followed my dad as he ran back home to find my grandfather not only drunk, but slamming my grandmother over the head with a shotgun butt. Fortunately, my dad got there fast and quickly grabbed the gun. Even luckier, an alert taxi driver, who had dropped my grandfather off at my house, had already unloaded the shotgun. He told my father that he hadn't fully bought my grandfather's "I'm going hunting with my son-in-law" story.

So, by age five I had been introduced to a stark reality. My sweet, precious grandmother had been forced to stare at what she thought was a loaded shotgun as her alcoholic and deranged husband pulled both triggers of the double-barreled gun. Only after the double misfiring did he try to kill her by bashing her head in. After this incident, my grandmother obtained a quick divorce. She lived for many more years, finally dying peacefully at age 97. However, my grandfather died of alcoholism at age 67.

As I grew older my mother and grandmother gradually revealed more details about their lives during the Great Depression of the 1930s and beyond. In those days, most women had no way to support themselves on their own with their children, so they ended up trapped by their circumstances. So it was for my grandmother. She and her eight children were forced to live with a severely sick, alcoholic man. Had my grandmother left him, she and her children would have had no place to live and no means to buy the basic necessities, even food.

Over the years, my mother and grandmother talked about the way they attempted to cover up his problems. Of course, they were embarrassed by his behavior, but they also lived with the fear that he would lose his job with the railroad. They also lived with his mental and physical abuse. Throughout my life, I noticed that my aunts and uncles, and my mother, eventually began to suffer severe depression, alcoholism, or both. The cycle of alcoholism renewed itself through the very innocent victims of it.

As I write this today, another generation of depression, alcoholism, and drug addiction has occurred in my maternal extended family—sadly, even another generation is in the making.

Within my maternal extended family, I also saw that the prevalence of severe depression and alcoholism included heavy tobacco use. Today, after studying the subject and having considerable experience with the issue as a doctor, I see how smoking may have contributed considerably to their alcoholism. As a child I heard stories from one alcoholic uncle who talked about getting into his dad's tobacco; even as a young boy, he "rolled his own." These stories were meant to be funny and innocent "family lore," but now I see how damaging these supposed childhood pranks were to his life. In fact, getting into the tobacco probably led to or accelerated his alcoholism. Predictably, he died of lung cancer. I'll discuss this important issue of tobacco again in other chapters.

My father rarely drank. Oh, he would occasionally put a bit of whiskey in some eggnog on a special occasion. However, a single bottle of whiskey sat virtually untouched on the top shelf of our kitchen cabinet, not fully consumed for many years. My dad grew up in a deeply religious family on a farm in rural Mississippi. A strict taboo against drinking alcohol existed both in the family and the community. For acceptable entertainment, the family gathered around the piano and sang gospel music. While he grew up with the typical privations of rural life in the 1930s, along with the strict Christian–based code of conduct that put limitations on having "fun," my dad and his family experienced a happy, stable, sober, and well-balanced life on the farm.

As a child of the Great Depression, my father had his first drink and saw his first movie theatre at age 17, after being drafted into the army. To my knowledge, none of his siblings or their children became addicted to drugs or alcohol.

After all this, A Change of Heart

By the time I reached high school, my attitudes against alcohol and drugs, and tobacco, too, were firmly entrenched. At least that's what I thought. As an athlete and a Christian, I would never have done anything to injure my health or that would hold me back from fulfilling my ambitions in life. Some of my friends would get drunk on beer, but I just pitied them and thought their behavior misguided. A small, fringe group of kids smoked pot, but they were considered weird and outcasts among the respectable—and respected—folk. Needless to say, I never drank or used drugs while in high school. I especially abhorred smoking.

College was a different story. I attended a major state university and along with most of my peers I joined a fraternity. During my college years, I interacted with the "best of our state," highly intelligent and competent young men and women who would become doctors, lawyers, engineers, and politicians. To my surprise, some of my new friends smoked tobacco and a few used marijuana, too. Virtually all of them drank, even to excess. Fraternity parties were characterized by free flowing booze and music. My frat brothers would have "beer busts," in which one could drink as much as he could, even to the point of becoming sick or unconscious.

Even at the time, I had difficulty reconciling that the "best of the best," individuals whom I greatly respected, were engaging in the same behavior as my grandfather, but without the violence. How could this be? I had thought everybody who drank was or would become an alcoholic, yet the future leaders of my state were partying like there was no tomorrow. In addition, I interacted with professors and other professionals who also drank alcohol. Although I didn't see them abuse alcohol, they seemed very nonchalant about drinking. Because of these experiences I reconsidered my conclusions about alcohol, but not about drugs or tobacco.

When I was nineteen I met a girl who became a big part of my life during my college years. Though a good person, she was not as inhibited about things as I was. One evening while we were out on a date she told me she had a surprise for me. Then she reached down and pulled out a brown paper bag. With a certain flourish she produced a bottle of bourbon and a cold soft drink.

The time had come for me to take the jump. As it turned out, the concoction my friend produced didn't taste bad.

Besides, it sure did make me feel good. That night I felt a euphoria that I'd never experienced before. Before long, I'd joined my friends and future leaders of America. We drank and had fun, sometimes even to excess.

Through my college and med school career I enjoyed alcohol just like everybody else. Though using it never led to legal or medical problems, I took advantage of every social occasion to have a drink. As I approached my middle twenties, however, I became bored with the bachelor life of partying and dating many different women. Instead, a life with a real partner, children, and a career in medicine became much more appealing. As I moved forward with my other goals, the importance of alcohol diminished.

Making Connections While at NRMC, Long Beach

Given my personal history, my experiences at NRMC, Long Beach, gave me a chance to observe others and draw certain conclusions. For example, I noticed how my college and med school drinking was similar to the drinking experiences of those in the group who were there for treatment. At first, this alarmed me, but as I listened to the many personal histories and drinking stories the patients told, several trends emerged.

First, to a person, each alcoholic began drinking very young, sometimes as young as 10 or 11, though this behavior was often done in secret and well-hidden from their parents. Tobacco often entered the picture early, and at some point in their young lives, pot smoking began. I also noticed that as they grew older, alcohol and drug abuse became an insidious *central theme*, gradually taking control of their lives. In terms of priorities, relationships and personal health and safety gave way to chemicals. I heard dramatic stories of car crashes, divorces, abuse, and other problems related to their addictions.

I also learned that their jobs were the last thing alcoholics or drug addicts jeopardized because they were the only way they could afford to consume chemicals and retain some self respect. As I attended these group sessions, I also heard painful accounts of how the participants' parents or spouses had also been alcoholics or addicts and how these individuals, now patients themselves, were victims of abuse and had suffered in other indirect ways from addiction. The stories of destroyed lives, sometimes going deep into the family history, were very sad indeed.

Questions Arise Within the Answers

Amidst this atmosphere of tragedy and sadness, the staff, many of whom were recovering alcoholics themselves, offered hope through the twelve steps of AA. But with each discussion, the alcoholic patients were cautioned that they were only one drink away from destruction.

One drink? As a physician, it made no sense to me that men and women could be properly diagnosed to have a condition and be treated for it, yet they could never return to social drinking. Besides, I asked, do people have uncontrolled drinking because it is a disease, or do they just lack the will to maintain control of their drinking? Based on 1970s knowledge, nobody could adequately answer this question. However, today's science offers clear explanations.

Alcoholism and drug addiction is a disease and, for sure, once addicted, one can never use addicting chemicals again without great risk of returning to the continued downward spiral that characterizes a life steeped in addiction. Toward the end of my two-week attendance at NRMC, Long Beach, I waited for the "punch line." You see, I reasoned that if a person becomes addicted to chemicals and, therefore, has an incurable disease, why not just prevent it? But, my two-week session came to an end, and I left, never having heard a word about prevention.

Still Waiting

I daily deal with patients and their families who have problems directly or indirectly related to chemical addiction, but I've been waiting since 1978 to hear about ways we can prevent these addictions in the first place. So, here it is, 2006, and I've found that very little has been written about prevention. I imagine you're familiar with the "just say no" slogan of the 1980s and school programs such as DARE. However, these initiatives and programs have done nothing to stem the tide of increasing alcoholism and drug addiction in this country.

The situation is not completely devoid of hope, however. We now possess the knowledge and the science to help us stop our young people from becoming victims of addiction. It's time we begin using it.

Points to Remember

• The model for today's successful addiction programs is the 12-steps of AA.

• Early life experiences with addicting drugs have a tremendous impact on the attitudes and decisions young people make when they are later confronted with the decision whether to use them.

• Though young adults may have similar drinking behaviors at first, those with a history of use at a young age tend to show a pattern of increasing use and progression to stronger addicting substances, while others show a decline in use.

• Drug and alcohol addiction may exist and progress for years unsuspected by friends and family because the addict's job performance may remain intact while all other aspects of life are failing.

• Until now, prevention has not received the degree of attention it deserves. Current prevention programs are largely ineffective.

3

A Lesson in Chemistry: What You Must Know

If you have questions about the addictive quality of a wide range of individual substances, then you certainly aren't alone. Based on my observations, considerable confusion exists among the general public about a variety of addictive chemicals. I hear this confusion among my own patients. However, you don't need to be a healthcare professional to see evidence of widespread misinformation about drugs, both addictive and non-addictive. Just listen to casual discussions about marijuana and you'll hear an odd collection of inaccuracies about the drug. For decades now, many adults—and young people, too—have spread the word that since you can't become addicted to pot, its use among teenagers is probably just a relatively harmless phase of "experimentation." In actuality, however, marijuana is quite addicting.

On the other hand I occasionally see discussions, even in supposedly respectable publications, describing medications such as Prozac using terms like "powerful, mind altering, and highly addicting." When it comes to Prozac, and a host of other useful medications, these statements simply are untrue. For example, when those suffering from depression take an antidepressant drug and begin to improve, they don't feel as they are under the influence of a mind-altering drug. They often are so pleased about feeling better that others around them are impressed by the "power" of the medication.

To gain an accurate understanding of addiction we must first understand what substances are truly addicting, and what that means in each case. The easiest way to understand this is to address categories of substances. I've listed them below, and you will see that some are considered drugs and some "spirits," while a few are industrial agents and others, conventional medications.

Alcohol: Perhaps the "Oldest" Drug

Without question, *alcohol* represents the best known addicting drug in the world. Evidence shows that it's been nearly universally used over many thousands of years, most likely because early cultures easily passed on their knowledge of how to convert sugar from grain and fruits into alcohol. This conversion can be accomplished easily enough using any number of techniques, none of which require "higher technology," or even complex knowledge. Because alcohol can lead to a pleasant euphoria, it's easy to understand how it could become a part of any culture, including our own.

As you know, many ancient cultures, including Jews and Christians,used alcohol. References to wine in particular appear in both the Hebrew Scriptures and the Christian Bible. We know that these middle-eastern cultures used wine in religious rituals and celebrations. Christians will recall the wedding feast at which Jesus performed the miracle of turning water into wine.

Of course, references to the problematic side of alcohol appear as well. In the Hebrew Scriptures (generally referred to by Christians as The Old Testament), we're specifically cautioned about alcohol. For example, *Proverbs 20:1* says, *"Wine is a mocker, strong drink a brawler, and whoever is intoxicated by it is not wise."* Indeed, these wise and divinely inspired men were aware of the alcohol paradox: Alcohol can be refreshing and enjoyable and it can destroy your life!

Medically, we classify alcohol as a mild brain depressant, which may provide a temporary burst of energy. Overall, however, it briefly relieves anxiety and makes the user sleepy. When taken in extreme "doses" or mixed with other depressants, such as even moderate doses of tranquilizers, alcohol can be so sedating that it can put you into a coma or stop your breathing, thus causing death.

You may have seen numerous reports about high school or college kids playing a drinking game at parties. The kids challenge each other to binge drink, usually downing shot after shot in a short period of time. These multiple doses of concentrated alcohol can literally be deadly. Tragically, a few students have ended up in the morgue, with alcohol intoxication as the cause of death. Investigations into these deaths usually turn up statements by friends who thought their drinking pals had only "passed out," so they left them to sleep it off in the bathroom or bedroom or some other place. In reality their blood alcohol levels reached "poison" concentrations.

When consumed in large amounts or used frequently over many years, alcohol can damage the brain, heart, stomach and liver. Alcohol can temporarily impair brain function, which we know has led to workplace accidents, and of course, tragic automobile accidents (and other transportation related events). For this reason, our society restricts or regulates the sale and use of alcohol.

Tobacco (Nicotine)

Tobacco is another substance that has a substantial history, and at least in our society, its "reputation" has made a complete 180 degree turn. This shift in attitude began about

1969, but the disastrous, yet unknown deadly impact of tobacco, began in the early 1900s. At that time, a doctor lecturing to his medical school class during an autopsy remarked that his students should take special note of a unique type of disease called lung cancer. Very rare at the time, he suggested to these students that they may never see another case in their entire careers. It was an uncommon disease because relatively few people used tobacco or they used it less frequently earlier in our society than occurred later as it made its way to wide acceptance.

It's safe to say that the lecturing doctor could have never have envisioned the glamorization of cigarette smoking that we saw in the movies in the 1930s and '40s or during World War II and throughout the 1950s. He would have had no idea that tobacco would be pushed into the mainstream of American life, and smoking rates would soar to up to 40% of the population.

Hard as it is to believe, in the 1950s, tobacco was advertised as a medical product of sorts. Some doctors were seen in commercials recommending smoking to "soothe the throat." In the early 1960s studies suggested the link between lung disease and cigarette smoking, but no one paid much attention to these early reports. In 1969, the Surgeon General issued the first warning that science showed very clearly that smoking led to cancer and heart disease, and by extension shortened life. However, even then we did not begin to see an effect on smoking rates for another five to ten years.

For years after the Surgeon General's first warning doctors, and almost everyone else, referred to using tobacco products, including chewing and pipe tobacco and cigars, as a "bad habit." However, acceptance of tobacco as an addicting substance has been widely acknowledged only over the past 10-15 years. My parents, both of whom were heavy smokers, warned me not to smoke because of the health problems it could lead to. Of course, I wondered why they said those things, if smoking was only a bad habit. But although my parents knew that it was harmful to their health, they didn't immediately quit. We have since learned that the nicotine contained within tobacco products is highly addicting. Neither of my parents could stop smoking because they were addicted. Both died prematurely of tobacco-related diseases.

How curious it is that even today we don't think of tobacco users as addicts. Yet, studies show that a person using tobacco will be hooked within days and even worse, it's as difficult to break nicotine addiction as it is to get off other addicting drugs. In fact, nicotine is far more addicting than alcohol. Paradoxically, our more benign collective attitudes toward tobacco are likely rooted in the centuries-long history of its use, not to mention its economic importance in this and other countries. Still, we don't associate tobacco use with other dangerous or damaging behaviors, although my mother could get quite cross if she ran out of cigarettes.

Nonetheless, for the past 50 years, tobacco (mostly through cigarette smoking) has been killing more people than alcohol and all other addicting substances combined. In the U.S. alone, it kills over 400,000 people every year and it reduces users' life expectancy by an average of 12 years. It is finally beginning to sink in that tobacco, which has had more social acceptance than other substances, is actually more dangerous than all other addicting chemicals used in our society. It's paradoxical, too, that other than the power to addict, nicotine is not harmful in itself; the other substances in tobacco, mainly tar, cause the cancers and heart disease linked to smoking.

The final paradox about tobacco is that it is the only harmful and addicting substance that no one uses to "get high." Sure, smokers may talk about smoking to relieve anxiety and improve concentration, among other mild effects, but it doesn't produce the euphoria associated with alcohol, for example. So, if that's true, why would a person choose to consume such an expensive product, when they don't get high and they know it shortens life by a dozen years? But, no one makes this choice; it's chosen for them.

Today, no sane adult would ever make such a choice. Put another way, how many 40-year-old first-time smokers do you know? Our children are a different story. Between their exposure to various media and observing their parents, other adult role models, and their peers, some young people are still persuaded to begin smoking because the natural appeal of adulthood and independence lures them into tobacco use. Unfortunately, once they begin using tobacco, these young people face tremendous difficulty when they try to stop using.

I deal with the sad facts about smoking every day in patients who have heart and lung disease and premature aging due to smoking. These adults want to stop but can't. When asked, they all tell me that they wished they had never been influenced to smoke when they were teenagers. Fortunately our society is beginning to get the message. The smoking rate is now about half what it was a generation ago, and death rates are beginning to decline as well.

While it is true that many people have stopped smoking over the last couple of decades, the smoking cessation rate remains dismally low and probably not too different from rates for recovery from drug addiction in general. Self-help and educational programs, "the patch," and Zyban, while helpful, have had little impact on overall rates of smoking cessation. This is why insurance won't pay for these methods to quit, and in addition, no solid proof exists that they work.

Many of those who finally quit smoking do so after developing a significant problem, such as experiencing a heart attack or receiving a diagnosis of emphysema. In these cases, many simply quit immediately, and then must cope with the damage done. Sadly, I have seen some adults suffering with terrible health effects of smoking, but they still can't stop!

More recent studies suggest that with each attempt to quit, the chances of success go up, and I tip my hat to any person who has succeeded. But, my stance in writing this book is to simply ask parents why they would risk letting their kids get hooked if there's about a 90% chance they will never be able to stop! For too long, the subject of addiction has been addressed through discussions about treatment and recovery. Yet, tobacco gives us another example in which treatment and recovery does not work well. While the rate of smoking is half what it once was, this is not because half of smokers have quit; rather, it is because many smokers are dying and they are being replaced demographically by non-smokers growing into adulthood. (More information about smoking appears later in this book.)

Opiates (Narcotic Analgesics)

We typically associate heroin with images of "skid row" addicts injecting themselves with dirty needles. Heroin is certainly the best known of this opiate group, but other drugs in this category can be medically beneficial, while also potentially addicting. To clarify, I've provided a list of common opiates, along with their uses.

- *Heroin*—an illegal substance, never used legitimately.
- *Methadone*—an oral opiate used to treat pain or assist addicts to stabilize or wean off heroin use.
- *Morphine and Demerol*—used mostly in the injectable form to relieve acute pain.
- *Codeine/Hydrocodone*—oral opiates commonly used to relieve moderate pain and to suppress coughing.
- *Other synthetic and atypical opiates*—these include

newer and often more potent pain relievers, such as Fentanyl, Oxycontin, and Dilauded.

Clearly, some opiates have valuable medical uses. However, all of them have the potential for abuse and users can become addicted to them. In fact, even some medical professionals have been known to become addicted to medicinal opiates such as codeine, morphine, and Demerol.

Heroin powder is typically melted with a small flame in a spoon, pulled into a syringe and injected into the veins. Initially, it causes intense euphoria, followed by sedation. Although heroin use has unfortunately developed an association with a certain "glamorous crowd," most users end up sharing needles, which carries dangers of its own. In addition, heroin users generally suffer from overall poor health. Beyond that, injectable opiates have a special danger not shared by other drugs in that, like depressants, they can depress parts of the brain, even the center that controls breathing.

General tolerance for these drugs in the brain, and at the breathing center of the brain, specifically, goes up exponentially and rapidly with repeated use. After the user stops for a period, the tolerance comes down again. Based on previous tolerance levels, users sometimes miscalculate the dose needed to get high and go straight to their old dose. This can be fatal. Because the street purity of the drug can vary greatly, many addicts have died suddenly when injecting what they thought was their usual dose to get high, but the dose turned out to be too strong.

Marijuana (Tetrahydrocannabinol)

Marijuana comes from the leaves of a type of hemp plant, and tetrahydrocannabinol (THC) is the active ingredient that causes euphoria and addiction. Marijuana is known by many names (pot, weed, reefer, and so forth) and is usually smoked.

While it can be ingested (i.e., added to food), it isn't well-absorbed through the stomach. This drug is plentiful and cheap, often grown in secret by its users or bought from dealers on the street—and not necessarily back alley streets. Though like other addicting substances it can have a euphoric effect, it's generally known that this diminishes with recurrent use. After a period of smoking marijuana, many users consider it a daily anxiety-reducing chemical. So, in order to get high, these individuals add other substances.

Marijuana has a mixed reputation, in that much of society seems to view it as not particularly dangerous or addicting, while others recognize its addictive qualities and influence on behavior. We've kept it illegal in this country, although it's either legal or its use decriminalized in several European countries. This drug fools people in some ways. On the one hand it has been clearly shown to be moderately addicting, but on the other, it doesn't appear to be as directly dangerous to one's health as other addicting substances. Many users eventually "graduate" and use more potent drugs along with marijuana and, therefore, they suffer health problems from the other substances. In addition, government statistics show that between 1993 and 2003, pot has increased from 3% to 16% as the primary drug addiction that is the cause of admission to treatment centers.

Those who stay with marijuana alone develop problems, too. For these individuals, marijuana usually becomes a daily tranquilizer to calm anxiety, but this enables them to avoid coping with and solving daily problems. They eventually seem to lose motivation and the mental will to accomplish necessary daily tasks. This attribute has become so well known that pot is commonly referred to as an "ambition killer." This habitual use can severely affect relationships and job performance. Notably, chronic users seem to have difficulty with short-term memory as well.

We've seen the growth of an active movement among users and others to convince society and governmental agencies that marijuana is safe and/or even necessary in certain medical situations. However, science is not on their side and no evidence backs these claims. It's clear to me that efforts to legalize or decriminalize the drug are linked with the desire to buy or sell it without fear of prosecution.

Stimulants (Cocaine and Amphetamines and Amphetamine-like drugs)

Cocaine is extracted from the coca plant found mostly in South America. Natives of South America have been ingesting it for many years without much danger. It was actually an ingredient of Coca Cola when it was first a medicinal drink concocted by a pharmacist. About a century ago, the federal government began to regulate addicting drugs and the Coca extract was removed from the product.

Cocaine has a good medical purpose and ENTs (Ear, Nose and Throat specialists) use it during certain procedures to constrict the tiny blood vessels in the inner surface of the nose, thus reducing swelling and bleeding.

During the 1980s, however, cocaine emerged as a "posh" drug, inhaled into the nostrils, often at glamorous parties. During this time, it was mostly an adjunct to alcohol use. Eventually, somebody figured out a way to purify it into "crack," which got its name from the crackling sound when cocaine is being cooked. Crack, this purified form of cocaine, is, like heroin, highly addicting. Crack users often lose weight and find themselves up all night getting high and then sleeping all day to recover. While it does not seem to carry the sudden death from overdose danger of opiates, crack addicts usually engage in dangerous criminal behavior and prostitution to maintain its use. However, we are beginning to get increasing reports of heart attacks triggered by crack.

Amphetamines and amphetamine-like drugs have been properly used and also abused for many decades without many problems, at least until recent years. In the 1920s, Benzedrine was the first amphetamine produced. It was first given to soldiers so they could remain alert during prolonged but critical periods of combat. Because of its stimulating effects on the brain, it has a history of abuse among truck drivers, who have used it to stay awake for long hauls; because it also suppresses appetite, women (mostly) have used it in attempts to lose weight. However, these once common "weight loss mills" using amphetamines have been shut down by state regulating agencies and I hear of fewer cases of this kind of abuse. Other attempts at finding "safer" appetite suppressants have not been successful to date, though some non-stimulant appetite suppressants are under study at this time.

Unlike marijuana and cocaine, amphetamines are produced chemically rather than extracted from a plant. For many years, these drugs have been legal, but available only by prescription. Below is a list of commonly used amphetamines and amphetamine like stimulants.

• *Benzedrine, Dexedrine (uppers, bennies)*—first used by soldiers to stay alert.

• *Adderall* (amphetamine) and Ritalin and Concerta (amphetamine-like)—commonly used for Attention Deficit Disorder (ADD/ADHD).

• *Methamphetamine (crank, crystal, meth, speed, ice).* Inhaled in a smoke form, it causes high levels of the active chemicals to reach the brain much faster than the ingested form listed above.

By any name, methamphetamines are highly addicting and usually produced in a home lab in a bathroom or garage. When you hear news reports about "meth" labs, this is the class of drugs they mean. Today, methamphetamine labs function much like whiskey stills back during prohibition. Users need only a little equipment and some raw materials to produce enough crystal to use and to sell—and at good profit.

Because meth is so common in the current world of addiction it has begun to affect sales of over-the-counter cold medicine market. Pseudophedrine, a safe medicine for nasal stuffiness, can now be manufactured into crystal meth in a simple "at home" lab, with the instructions for producing it available on the internet. The problem has become so serious that most states now monitor and control the sale of pseudophedrine containing medication, such as Sudafed.

Depressants (Minor Tranquilizers (anxiolytics) and Sleeping Pills (hypnotics)

Depressants include four main groups of chemicals: *barbiturates, benzodiazepines, non-benzodiazepine hypnotics, and alcohol.* Longer acting barbiturates such as Phenobarbital, used primarily to control seizures, are not easily abused. However, Seconal and Turinal can be abused and are rarely prescribed anymore due to their many side effects and problems. Their use has been almost completely replaced by benzodiazepines and non-benzodiazepine hypnotics.

Benzodiazepines are divided into two groups: *Minor tranquilizers (anxiolytics/muscle relaxants)* represented most by such brands as Xanax, Librium, Ativan, Transene, and Valium, and *sleeping pills (hypnotics)* represented most by Dalmane and Halcion. A newer, non-benzodiazepine group of sleeping pills (hypnotics) are represented most by Ambien and Sonata. Their affect on the brain is similar to benzodiazepines.

The drugs from these four groups cause euphoria, they reduce anxiety, and they have a sedative effect. They are also addicting. At higher doses they can affect short term memory.

Individuals in AA refer to this brief amnesia as a "blackout."

Some drugs in these groups act more rapidly than others, and likewise, some have greater sedating effect, but they have the same basic effect on the brain as alcohol. We see further proof in that doctors must wean heavily drinking alcoholics gradually to avoid the dangerous withdrawal syndrome, delirium tremens (DTs). While we could use smaller and smaller doses of alcohol to do this, it's safer and easier to wean the alcoholic with benzodiazepine drugs like Librium.

Alcoholics know this crossover effect between alcohol and depressant medications very well. In fact, alcoholics have often asked me to prescribe Valium or Xanax after they have stopped drinking because they want something to take away the craving for alcohol. However, unless these individuals are being treated as inpatients, I refuse these requests because these individuals may begin to drink and take pills, an extremely dangerous combination.

Sometimes people who never even consider drinking alcohol—and don't condone its use by others either—will sometimes ask me to prescribe some of these minor tranquilizers or sleeping pills. I must admit I enjoy their response when I explain that if I prescribe one of these medications for anxiety or insomnia, they will be taking a "martini" in pill form. And this is not an overstatement!

I once encountered an elderly lady in a hospital cafeteria and observed her staggering around, appearing confused, but also quite happy. At first I thought she was sick or having a stroke, but it suddenly occurred to me that she was drunk! I spoke with her daughter, who explained that her mother was visiting a relative who was having surgery. Her mother took Valium on a regular basis to manage anxiety. However, that day she took an extra Valium because of increased stress. I would say she was "feeling no pain." The extra Valium she took was comparable to drinking an "extra" glass of wine in that it made her "tipsy."

Not only does depressant medication act on the brain like alcohol, it actually magnifies the effect of alcohol. For example, people can drink themselves into alcohol toxicity by consuming high doses over a short period of time. While they will lapse into unconsciousness, after throwing up they'll probably be fine after the alcohol wears off in a few hours. We call that "passing out." On the other hand, even moderate doses of alcohol taken with moderate doses of depressant medication can cause coma and death.

In recent years, we've seen reports about women who have been raped after given a drink of alcohol secretly laced with a dose of rohypnol, a depressant. This combination first removes the woman's inhibitions, renders her unable to protect herself, and then it erases short term memory. Even worse, the potent combination of alcohol and a depressant can kill! As a possible example, some have speculated that Natalie Holloway (the young woman who was reported missing in Aruba and at this writing has not been found) may have fallen victim to this dangerous combination or one similar to it. It is possible that the combination of alcohol and rohypnol depressed the breathing center of her brain to the extent that this young woman slipped into coma and died, thus killing her unintentionally. A combination of alcohol and any drug in the depressant and opiate categories can give the same result.

Nitrous Oxide (Laughing Gas)

Administered through a mask, anesthetists and dentists give this drug to patients during painful procedures because it provides sedation and pain relief. It also has a euphoric effect, thus the term "laughing gas." When abused, it can be very dangerous. For example, death can result from an increase in the concentration of nitrous oxide, when not properly monitored, to the point that the oxygen is displaced within the lungs. When this occurs, the person becomes unconscious and dies from lack of oxygen.

Inhalants

Inhalants include a considerable number of little known compounds available for daily use, including two of the most common, glue and spray paint. Users commonly refer to this practice as "huffing," "sniffing," or "chroming." Based on current knowledge, kids tend to favor the glue used for constructing model cars and airplanes and get high by spraying or dripping the substance into a bag and then inhaling the fumes. Fortunately, many stores now restrict the sale of glue only to adults.

It's important that parents realize how dangerous to sensitive brain tissue and highly addicting these chemicals are. To give you just one example, I once saw a young adult patient who had sniffed glue as a child. He was so disabled that his level of functioning is best described as a combination of being both schizophrenic and mentally retarded.

Steroids

Though abused for several decades, *steroids* are beginning to receive the attention they deserve. To clear some confusion, there are several hormones in the human body that are considered "steroids." Estrogen (female hormone), testosterone (male hormone), and cortisol are but three of the naturally produced hormones known as steroids. *Anabolic steroids* are laboratory created testosterone, and these are the abused steroids. Healthy men produce testosterone normally from their testicles, but difficulties occur when *additional* male hormones are taken by young male athletes in order to enhance their athletic prowess or physiques.

Anabolic steroids are usually taken several times daily by injections and/or orally. While they definitely work, a fact to which any spectator at a bodybuilding contest can attest, they also are dangerous. Among other things, anabolic steroids cause acne, hair loss, and liver damage. Because the testicles of the steroid user are no longer needed to produce testosterone internally, the testicles may shrink and stop working at all, thereby causing sterility.

These steroids also can have severe side effects known as "roid rage," in which the user is unable to control his temper. Though not well explained, there appears to be an addiction syndrome caused by steroid use. It may be that users don't want to lose their massive "pecs," broad shoulders, and trim waist, or it could be that mild euphoria reported by users may point to a more conventional type of addiction. At this point, we need more research to clarify the nature of this addiction.

Who uses anabolic steroids and how broadly is this class of drugs used? At this point, this hasn't been well studied, but numerous reports outline fairly common use among middle school and high school boys. It is easily found on the "black market," typically through stores that sell nutritional supplements, or through fellow athletes and sports trainers.

Steroid use is extremely common among college and professional athletes. However, recent data suggest that contrary to the athletic association with steroid use, many teen users aren't involved in sports at all and are *more* likely to engage in drug and alcohol use. Finally, I am sad to report that even girls have begun using anabolic steroids. Apparently, there really is no end to what people in our society will do to enhance their body image or athleticism.

Other Non-addicting but Abused Drugs

Fortunately, drugs in this category do not enjoy wide use, though Ecstasy appears to be growing in popularity. They are neither prescribed nor grown but must be manufactured in a black market lab. Hopefully their production will remain too complex to be so widely produced as crystal meth which is found in home labs across the country.

Some substances are abused and dangerous but not addicting. *LSD (lysergic acid diethylamide)*, also known as "acid" was used in the 1960s and '70s, but is not as commonly used today. It's touted as a hallucinogenic agent, and kids abuse it to experience these visual hallucinations, which can sometimes be pleasant. However, it's dangerous because users have been known to feel invincible and behave strangely and do things like leap from buildings. In addition, mental illness can result from its use.

PCP (phencyclidine), commonly known as "Angel Dust," was originally designed in the 1950s as an anesthetic for humans, but because of its side effects was converted to animal-use only. However, it had too many problems even for that and has never been approved for any legitimate use. In the 1970s, it became popular among teenagers. Because it's a powerful stimulant, hallucinogen, and anesthetic, and also affects judgment, it is the "perfect storm" as far as dangerous drugs of abuse are concerned. For example, users can become very dangerous and difficult to control and legends abound about feats of superhuman strength.

I witnessed a case in which a US Marine took PCP and later drove a truck into a ditch, injuring himself and killing others. While in the hospital he grabbed a long pair of pointed scissors and proceeded to kill a number of patients in the hospital. He was subdued only after three bullets were fired through his chest and into the wall and eight MPs held him down to put him into restraints.

Ecstasy (MDMA) is a more recent addiction to the drug list. A so-called designer drug, it has properties of LSD and amphetamines and a well-documented ability to destroy brain

51

cells. Despite that, no "Rave party" would be complete without Ecstasy.

Dextromethorphan is a non-prescription synthetic opiate found in a number of cold preparations in any pharmacy. (Robitussin DM and Nyquil are two well known brands.) Its medicinal purpose is to suppress coughs, but its abuse among kids across the country has come to light only recently. In street slang it's called "dex," "dxm," and "robo." While it causes a mild euphoria when taken in high doses, kids abuse it in order to create an LSD-like "out of body" experience, a kind of mild hallucinogenic effect. Because it is quite toxic when taken in overdose and even can be lethal, I recommend that you not stockpile these cold medications. In addition, watch for signs that your teenager takes an unusual interest in its use.

Drugs not Abused, but Thought (Incorrectly) to be Harmful

I included this discussion only because these drugs are thought to be addicting or capable of being abused—or both. Neither is true, however. Though like any medication they can produce side effects, these drugs have helped millions of people and their use should not be avoided or condemned just because some misinformed people say they are dangerous or addicting.

Prozac, the best known drug in this group, also is the first of the modern antidepressant medications called SSRIs (selective serotonin reuptake inhibitors). Other antidepressants, such as Elavil, Tofranil, and Sinequan, have been around for many years, and although they have considerable side effects, they cannot be abused. Prozac and others in its class of drugs were developed to provide relief and benefits to depressed patients, but without some of the significant side effects experienced with the older antidepressants.

For a variety of reasons, Prozac gained some undeserved political attention, even becoming something of a "lightning rod" within discussions of mental illness. As you may know, The Church of Scientology has used some misconceptions about the drug to attack it and other drugs used to treat mental illness. Some within that organization have targeted psychiatrists and psychiatry in general. But, let's just say that claims that Prozac is addicting or mind-altering are ludicrous. However, it and others in its class have taken a hit lately, primarily because well-meaning researchers have suggested that these drugs may trigger suicide in depressed patients, especially teenagers.

For centuries we have known that depression can lead to suicide. In addition, however, doctors have known for decades that antidepressants can, on a rare occasion, "trigger" suicide in severely depressed patients who may go through a "suicidal window" as they improve.

Obviously we have to balance the risks and benefits. Patients using these drugs should use them carefully and doctors need to closely monitor patients who are severely depressed or suicidal. But should we deprive millions of people relief derived through this wonderful medication, just because of this unusual response to treatment? Over the years, I've had a number of patients who would have benefited from taking Prozac, but who have refused it because they believe some of the bad publicity it has received.

Other drugs in this category are Celexa, Lexapro, Zoloft, and Paxil. Other modern antidepressants in other classes include Cymbalta, Effexor, Desyrel, and Wellbutrin. All these and other commonly used antidepressants are safe and help the many millions who suffer from anxiety, obsessive-compulsive disorder, depression, and many other disorders.

The major *tranquilizer (anti-psychotic)* drug group deserves attention, too. Though very powerful, they are not abusable or addictive. In fact, the biggest problem their use poses involves keeping patients on these drugs. What I mean is that those who must take them often don't like the side effects and once they feel better (because the drugs do their job) they may believe they don't need the drugs. Many of the "street people" we see today are psychotics who have refused to take effective medications and, therefore, can't function in society or hold a job.

Schizophrenia and severe bipolar disorder are the most common psychotic disorders treated with these drugs, including Prolixin, Throrazine, Haldol, Risperdal, Zyprexa and Seroquel.

And What About Caffeine?

No addiction discussion would be complete without talking about caffeine. We can blame it on Starbucks and other premium coffees served in coffeehouses—even rest stops on the highway may have a cappuccino machine. Overall, we're consuming caffeine in ever increasing amounts, especially because so many soft drinks contain caffeine, too. A number of studies have been done on caffeine to determine its addiction capability and possible harm.

So, far, I'm happy to say that no study has found a significant health risk from using caffeine. Ardent coffee consumers should be aware, though, that extreme doses can lead to benign episodes of rapid and irregular heart rhythms. As you may have experienced first hand, sudden withdrawal can lead to temporary headaches.

Users beware! Many of the current caffeine drinks contain high-calorie ingredients and may threaten your waistline. They also threaten your wallet! Still, if you want to consume over-priced coffee with odd names like lattes and frappes, then just monitor the calories.

Relative Addictiveness of Drugs

With our list of substances complete, we need to address the relative addictiveness of these drugs. With the notable exception of tobacco, we consider the general rule that the higher the euphoria created by a drug, the faster and stronger the addiction. However, the overall danger of the drug must be analyzed by considering other factors, including, for example, unintended substances, such as tar in cigarettes, which is ingested or inhaled along with the nicotine. In the case of heroin taken by injection, one has to consider the risk of exposure to someone's diseased blood when sharing needles.

The exact ranking of the drugs on this list is subject to more discussion and study. However, I created the list for parents to use as a guideline to help them better understand drugs and drug addiction.

Lower Addiction Capacity
Alcohol
Amphetamines (oral)
Minor tranquilizers/Sleeping pills

Middle Addiction Capacity
Opiates (oral)
Marijuana
Cocaine (powdered)
Inhalants
Gases

High Addiction Capacity
Crack Cocaine
Heroin
Crystal (methamphetamine)
Tobacco

Points to Remember

• Nicotine in the form of tobacco is proving to be the most dangerous drug of all because of its impact on health.

• Alcohol and marijuana rate moderate to low in the euphoria and addiction scale, but when used by young people, they often lead to much more addicting drugs.

• Tobacco, while not causing euphoria, is highly addicting and also may enhance the effect of alcohol and marijuana in leading to more addicting drugs.

• Drugs in the antidepressant and antipsychotic group are not addicting.

• Drugs fall into different levels of addiction. Keep in mind the general rule: *the higher the euphoria, the faster and stronger the addiction.*

4

A Child's Developing Brain

You no doubt chose this book because you, too, are aware of the current situation with addiction in our society, especially that affecting young people. Unfortunately, a level of superficial awareness is where many people—parents, teachers, law enforcement professionals, counselors/therapists, and even physicians—become stuck. This occurs because these individuals don't understand how these substances actually work on the brain, so even chemical dependency specialists have had limited knowledge. However, recent advances in neurological science provide us with insights we haven't had before.

In the 1970s information began to emerge that allowed us to peek into the microscopic workings of brain cells (neurons), which led the way to explanations about the nature of addictive diseases. So, we find ourselves in a situation in which science is on its way to solving the mystery of addiction, but the cure is still not in sight. This is why I remain even more convinced that *preventing* addiction is the way of the future.

Welcome to Science Class

After studying human anatomy and physiology as a medical student and spending over 30 years treating thousands of individuals for a variety of diseases, I continue to view the body with childlike awe. No matter how scientifically and technologically advanced we become, nothing can compare with the sublime brilliance of the inner workings of the human body. Every day, as I practice medicine, I am reminded of the reality that only a being with a much higher order of intelligence and power than humans could make these bodies—and the many other things in our world—possible. So, when it comes to the story of the universe, God is the script writer and scientists are the script readers.

The Nervous System, an Organ of Duality

In order to get a clear picture of the effects of addicting chemicals on the brain, you need a very basic, overview of the nervous system. This amazing organ has two main components:

• the brain, also known as the central nervous system (CNS), and

• the spinal cord and nerves going to organs, called the peripheral nervous system (PNS).

The CNS is the command and control center of the body and the PNS delivers these commands to our organs and, through its sensors in the organs, sends responses or "feedback" back to the CNS. This is the system by which the control center makes millisecond by millisecond adjustments in order to maintain optimal functioning.

The CNS is also divided into two levels of operation, *conscious* and *unconscious*. Conscious functions require decision making and, at times, the intellect. For instance, during a school day children make a number of conscious decisions, including who they will talk to or kid around with and what to eat for lunch. More importantly, they try to learn material in their various classes, which they apply later during tests or in some cases, in life outside of school. These day to day activities are performed consciously.

However, the unconscious is in play, too. While making

conscious decisions, other parts of the brain, such as the hypo-thalamus, are busy controlling functions we aren't aware of moment to moment, i.e., secreting needed levels of various hormones, the onset of hunger, and, even when to breathe (a function controlled in the brain stem).

Conventional wisdom suggests that the conscious part of the brain should override or otherwise control the unconscious part of the brain. However, this is not always the case. Let's say that you are on a diet to lose weight. The conscious part of your brain may make this decision because your waistline has expanded, and you know that you need to shed a few pounds. Yet the sight of an ice cream parlor may trigger a desire for a chocolate milkshake and you find you simply can't resist. Even when using your intellect and your conscious will, you may experience this temporary dieting failure. This uncon-scious, yet powerful brain function will be an important part of our later discussion of addiction.

The Nervous System: An Organ of Balance

Another amazing but fundamental characteristic of the nervous system is the way it balances itself. A constant, millisecond by millisecond push and pull operation goes on throughout the nervous system. For instance, the simple task of picking up a glass of water and drinking it involves millions of brain cells giving delicately balanced commands that make it possible for you to reach forward, grasp the glass, lift it to your mouth, and swallow the fluid without choking. Should your nervous system not be in perfect balance, this simple task may prove to be awkward or impossible.

Some brain cells "push" while others "pull." Or, more specifically, some brain cells activate bodily functions and movements while others simultaneously inhibit them. This activation/inhibition system gives us the balanced, desired action performed in a smooth and sometimes skilled way. Consider a concert pianist or a talented artist. Can you imagine the wonderful interaction between conscious intellect, unconscious brain operations, and the activation/inhibition process that leads to their desired results?

When the Balance is Flawed

Parkinson's disease provides an example of an out-of-balance neurological system. In this disease, certain parts of the brain become damaged and cannot respond by activating or inhibiting certain functions, which is why a patient with Parkinson's disease may have considerable problems with simple tasks such as lifting a glass of water and drinking it. This occurs because certain parts of the nervous system may be activating, while others are not properly inhibiting or vice versa, and, therefore, the person experiences the absence of balance.

Attention Deficit Hyperactivity Disorder (ADHD) is another excellent example of this problem. This disorder is very much misunderstood, even by well-educated individuals. Many believe that kids with ADHD have too much energy and that doctors erroneously prescribe depressant medications to slow them down in order to "make them behave." I know this myth is widely held because of the way it often is characterized in the lay media. Furthermore, from time to time, an exhausted mother will bring her energetic preschooler for treatment of ADHD thinking the child is "overactive."

In truth, the situation with ADHD is just the reverse. A relatively small percentage of kids (yet a large cumulative number) in this country inherit a problem in which a part of their brain is *under*-active. In this case, the under-active center is the part that controls attention span. So, when the attention span center is under-active, it stands to reason that the child may have difficulty concentrating and by extension, is easily distracted. This easy distractibility is often incorrectly perceived as *over* activity, because the child is unable to focus on one task but a few seconds.

We treat this problem with stimulant medication such as Ritalin. For the specific period the child takes this medication, the under-active attention-span area of the brain is "awakened," which results in normal ability to concentrate. When treated, these children may appear less active because they can focus and learn. As you can see, treating this disorder in properly diagnosed children is anything but drugging them to behave or to calm them.

Paradoxically, treating kids early and properly with Ritalin and other stimulant medications that are potentially addicting appears to help prevent drug addiction. This is supported by early studies on this question. Two factors clarify this. First, at the doses given to children, and the form of intake (pills), they experience no high or euphoria, and, therefore, no abuse and no addiction occur. Second, as children are better able to learn and experience success in school and, as a result, are less likely to drop out of school, they also are less subject to the other influences of addiction, including below normal levels of both education and income. As you learn more about addiction, don't forget about the importance of balance and the activation/inhibition nature of the nervous system.

It's all About Brain Chemicals

You expect your computer to have components that communicate with each other. Logically, you know that if your computer keyboard did not communicate with your hard drive or your hard drive with the memory board, your PC wouldn't work. Take that same principle and apply it to your nervous system. The CNS must communicate with the PNS and with its other components and vice versa. If it doesn't, it can't function properly. Just as importantly, it must do so within milliseconds.

Communication in your PC takes place through low voltage electricity. In your nervous system, communication occurs through a combination of very low voltage electricity in some places and through small traces of chemicals (neurotransmitters) in others.

Individual cells in the nervous system, the *neurons*, specialize. Some neurons allow vision, others move your limbs, and others are used to enable thought processes. Microscopic in size, neurons bundle with other neurons to form nerve tracts in order to accomplish their specialized functions.

Neurons must communicate with each other, and to accomplish this, they need two structures, *dendrites*, which receive information from other neurons, and *axons*, which send information to other neurons. So, to function, a neuron must send its signal from its nucleus down its axon, which you can think of as a transmitting arm, literally a tentacle-like extension. It accomplishes this through very low voltage electricity.

Once the signal gets to the distant end of the axon, it transfers the signal to the other neuron's dendrite, the receiving arm, which is also a tentacle-like extension. The gap that exists between the axon of one neuron and the dendrite of the other neuron is called a *synapse.* Using the PC computer example, a synapse (a connection between two neurons) would be equivalent to a junction between two wires.

As far as the study of addiction is concerned, the synapse is by far, the most important part of the neuron. You see, in order for the signal to move from one neuron to another it cannot simply jump through this gap, the synapse; it must use another vitally important system of communication. This

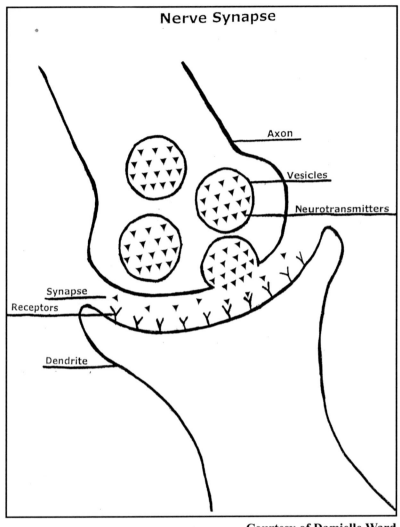

Nerve Synapse

Axon

Vesicles

Neurotransmitters

Synapse

Receptors

Dendrite

Courtesy of Damielle Ward

system requires the use of trace amounts of the chemicals, the neurotransmitters, mentioned before.

This signal or activation begins at the nucleus of one neuron, travels by electricity down to the distant tip of its axon where it triggers a release of certain chemicals at the edge of the synapse. These chemicals then travel across the synapse to the distant tip of the dendrite of the next neuron. The second neuron, the receiving neuron, has special receptors that only these chemicals can stimulate (or inhibit), so the chemicals bind to these specialized receptor sites. At that point, a new electrical signal begins at the end of the dendrite, which is relayed electrically to the nucleus of its neuron. In turn, the second neuron relays its signal on to the third neuron . . . and so it goes.

You probably have heard about neurotransmitters in connection with conditions such as depression, obsessive-compulsive disorder, or other mental illnesses. These disorders are often described in terms of "chemical imbalances," or more precisely, an imbalance of neurotransmitters.

Antidepressant Medications: The key to Understanding Neurotransmitters.

For many years, doctors prescribed antidepressant medications, but didn't understand how they worked. Like most medications discovered before the 1950s it was pure, dumb luck that led us to the discovery that medications like Elavil and Tofranil help people with depressive disease. Fortunately, scientists exploited this luck by performing research on the brain and antidepressants, which over time has led us to our current understanding of neurotransmitters.

Discoveries in the 1970s clarified depression as a condition caused by an imbalance or deficiency in certain neurotransmitters. Since then our knowledge of neurotransmitters has enabled us to provide better help to depressed people. A dividend of this research has been increased knowledge about the role of neurotransmitters in addiction.

Although antidepressants can restore low neurotransmitter levels back to normal, they are unable to cause abnormally high levels of neurotransmitters, no matter how much you take. The explanation for this is outside the limited scope of this book, but it is related to the enzymes that break up the neurotransmitters after they have been released.

While antidepressants don't increase neurotransmitters, they do make sure plenty are available. Therefore, since they don't trigger excessive amounts of neurotransmitters, antidepressants cannot cause addiction. Not one documented case exists of an antidepressant causing euphoria or addiction. I mention this to allay any lingering fear that any of the many antidepressant medications cause addiction.

Neurotransmitters on the Move

Neurotransmitters sit in sacs, called *vesicles,* located at the terminal end of each axon. When a signal comes down the axon and reaches the synapse, the vesicles release the exact amount of the specific neurotransmitter indicated by the intensity of the electrical signal that reaches the vesicle. As the neurotransmitters flow into the synapse space, they are quickly picked up by receptors at the tip of the dendrite on the next neuron, that is, on the other side of the synapse space. Any leftover chemicals are quickly "swooped up" by enzymes, and then broken down to be reconstructed into neurotransmitters again, and they "live" in the vesicles and await future use.

Neurotransmitters and Receptors: A Lock and Key

A neurotransmitter acts as a key, and its corresponding receptor acts like a lock. Neurotransmitters bind with and activate or inhibit only those receptors designed to receive them. If the wrong neurotransmitter hits a receptor, no binding occurs because the unique "key" will not fit into the "lock." True to the balanced nature of the brain, some of the neurotransmitters cause activation of neurons and some cause inhibition of neurons.

The specific nature of receptors comes into play when we discuss various drugs. In the case of addicting substances, each one either triggers the release of abnormally high levels of specific neurotransmitters or binds to and activates or inhibits receptor sites directly (like a neurotransmitter) or both.

Addicting Drugs . . . False Messengers

In 1997, *Time* magazine published a comprehensive discussion concerning the then-emerging information about the way addicting drugs can affect the brain by affecting neurotransmitters and their receptors—and with tremendous force. The author of the article, J. Madeleine Nash, suggested that getting high and ultimately becoming addicted to drugs resulted from the impact of addicting drugs on the nerve cell synapse. According to Nash, scientists had determined that a drug appears to produce a high or euphoria by overwhelming the receptors with intense stimulation many times above normal levels.

More importantly, this new research was able to demonstrate permanent changes in the addict's brain chemistry, which finally gives us the science behind the axiom, "once an addict, always an addict." This information changes the dynamics of the debate about addiction: Is it a disease or is it all a matter of self-discipline? This ongoing debate exists because no one had adequately explained why drug addicts continue to compulsively use drugs regardless of their damaging effects. Now, however, the scientific community can prove that addiction is a disease and, for the most part, those afflicted with it, addicts, can't stop using without help.

David P. Friedman, PhD, and Sue Rusche coined the term "false messengers" in their 1999 book of the same name (See Resource List). This term denotes the way addicting drugs, including alcohol and nicotine, bind to specific nerve cell receptor sites *as though they were neurotransmitters secreted by the body,* and hence, are false messengers. These addicting substances are actually naturally occurring or synthetically produced substances that mimic neurotransmitters by binding to their receptor sites. In some cases these drugs bind to the receptor and activate neurons, and in some cases they bind to receptors and inhibit neurons. In still other cases, they do both.

The latest studies of nerve cells show that each drug appears to affect a particular group of neurotransmitters or their corresponding receptor sites or both. What an amazing coincidence! A natural or synthetic substance contains the exact "key" to open the "lock" of microscopic receptors. Or is it really a coincidence?

If you have ever been given a narcotic medicine for severe pain or have had general anesthesia administered during surgery, then you know how wonderful pain-relieving drugs are. Were it not for these drugs, many common and miraculous surgeries would be impossible to either undergo or perform. In my opinion this is no coincidence at all. Only a higher power and intellect could have created a world in which substances like opiates grow naturally. Then, when taken into the body, the substances uniquely bind with receptors at certain synapses of neurons specifically designed to relieve physical pain. Oddly enough, to understand how drugs help relieve pain we need to look at what causes pleasure.

The Reward or Pleasure Center of the Brain

Many things that don't involve using drugs give us pleasure in life. Consider such common experiences as eating a delicious dessert, watching the sunset, or having sex. Yes, don't forget about sex! Sex is the most intense pleasure that mammals experience without taking drugs. And by sex I don't mean just intercourse. Think of the pleasure of your first kiss.

When we have sexual experiences our pleasure center goes wild. Just imagine all the neurotransmitters released during sexual excitement.

Why do we have such a natural but intense form of pleasure? Well, our Creator knew that our species would need to survive through very difficult times. He gave us several biological and yet practical reasons to procreate: our love of children, the desire and need to bond, a need for laborers, and most of all, the pleasure of sex. Of course, in recent times, epidemic diseases are uncommon and food is plentiful, circumstances which have led to a fully populated world. Since our Creator's mission of populating the world has been accomplished, one could argue that in recent history activating our pleasure center through sex tends to cause society more problems than benefits!

However, the pleasure center of our brains is responsible for the warm, euphoric feeling, a sensation that can be evoked by natural experiences as well as drugs. This center is located in the *ventral tegmental area (VTA)* which is a small area deep in the center of the brain. Without it we would lose the ability to have pleasure, which would be a terrible existence indeed. On the other hand, without it we probably would see no drug experimentation or addiction, because intense stimulation of this area of the brain is required to get high.

Introducing the Locks and the Keys

I realize that discussions of neurotransmitters can be complicated and confusing, but the details are not as important as the basic concept that the addiction to drugs permanently produces enormous changes to the brain. I'm providing the following explanations in order to help you sort through the various drug groups and the specific way they alter brain chemistry.

Depressants including alcohol

This class of drugs generally affects nerve cells by activating *Gamma-aminobutyric acid (GABA)* receptors. GABA is a neurotransmitter that inhibits nerve cells. Depressant drugs either increase GABA directly or the GABA receptors are "fooled" by the depressant drug when it binds to and "unlocks" the GABA receptor. No matter the mechanism, this group of substances inhibits different CNS functions. GABA inhibits the *inhibiting neurons*, so paradoxically, users also may experience excitation. Overall, however, they feel sedated because of the inhibition effect of GABA. This explains why some intoxicated people become agitated (fighting drunk) or seemingly very "alert." But eventually, even the agitated user will succumb to the sedating effects of the drug.

In general, drugs in this group reduce anxiety. They also produce a mild euphoria. However, to cause euphoria and thus to be addicting, depressants must affect our pleasure center to some degree. Like every other addicting substance it must stimulate the VTA, perhaps through the neurotransmitter, dopamine, though less intensely than many other addicting drugs.

Nicotine

Nicotine (from tobacco) binds to one of several types of the *acetylcholine* (a neurotransmitter) receptors, fooling them to think they are getting acetylcholine secreted from the body. In addition, through a complex mechanism, *dopamine* is increased in small amounts in the VTA, and in turn the user receives a mild pleasure sensation and, briefly, reduced anxiety. It remains a mystery to me that nicotine is so addicting when it causes relatively little euphoria.

Opiates

Opiate drugs contain certain protein components that "coincidentally" directly bind to *opiate* receptors and inhibit them. These receptors are found throughout the central and peripheral nervous system. For instance, they are present in the nerves of the gastrointestinal system, and in the alertness and breathing centers of the brain. With low doses of opiates, inhibiting these receptors results in constipation; at higher doses, the user experiences sedation; and at even higher doses, breathing may stop. However, opiates also trigger release of dopamine, which is their most important effect. Through a complex set of actions, both direct and indirect, opiate use leads to the release of dopamine at high levels into the pleasure center of the brain. Naturally, the amount of pleasure and the rapidity of the onset of addiction are directly proportionate to the dose, method of intake, and the potency of the opiate.

Marijuana (tetrahydrocannabino, THC)

Like other addicting drugs, THC binds to specific receptors sites called *cannaboid* receptors. However, unlike the knowledge about opiates, scientists have not figured out exactly how THC affects the brain. However, since we do know that marijuana clearly reduces anxiety and increases euphoria and is addicting, we have no doubt that it affects the pleasure center in some way.

It's commonly noted that cannaboid receptors have a role in appetite, and marijuana users talk about the "munchies." This probably explains why it has been used to reduce nausea in cancer patients. A drug recently released in Europe binds to the cannaboid receptors that govern appetite. This medication has been specially engineered to act on the cannaboid receptor in the opposite way as marijuana, thereby decreasing appetite in order to assist in weight loss. This drug shows great promise as it is touted as not abusable and also may be helpful in smoking cessation.

Stimulants

These drugs have both direct and indirect activation effects on dopamine. As with opiates, stimulants increase levels of dopamine (the pleasure chemical) in the pleasure center. Drugs like methamphetamine (stimulant) and heroin (opiate), though in different drug classes, have much in common. They both cause tremendous euphoria by producing high levels of dopamine in the ventral tegmental area and both are extremely addicting. They differ in the mechanism in the brain through which they increase dopamine and thus, euphoria. Opiates do it through a combination of activation and inhibition, whereas stimulants do it through pure activation. This explains why the characteristics of their use and side effects are different, but their intense addiction properties are very similar.

In summary, when you think of euphoria and addiction, think of the pleasure center of the brain, the VTA, and its corresponding neurotransmitter, dopamine. Addicting drugs affect various other neurotransmitters, mostly responsible for relieving anxiety, that contribute to the abuse of the drugs. But, as stated above, their effect on dopamine and the VTA is what makes it so difficult to stop using these addicting drugs.

The Progressive Stages of Addiction

Think of the above discussion as the "who" of addiction in that the substances have certain names. What follows is the "how" piece that describes addiction and neurotransmitters. We can start with information we've known for a long time.

The six classical steps to addiction are:
Drug (and alcohol) experimentation
Increasingly regular use
Tolerance
Physical dependence
Psychological dependence
Addiction

It may take an individual several years to complete these stages or the stages may rush to completion, almost in one episode of use. For instance, because of its lower addiction capacity, alcohol abuse may occur for years before the user becomes fully addicted. On the other hand, addicts often report that with the *first use* (experimentation) of crack, heroin, or crystal they felt an intense psychological compulsion (psychological dependence) to continue to use. They also report that within days they had to continue to dose themselves just to prevent withdrawal (physical dependence). With each use of the drug, less euphoria was experienced at the same dose (tolerance).

In general, it appears that the length of time from experimentation to addiction is shorter with more potently addicting drugs. Priming from "introductory" drugs also appears to accelerate the addiction timeline. In other words, individuals, often pre-teens or adolescents, may use alcohol, marijuana, powdered cocaine, or a combination for months or years before trying higher potency drugs. As they may already be addicted to the lower potency drugs, just one use of crack, crystal, or heroin may trigger a full-blown serious drug problem. I consider this scenario typical, and as a physician I rarely hear a history in which the addict chose heroin, crack, or crystal without having been a regular user of at least one of the lower potency drugs like alcohol, marijuana, or powdered cocaine for a significant period of time. Tobacco, discussed later, appears to be a factor in priming as well.

The Compulsion to Keep Using

We now can explain the compulsion to keep using, and it's related to the VTA, which, as I explained, is the pleasure center of the brain. All mammals have this center, and scientists have been able to reproduce in some animals what happens to humans in addiction. Researchers have shown that if you put a tiny, electrical probe into the pleasure center of a rat and connect it to a button, you can teach him to push the button with his nose to electrically stimulate the probe. Once he learns that pushing the button causes pleasure, he becomes ardent and energetic at continuing that behavior.

Clearly, rats can become conditioned to push the button to bring on pleasure. Even more interesting, they push the button with increasing frequency, and will do so to the exclusion of eating, sleeping, play, or having sex. They continue until they collapse from exhaustion. Is this beginning to sound like addiction?

As humans we stimulate our pleasure centers when we use addicting drugs. The more drugs we take and the higher their potency to give euphoria (pleasure), the more we will succumb to compulsively seeking to take drugs at every opportunity.

So, Why Can't Addicts Stop?

Several dynamics are in play to keep the addict using. First, as we've seen, various studies of addicted brains show that nerve cells undergo permanent changes. These changes include the amount and type of neurotransmitters, the number of corresponding receptors at the synapses, alteration of metabolism of the brain, and a reduced number of neurons in the brain. Therefore, after all these permanent changes, the brain is different! If the brain can change, so can the personality.

In everyday terms, addicts may be known as honest or

loving or caring individuals during their pre-addiction years, but changes to the brain invoked by addiction may cause personality changes as well. These are usually negative changes, which leads us to ask why that would be the case. Again, we find the answer within the workings of the brain. With each episode of pleasure or euphoria, especially in the adolescent brain, the brain is being reprogrammed, not unlike introducing a virus into a computer program. The computer may operate and look like normal, but you may notice some problems with the computer operations once the virus has entered. Likewise, addicts may gradually begin to show personality changes, and this "Dr. Jekyll and Mr. Hyde" effect may be short term, long term, or cyclical. As tolerance to the drugs builds, addicts find their world turning upside down.

Addicts will say that in the beginning their lives feel normal most of the time, but are punctuated by periods of great pleasure when they use drugs. So, they continue to use, but their tolerance to the drugs builds. Highs get lower and flatter and lows become deeper and deeper valleys. During the low periods, defined as times that addicts take a break from using, they become irritable, depressed, and uncomfortable. Before long, they must up the dosage and use more often just to feel "normal," which then drives them to use even more drugs.

As addiction progresses, addicts increasingly lose control over their lives and drugs begin to unconsciously take over decision making, and this can become extreme. Addicts often say that at some point they will "beg, borrow or steal" to get the drugs, especially if they can no longer hold a job to finance their addiction. They do this because to their brain, nothing is more important than getting high or just becoming comfortable. The stronger the drugs used, the more intense the effect.

Soon addicts become so obsessed with drugs that they

think of little else, and during most of their waking hours they compulsively spend most of their time trying to acquire and use them. We hear about "crack whores," women and men who trade sex for drugs, and adults who live with their elderly parents while systematically stealing their cash, pilfering their accounts, or hocking their belongings.

Who would do such horrible things? Well, only those individuals desperate to get high or at least desperate to avoid the pain of withdrawal could act so outrageously or self-destructively. On the extreme end, we see violent crime or suicide, both of which are common with addiction, all because the brain has been gradually reprogrammed by drugs. As the addictive disease progresses, the addict becomes more and more willing to do more and more desperate things just to get high or stay comfortable. At this point the unconscious function of the brain has taken full control over the conscious function.

I Won't Use Drugs (or Drink) Again—I Promise.

Have you ever heard an addict make promises to shape up and never use again? You probably believed the promise. You believed it for two reasons. First, you wanted to believe it and second, the addict was so convincing—and that's because addicts believe their own promises, too. I have heard alcoholics, drug addicts, and smokers say, "I have quit a thousand times." Yet they keep using. Pretty soon you neither believe nor trust them, at least when it comes to promises or other pronouncements related to their addiction.

These issues of trust and an addict's promises take us back to the conscious versus unconscious functions of the brain. Alcoholics or drug addicts come to a moment of clarity when sober, often when confronted with a loss of job, damaged or destroyed relationships, or a health crisis. At times of clarity, many make a conscious decision to stop using. This same phenomenon occurs with smokers. Almost daily I diplomatically confront patients who have heart or lung disease due to smoking and ask them to stop. They usually respond by saying they should or will stop, but often this simply doesn't happen.

The alcoholic, the drug addict, and the smoker are all well-intentioned people and when they make promises they truly mean them. They want to stop and intend to stop, but they can't. At least they can't without considerable therapy in the case of drug addicts and without tremendous motivation in the case of tobacco users.

Addicts find themselves in the same dilemma as the dieters, mentioned earlier, who are bedeviled by their unconscious brain processes. As dieters pass the ice cream store, or see the potato chips in the cupboard, they begin eating the item, thereby breaking their diets even before they realize what happened. An alcoholic once told me that before entering treatment, he realized he had a drinking problem when it occurred to him that drinking a dozen beers each evening was not good for him. He made pledges to himself to stop or at least cut down on his beer drinking, but after he broke that commitment to himself, he posted a sign on the refrigerator that read, "Do not drink beer." That didn't work either.

"Denial ain't just a river in Egypt" (Mark Twain)

This increasing dishonesty on the part of the addict, both to himself and others around him, is an important symptom of *every* drug addict. This progressively enlarging gap between what addicts say or promise and what they actually do is called *denial*. Remember this important symptom of addiction because it represents the "roadblock" in the addict's soul between conscious will to stop using and the reprogrammed drive of the unconscious mind to continue using drugs.

So, for addicts and dieters, strong, unconscious forces compulsively compel them to overcome their conscious will to stop. Logically and consciously, addicts know that drugs hurt them and they shouldn't use them. But once the brain has been trained by addicting drugs that intensely stimulate the pleasure center and is physically reprogrammed to constantly seek drugs, addicts must just as constantly battle those unconscious forces. Meanwhile denial allows them to avoid self-awareness and ignore reality. Dieters must fight the good fight until they lose those extra pounds. Addicts must battle the unconscious forces for the rest of their lives. It's no wonder that addicts continue to use drugs, even to their detriment; even after treatment, it's no wonder so many give in and use drugs again, sometimes returning to drug use before they are even conscious of doing so.

Don't Count On Treatment

I hope you now understand why it is unrealistic to expect addicts to quit using on their own. And, even if they do quit using with therapy, chances are overwhelming they will use again some day. This frustrating and poor prognosis has the biological basis I've outlined here. Sure, thousands of people are helped each year through drug addiction treatment, but most addicts never get treatment or respond to it if they do. So, wouldn't it be better if we prevented addiction in the first place?

Unfortunately for addicts, bad news prevails. Statistically, it is extremely unlikely that they will ever stop using drugs without significant therapy. And even with therapy, they have a 90% chance of returning to drug use. Even worse is the irreversible brain reprogramming that will never free them from a lifelong, unconscious desire to get high.

This knowledge should empower you to confront the key

question: Would you rather take the risk that your kids will become addicts or tobacco users and then try to treat them later, or prevent addiction in the first place?

Points to Remember
- The human body and the universe in general are sophisticated and complex systems and could be designed only by an intelligence and power much higher than ours.
- The nervous system is made up of elements that activate and elements that inhibit. This creates a beautiful balance that makes it efficient and responsive.
- Addicting substances interfere with nervous system functions by greatly altering the amount of stimulation of neurotransmitters and their corresponding receptor sites.
- Euphoria or "getting high" on drugs is caused when the pleasure center (VTA) of the brain is highly stimulated. Conversely, the stimulation of the pleasure center with frequency and intensity causes addiction. Dopamine is the main neurotransmitter mediating the sense of pleasure, and thus, addiction.
- Other neurotransmitters and their receptors play a secondary role in addiction by offering relief from daily anxiety.
- The permanent modification of brain structure, function, and metabolism by addicting substances leads to the reprogramming of brain processes.
- As their disease progresses, addicts' unconscious desire to get high or stay comfortable progressively overrides their conscious brain functions.
- Addiction is chronic, progressive, and incurable. But it is preventable!

5

"Imprinting" and Addiction

You now have basic and essential information about the brain, specifically, the substantial impact of addicting chemicals on neurotransmitters and synapses. The next step involves examining some additional effects of these chemicals on young, still developing brains. First, keep one thing in mind: *Evidence shows that addiction almost always begins during childhood or adolescence.*

Not only that, but *every child is potentially a future drug addict.* I'm sure you'll agree that's a sobering thought! (No pun intended). You've no doubt heard about the impact of genetics on drug and alcohol addiction, and many assume that a link between the two always exists. However, just because addiction runs in families, genetic influences may be the weakest link, or in some cases, not a real causative factor at all in becoming addicted to a particular substance. By the same token, just because you can't point to past or current addictions within your immediate family, that doesn't mean your children are protected from addiction.

The human brain is not only a complex and beautifully functioning organ, it is sensitive to external stimuli, which may cause significant changes. Moreover, if we introduce addictive substances into a developing brain, the changes may be devastating and permanent. Evidence that shows that substances such as alcohol and marijuana, which many consider "benign" chemicals, can create a devastating addiction cycle in developing young brains.

The Concept of Imprinting

If you took a basic course in psychology, you may recall learning about Konrad Lorenz, a twentieth-century Austrian biologist, well known for popularizing the concept of *imprinting* in graylag geese. He demonstrated that within a narrow, 36-hour window after birth, geese (and several other species of birds) identified almost any moving stimulus as their mother. Famous pictures of Lorenz show him wearing wading boots and walking with a line of geese following him; these goslings were imprinted after birth to think *he* was their mother.

Obviously, the human brain is far more complex and less stereotypical in its response. However, it also can be influenced by environmental stimuli and we can apply the concept of imprinting to developing human brains. To be sure, most adults understand that a young brain is sensitive to stimuli far more than an adult brain is when it comes to learning. Parents and teachers understand this through experience, but child psychologists have also established this concept through research.

For example, we know that early childhood experiences (of varying degrees of significance) create a permanent change in the personality and thinking processes of children's brains. For example, adult sex offenders often recount a history of childhood sexual abuse, thus suggesting that young victims of abuse are at risk for becoming abusers. Another recent example I can cite is that of an adult woman who was allowed to see a pornographic movie as a child. As an adult, she has suffered from a phobia to male genitalia.

I use these examples to more clearly exemplify my point

about external stimuli and the immature brain and the lifelong results that can occur. However, in day-to-day terms our children are being shaped by many external stimuli, positive and negative. These stimuli include subtle and subconscious "inputs," as well as dramatic and life-changing stimuli mentioned above. Most importantly, alcohol, marijuana, and inhalants serve as important external stimuli to the immature brain.

In fact, the most important concept I want you to take away from this book is the *imprinting effect that any addicting substance can have on young, developing human brains.* Earlier in the book I discussed my personal experiences with my maternal grandfather, whose story raises important questions. For many years I wondered why he developed into a terrible alcoholic, while my father rarely drank alcohol throughout his life. In addition, why did I use and abuse alcohol with my friends while in my early twenties, but later consider alcohol irrelevant in my life? At the same time, why did so many of my friends progress to heavier drinking and addiction to various drugs? Finally, in my medical practice I frequently observe that virtually all addicts, including those who use tobacco, have a history of *early* first use, sometimes as young as age eight, but almost always by age 15.

The Age of First Use

Based on what we know today, the main factor that differentiates addicted and non-addicted adults is *the age of first use of addicting substances.* Put another way, when we look at non-addicted individuals, what they have in common is the *delay* of first use of addicting substances, mainly alcohol. To bring this point home, I've looked at my grandfather and other addicts I've known, and after examining their history, virtually all began using some kind of addicting substance at a surprisingly young age. On the other hand, my father had his first opportunity to consume alcohol at age 17, after being drafted into the US Army. As for me, I took my first drink of alcohol at age 19. Neither of us developed a drinking problem nor drug addiction.

Researchers have raised similar questions about who is addicted and why, and in recent years we've seen results of a number of studies on this issue. Increasing data provide answers to important questions about childhood use of addicting substances and its relationship to adult addiction later in life.

By way of explaining the research, consider that for all addicting substances except alcohol, the term "age of first use" means just that, the first-time research subjects used the drug. However, the situation for alcohol is slightly different. The "age of first *intoxication*" is the critical event when comparing early alcohol exposure and later addiction. I believe this distinction makes sense. Apparently, for a substance to create imprinting on the young, developing brain, some form or degree of euphoria is needed.

Why is this important? We can look far back into human history for the answer. For example, 13-year-olds who take a single sip of wine in church during communion, or as a part of other religious ceremonies, are unlikely to experience euphoria and thus addiction. Indeed, wine in particular has been a part of Judeo-Christian religious rituals.

On the other hand, if the same 13-year-olds were to smoke a joint, they would undoubtedly get high. Moreover, let's face reality: when young teens or pre-teens secretly use alcohol or drugs their purpose is almost always intoxication, and they repeat the behavior any number of times. In other words, this secret early first abuse of alcohol or other drugs, such as marijuana, is usually linked to not only intoxication, but several repeated uses, often within a span of weeks. This provides plenty of exposure to begin the imprinting process for addiction.

Practically speaking, the age of first use should actually refer to the *first experience of euphoria* from the addicting substance. Of course, it seems every rule has its exception, and in this case, it's tobacco. Although tobacco does not cause a true euphoria, the age of first use is just as critical as other non-alcoholic addicting substances.

Statistics Back the Concept of Imprinting

The U.S. Department of Health and Human Services keeps statistics on addiction. Based on large populations, these numbers provide, among other things, some facts we need to know about children and later addiction in adults.

• Of the 14 million people addicted to alcohol in the U.S., 95% began drinking before age 21 (2003 figures).

• Those adults whose first intoxication with alcohol was before age 15 were 5 times more likely to become addicted to alcohol as adults (2003 figures).

• First intoxication with alcohol before the age of 15 among males was twice as high as females (24% vs. 13%).

• Among adults, men were twice as likely to be addicted to alcohol as women (10% vs. 4%). This is not surprising considering the previous statistic.

• The graph on the next page shows that the younger the person at first abuse of alcohol, the more likely he or she will need treatment for addiction as an adult. Note that the rate falls dramatically after age 18.

While the data listed on the chart provide *indirect* evidence of the effect of addicting substances on the youthful, developing brain, the information is compelling. Of course, we need more research to better define these issues, but ethical limits

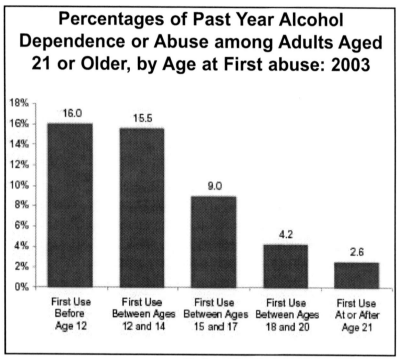

Percentages of Past Year Alcohol Dependence or Abuse among Adults Aged 21 or Older, by Age at First abuse: 2003

National Institute on Drug Abuse 2003

exist, too. For example, we could never select a group of children, give them addicting drugs, and measure the response of their brains. No research committee would approve such an experiment, and likewise, ethical scientists would never suggest it. However, while I find the statistics compelling, other knowledge backs the notion of imprinting.

The Latest Wake-up Call

In July 2006, the *Archives of Pediatric and Adolescent Medicine* published an article reporting the results of a large-scale study that included 43,093 adult subjects (their average age was 44). These individuals had face-to-face interviews about their past drinking histories. Here are their findings:

• Those who began drinking prior to age 13 drank to intoxication much more than others, even during high school.

• 47% of those who drank before age 14 eventually became addicted, versus only 9% of the group who began drinking after age 21.

• There appears to be a direct linear relationship between the age of first intoxication and the ultimate chance of adult alcohol addiction.

• The time span between the age of first intoxication and later addiction is shorter among younger first-time drinkers than older ones.

• The severity and number of addictive symptoms were worse among the younger first-time drinkers.

• These trends existed even after all social and genetic factors were eliminated, which suggests that environment, specifically the age that drinking began, was the most reliable predictor of future addiction.

How can we interpret these data? Basically, what this study tells us is that the younger kids begin drinking, the more likely they will become addicted to alcohol. In addition, kids who begin *drinking alcohol before age 14 have a 50% chance of becoming an alcoholic*. Finally, the younger a child begins drinking, the faster he or she becomes addicted and the worse the addiction, regardless of genetic or socio-economic background.

The Developing Brain Provides Answers

To understand the statistics, we again return to what we know about the developing brain. In newborns, the brain is proportionately quite large, as compared to the adult brain. However, it is immature, meaning that at birth, infants have a significant amount of unused brain tissue. So, while the head is large and is filled with brain tissue, neurologically speaking, the infant can do little more than eat and sleep.

As children mature, developmental milestones, such as walking and talking, begin to reflect the maturation process of the brain, but not its growth. This trend continues through the onset of adolescence, when the body undergoes dramatic growth and development. However, the brain grows very little in size and doesn't mature nearly as rapidly as the body. So, by the time adolescents reach age 16, they are adult-sized humans with child-like brains—and that, as you probably know, is a precarious combination. Most importantly, we must recognize that a great deal of brain maturation occurs *after age 16*!

How does the Adolescent Brain Mature?

The brain must undertake several key processes in order to mature. One involves the progressive coating of axons and dendrites with a fatty substance called *myelin*, which makes nerve cells function faster and more efficiently. The second process in the maturing brain is the creation of considerably more connections between neurons, a process by which it creates a better neuronal network. A third process, *pruning,* is in simple terms, the "use it or lose it" function of brain development. Over time, our brains have a remarkable ability to decide which portions of the brain are useful and which are not. In other words, some nerve bundles in the brain may lose some function while others undergo enhanced function. These changes serve the adaptation process that allows the brain to efficiently meet the unique and individual demands made on it.

Sometimes this adaptation process goes awry. Think of what we call "lazy eye" (amblyopia), a condition in which some young children have a single eye that turns inward or outward and causes the brain to see two images. Unless the two eyes are brought into alignment through surgery, the brain will adapt and destroy nerve tracts assigned to one eye, thus causing blindness in that eye. This occurs because the adapting, maturing brain "knows" that seeing two images is not beneficial for survival.

On the other hand, some adaptation is deliberate. For example, in a young piano student, certain portions of the brain responsible for intricate finger articulations may become highly developed through years of practice and performance.

So by age 18, the adolescent brain still has a long way to go before these processes of maturation are complete. Many adults may be well into their twenties before maturation is complete. Meanwhile, personalities, interests, and goals can undergo "last minute" changes on the way to maturity.

When we examine the data in context of the big picture of young adulthood we can provide scientific support for certain suppositions. For example, our fairly recent knowledge helps explain why statistically, teenage and young adult marriages have a poor success rate. People in this age group usually have self-centered and juvenile goals and motivations, and they don't yet have adult coping skills. So, within a few years couples may "grow" apart as brain maturation leads them, individually, to differing interests and goals.

As an aside, this phenomenon has served as a convenient explanation of what my wife has described as my reluctance at age 25 to move our courtship toward matrimony. I usually respond by pointing out my naturally delayed brain maturation. She quickly agrees with the observation, but doesn't accept it as a reasonable excuse.

Adolescence, a Neurological Conundrum

We've often heard teenagers described as children in adult bodies, and given what we know about brain development, that's certainly true. Understanding this helps us see why these young people are caught in a difficult situation that we former teenagers can appreciate. They really are betwixt and between.

They often feel like adults, look like adults (sort of, anyway), and they want to be adults, but these feelings and longings take place within an immature brain. The brain-body mismatch may get them into trouble, and it most certainly plays a significant role in allowing addiction.

Characteristics of this child brain/adult body syndrome that contribute to drug abuse and addiction include:

- Impulsiveness
- Rebellion
- Feeling of immortality
- Lack of judgment
- Inflated sense of knowledge and intelligence
- Idolizing adulthood
- Pursuit of independence
- Pursuit of novel experiences

Based on this list, it's easy to see that tobacco, drugs, and alcohol can represent a strong allure to teenagers. To them, addicting substances appear exciting, fun, stimulating, rebellious, and adult-like. Teenagers just naturally believe they are "indestructible" and far "too smart" to allow anything to harm them.

Our teens aren't alone in their confusing predicament. Never far away are savvy advertising media ready to exploit teenagers' feelings and beliefs. Books, magazines, movies, television, and more recently, the internet, are often filled with messages directed to young people and intended to influence them to experiment with addicting substances.

On balance, as tough as it is, it's important that adolescents go through this stage of development. If they didn't, then they would not be able to make the transition to adulthood.

Let's Summarize

So, to briefly restate, we know that addicting substances act upon the neurotransmitters and synapses to create an artificially, chemically-driven euphoria at the VTA (ventral tegmental area) in the brain. This creates a permanent change in brain structure and chemistry, especially in maturing brains. The brain becomes reprogrammed to act through its unconscious mechanisms to repeatedly regain euphoria and escape the pain of withdrawal. This process becomes a vicious cycle; with each round of drug use, the brain unconsciously compels the addict to use drugs again and again at increasing doses, despite his conscious and intellectual will to do otherwise.

This chapter explains the maturing brain's great sensitivity and adaptability to outside stimuli. These stimuli include almost any significant experience. Intense euphoria created by addicting substances offers an example of the most powerful imprinting effect of all, especially to the young brain.

What is the Role of Introductory Substances?

Some individuals regard the concept of introductory substances with some skepticism, which adds a note of controversy to discussions within the field. However, I believe the evidence supports the concept of introductory (also known as gateway) addicting substances and also fits well with the concept of imprinting.

Introductory addicting substances may be defined as at least somewhat socially acceptable, lower potency, easily available chemicals that usually are the initial drugs used by youths. We can include alcohol, marijuana, inhalants, and in my opinion, tobacco. Individuals may become addicted to one or more of these substances, but most who use these introductory drugs would not have initially used the more potent drugs. However, a certain percentage of these users will progress to more potently addictive drugs because of the tolerance they develop to the introductory substances.

If you're familiar with the old hand pumps used to pump water from a well, then you're familiar with the concept of *priming*. Farmers used to talk about "priming" the pump, which means putting some water into the pump to displace the air trapped within it. If they fail to prime the pump, then the pump itself will fail because the trapped air bubble will block the flow of water from the well into the bucket. Introductory substances prime or sensitize the brain to respond to the built-in mechanisms already existing that make the brain susceptible to addiction to even more potent and dangerous drugs.

How does the Priming Process Work?

Typically, children or adolescents are either unwilling or unable to experiment with strongly addicting drugs, such as heroin, crack, or crystal. They are unwilling because they've heard negative things about them and they understand there is a taboo against their use. In their non-addicted state, kids and teens are sensible enough not to try these drugs. Generally speaking, the strongly addicting drugs are not immediately available to most kids. By contrast, many young people have access to an ample supply of alcohol. In any given group of friends, kids usually manage to sneak alcohol from someone's home or easily purchase it with a fake ID card. Similarly, marijuana may be nearly as available from friends.

Many kids have an erroneous belief that alcohol and marijuana are benign and non-addictive, which is why kids will often use them to the point of intoxication. But, make no mistake, inhalants such as glue and spray paint are widely available, especially to the youngest of our kids.

Currently, I'm hearing increasing reports that some adults give alcohol to their kids. There seems to be a misguided belief among a number of parents that they should facilitate the "right of passage" into the adult world by allowing kids to use alcohol or even buying it for them. This is particularly true of special occasions like prom and high school graduation. In some cases parents show little or no concern about their kids' drug use, as long as the drug is "just pot." The rationalizations for this often center around the belief that getting drunk or high under parental observation is safer because they would not engage in risky behavior like driving while intoxicated. They argue that since the kids will get drunk or high anyway, they're protecting them from harm.

By these actions, parents give tacit approval of their kids' behavior, and it's essentially outright enabling. Some parents become upset when they learn their kids are smoking, but then are relieved when they find out it's "only pot." Such is the level of confusion and even ignorance among some parents today.

I will address this notion of allowing kids to use certain substances like alcohol under adult supervision later in this book in order to explain in greater detail why this is a truly unwise and dangerous practice. Suffice it to say for now that parents who would never find it acceptable for their kids to use crack, heroin, or crystal often unknowingly encourage them to do just that. By allowing or not vigorously discouraging the use of alcohol, marijuana, or inhalants at a young age, they are accelerating their young brains to seek out these potent and dangerous drugs in the future.

When Boredom Begins

After partying with these introductory substances for weeks, months, and sometimes years, the novelty and euphoria begins to wane. That response shows the first signs of tolerance to the drug. In order to attain the fleeting sense of euphoria experienced in the past, young users are confronted with a choice. They may reason that alcohol and marijuana aren't that great anymore, and complain that they don't get the old highs they once anticipated. However, they still insist they aren't addicted. But by this point they probably use alcohol and/or marijuana several times a week just to keep their growing anxiety under control.

In order to feel that great euphoria again, they begin to consider things that were unthinkable in the past. Why not try cocaine? Why not try crack? Why not try that combination of drugs their friends talk about? Again, these young users engage in rationalizations. After all, they reason, if they can handle (not become addicted) the lower potency drugs, they surely can handle the stronger ones. Besides, their friends now use those drugs and they give all kinds of assurances that they aren't hooked. By this time these teenagers have reached a point where the old taboos about drugs have lost their power, and the teens are driven to seek greater, more intense euphoria. Because of past drug use, young users generally have made connections with those who can supply any drug they want.

Young addicts begin to reason that they should try crack just once to check it out, but when once they do, they experience a high they never felt before. At this point, they are hooked and don't look back. They are full-blown addicts whose every waking moment is spent thinking about their drug of choice. For most of the day, they plan ways to find the drug and pay for it, all the while anticipating what it will feel like when they can use it. These addicted teens can *never* return to a non-addicted state.

Clearly, teenage addicts cannot see that what looks like "baby steps" are progressively moving them from drug experimenters to drug addicts. Often, their parents and friends don't see it either. This phenomenon occurs every day all across the U.S., and it's happening to thousands of young people. There's a *10%* chance that *your* child is somewhere in this progressive process right now.

The Role of Nicotine—Tobacco

I contend that we've greatly underestimated tobacco's role as an introductory drug. Unfortunately, I can find very little written about this issue. However, we do know that nicotine is even more addicting than alcohol and marijuana. It seems very logical to me that it can prime the "addiction pump" for the same reasons other introductory drugs do. In addition, the incidence and intensity of cigarette smoking is inordinately high among drug addicts, a fact that speaks volumes. Finally, regular tobacco use among adolescents is higher than addiction to other substances. Recent evidence suggests an upward trend for cigarette smoking and other drug addictions as well. So, it is reasonable to expect that preventing cigarette smoking among young people may help us prevent addictions of all forms. We need research in this area of adolescents and addiction.

Are You Convinced Yet?

Thus far, I've tried to connect the dots of addiction. By now you should be aware of the early onset of addiction, much earlier than most parents realize. In addition, drug addiction is a disease with a poor prognosis. So is there any question that prevention presents a much better option than treatment? If you ever doubt the critical importance of prevention, then fall back on what you now understand about the way chemicals work on the nervous system: each chemical use reprograms the user to want even more addicting substances.

Finally, I hope that you are impressed with strong evidence supporting the idea that *if we can keep our kids from using addicting drugs, at least until they are 18-21 years old, we dramatically increase their chance of avoiding addiction altogether.* Now, if you can lock up your children until they turn 21, then you can put this book down and read no further. On the other hand, if you find that strategy impractical, as I am sure you do, read on and find out how you can prevent addiction in your youngster.

Points to Remember

• The young, maturing brains of children and adolescents are highly sensitive to experiences of all types.

• Intoxication by even the mildest of addicting substances can "teach" or program the young, maturing brain into beginning the addiction cycle. This process can be referred to as *imprinting*.

• Studies show that the younger a child experiences a chemically derived euphoria, the greater his or her chance to become an addict, even from "acceptable" forms of drugs like alcohol and marijuana.

• Substances known as "introductory drugs," which are not considered dangerous or highly addictive, may lead to the most serious addictions to other drugs through priming or sensitizing the maturing brain.

• Nicotine in the form of tobacco appears to play a priming role as well, though this currently is not well measured or understood.

• Young, maturing brains have many other characteristics that make them susceptible to drug experimentation and addiction.

• Everything that we know about maturing brains and addicting chemicals suggest that the most effective strategy to prevent drug addiction involves preventing even alcohol and marijuana use, at least until ages 18-21.

6

Treatment of Addiction: Cause for Hope or Fruitless Effort?

By now you probably see a pattern in that I'm again posing this single critical question: *Why not prevent addiction rather than treat it?* I can offer one reason this question often doesn't appear to hit home with parents with as much force as I'd like. Based on my observations, parents rarely worry that their children will actually become drug addicts. I can't provide a definitive reason for this attitude, but perhaps most parents believe that for one reason or another, their kids are insulated or otherwise exempt from developing this problem. Or is it possible that most parents think they've done a good enough job of educating their youngsters to "say no" to the drug dealer? Maybe these parents are confident that they'll recognize "early signs" and then quickly intervene before their child becomes addicted.

Another reason comes to mind and it arises from the medical field itself. Perhaps physicians and other health professionals have accomplished so much in medical science that we have created an unrealistic expectation that we can "fix" any type of drug problem that shows up.

After giving the addiction conundrum a great deal of study and thought, I'm convinced that parents who have only a casual concern about drug addiction are ignoring an extremely dangerous threat. It's no exaggeration to say that their attitude puts their child in peril. For this reason, my medical expertise and my deep concern for parents have led me to undertake a mission. My intention is nothing more or less than strengthening your desire to prevent, in every way possible, addiction in your youngster.

Now that you have a foundation of information about addiction and the brain, I offer my take on the danger addictive chemicals pose to your kids and mine every day.

My Experience with Hope Unrealized

When I was five years old, I eagerly waited for my mother to come home from the hospital with my "brand new" baby sister. When I saw my father pull into the driveway, I quickly ran to meet them so I could hug my mother and kiss the baby. However, even as such a small child, I could see something different about my mother. She seemed detached and not at all her usual affectionate self. As happens often with young children, I thought that perhaps she was mad at me about something.

My mother's response to me was unusual, but subtle, too, and left me perplexed because she'd always been an ideal mom. This sounds like a reflection of childhood idealization and bias, but in my young life other people talked about the Flemings as a "perfect" family. My father was considered handsome and hard working, my mother beautiful and nurturing. I recall my mother reading to me each night and saying prayers together. With others, she was kind and generous and spoke to everyone in a manner that reflected her refined qualities. As far as I knew I had a perfect mother and I lived in the perfect middle class home.

Within a few weeks of my sister's birth, my mother was in a straightjacket in the psychiatric ward of the state mental hospital. She'd suffered a precipitous "nervous breakdown," triggered by post-partum depression. I remember that in the days leading up to this psychiatric admission she'd became increasingly agitated, unable to sleep, and combative with my father. My mother also began to hear voices and obsessed over crazy ideas; then we'd hear her loud screams as she tried to drown out these audible hallucinations.

In my perplexed child's mind, I sensed something was terribly amiss. All I wanted was for whatever was wrong to go away. My mother needed to stop being strange and distant and go back to the way she'd been. When she was hospitalized, I longed for her to come home and take care of me and my baby sister. To their credit, my dad and grandmother told me she had a sickness with a name, schizophrenia, and that she would take medicine and be better one day.

After some weeks of hospital treatment, my mother returned home, but she was still not the same person. High doses of antipsychotic medication had caused considerable weight gain, and mentally, she was still very sick. I waited for her to get well; weeks turned into months and months into years, while my mother's mental illness waxed and waned, leaving our home in a state of tension.

As time passed, I feared my dad would leave us. At other times, my sister and I went to stay with other relatives during my mother's hospital stays. Through all of this I longed for, hoped for, and expected to again see my mother as I remembered her before her illness.

Eventually, with tremendous amounts of medication, my mother became sufficiently functional that our home situation stabilized. Then, when I was eleven, my mother gave birth to my little brother. Within weeks of his birth and despite the medication, my mother fell into her worst psychotic episode ever, thus beginning once again the entire psychotic cycle and process.

Over the years my mother's schizophrenia settled into a chronic, disabling disease, yet I maintained hope that someday she would be her "old self" again. That hope aside, every day still brought a crisis of some kind. My mother's behavior and appearance embarrassed me, and her illness caused delusional thinking. She often accused other people, including her family and even the neighbors, of various "wrongs" and that meant she cursed us, too. In stark terms, living with my mother was hell.

When I was about 15, I received an epiphany, a realization that she would never be normal again. The beautiful woman of my youngest years, the mother from whom I received such love and nurturing, had disappeared, was gone and wouldn't be back! Even worse, my brother and sister never even knew that wonderful person. This epiphany didn't necessarily bring me a sense of peace. In fact, I felt angry because the doctors couldn't cure her.

As I grew into adulthood, however, and began to process all that had happened over the years, and what it left in its wake, I became philosophical. Finally, I was able to intellectually reconcile that my mother had a chronic, neurological disease that affected her brain. Once I began to accept this reality, I lowered my expectations about what she was capable of in relation to me, and accepted that a chronic, incurable disease made the situation what it was. When I was 35, she died of an unrelated illness, and while I loved her very much, she had never again been the mother I had once known.

I can understand that you might wonder why I'm telling this painful, personal—and family—story. Well, although my mother was not a drug addict, I call upon this experience when I hear sad family stories about drug addiction. I know exactly what the mother of a teenage addict is hoping and praying for. I feel the embarrassment of adults whose spouses act disgracefully when abusing drugs or alcohol. I know the longing every family has as they imagine the day when their loved one will stop using drugs and return to his "old self."

I Wish I Could Offer Reassurance

I, too, have had friends, relatives, associates, and others in my life, who have been addicted to drugs. These relationships have caused me great pain, but none as much as what happened to my beloved mother. Those experiences, however, constantly remind me that for the addict, addiction is chronic, progressive, and mentally disabling, not unlike what schizophrenia was for my mother.

So, if someone in your family is an addict, I empathize with you, and you have my sympathy. But I cannot reassure you. Your addicted loved one, whether diagnosed or treated, has changed permanently and, like my mother, will never be the same again. No matter how young or old, he or she will suffer from the disease of addiction until death.

So, to be completely straightforward about this, you must understand that addiction indeed is a chronic, progressive, and *incurable* disease. I tell you this so that you will come to the same realization I did—and as quickly as possible. The sooner you understand and accept this reality, the sooner your healing and survival will begin. Otherwise, you will continue putting your life on hold, awaiting the day your addicted love one will return to you completely normal again.

Should We Give Up on Addicts?

As harshly and starkly as I talk about the realities of addiction, don't take my statements as hostile to or unsupportive of addicted individuals. On the contrary, the reason I have such passion about this subject is that my heart breaks for addicted people. I know they go through as much or more pain than their family and friends experience. In addition, some addicted friends of mine have made great progress in their recovery. They do extremely well and are highly functional individuals. However, with the clarity recovery brings them, they would be the first to tell you that only a single moment with an addictive substance can be their downfall—a single beer could be their undoing, robbing them of precious recovery.

Addiction is Incurable, but what about Remission?

Since addiction is incurable, those familiar with the disease never talk about cure rates. Currently, it's unrealistic to expect a cure for addiction because of the permanent changes to the brain caused by using addictive drugs. However, there is something called *remission*. Remission in drug addiction can be defined as a period of time during an addict's life when he stops using addicting substances, longer than his usual interval between uses. Therefore, technically speaking, addicts who stop using for a few weeks or for 20 years, or even the rest of their lives, do so because they are in remission, not because they are cured.

Recovery is another term associated with addiction treatment. It's defined as the period during which addicts have not only stopped using, but are working (through some type of therapy) to deal with their addiction. Because remissions can be spontaneous, one can have remission and not recovery. Most episodes of remission without some type of therapy (recovery) will lead the addict to begin using again. Willpower, that is, the will of the conscious mind, is simply too weak to fight the unconscious compulsion to use drugs. Remember that the drug(s) has powerfully reprogrammed the addict's brain to continue to use the drug over and over.

Those of us who are not addicted have great difficulty understanding this programmed compulsion to use. Since we don't have the "reprogramming virus" that afflicts addicts, we can easily choose not to use. The addict must forcefully and daily *un-choose* to use.

If Addiction is a Disease, are Addicts Responsible for their Actions?

Addicts must be held responsible for their actions. If we were to allow drunk drivers to go unpunished, we would remove an incentive to avoid drinking and driving. The same applies to any chemical use linked with any action that breaks the law. Using the fact of a disease to let addicts off the hook for their actions only enables more of the same. They break more laws and get even sicker, which is why we must remember that the disease is progressive.

On the other hand, many sober, recovering, and functional addicts accepted help because they were forced to. Every year the criminal justice system leads thousands of addicts to therapy and help. In addition, we've seen that both the threat of job loss and family interventions are potent forces, too.

In addition, as members of society we have an obligation to protect innocent people. So, even if drunk drivers fail to seek treatment or violent drug offenders fail to change their lives, we must incarcerate these offenders to protect potential victims. Of course, legal questions arise; specifically, should we punish people who break laws when they do it because of their disease?

I'm not a lawyer, but I think my reasons for holding addicts responsible for their behavior are correct. Addicts, just like non-addicts, always have choices, and we are all accountable. For example, alcoholic individuals may be unable to stop drinking, but they don't have to get behind the wheel of a car. They have the choice not to endanger others, and if they choose to drink and drive, society has an obligation to punish them if caught. What we hope is that along the way they will receive treatment too.

How Effective is Treatment for Addiction?

This is a difficult question, and fundamentally, even with treatment, the chance an addict will stop using is low. The difficulty of assessing treatment results rests with the problem of defining "success," at least in terms of interpreting the way treatment centers measure and report success. For example, a treatment center might conduct a phone survey a month after a patient is discharged. How reliable is this method? If addicts have not used during the first month after treatment and report this in a phone call, this is reported as a success. But what if they begin using in the second month?

When I researched success rate claims among various treatment entities, I found astounding claims. Some report success rates of 75% or 85%, which are ridiculous figures. They go against what everyone with experience in the field knows to be true. I even found some centers comparing their inflated figures against the inflated figures put out by their competitors, thus causing further inflation of success rates. Obviously in the for-profit setting, tremendous financial incentive provides motivation to make these absurd claims of success. But even in the not-for-profit setting, reputations and payroll often depend on claimed success rates.

In reviewing the federal government's Department of Health and Human Services website, I found an additional viewpoint. We could reasonably expect that the government would have no reason to inflate success numbers, but their perspective of success appears based on decline in episodes of use of drugs among addicts. So, based on those figures, getting high less often is a form of success! To clarify, we can find some validity in that perspective of "success." For example, studies do show that reduced frequency of use correlates with increased numbers of treatment episodes. Besides, based on our understanding that addiction is chronic, progressive, and incurable, then reduced drug use is better than increased use. Still, we have to ask ourselves if this limited result of multiple treatment episodes is particularly cost effective.

Standards of success are all over the map and incentives exist to inflate figures, which makes it difficult to get reliable information. Given this situation, I believe that nobody really knows how successful treatment is. However, most authorities on the subject believe that less than 10% of *treated* addicts will stop using drugs for good. Even among that "golden" 10%, I've observed that many often temporarily backslide, but quickly spring back to sobriety. Or, they may "prop up" their sobriety with another, less abusable drug and remain functional, sometimes for a long time.

Many years ago a prominent, widely admired man in my community came to me for medical care. He'd been a recovering alcoholic for many years, even helping to establish and lead a local AA group. Among other medical issues, he asked me to refill a prescription for Valium (an addicting tranquilizer). He'd been taking it for many years, which surprised me. I'd been taught that AA is a "non-drug" treatment concept and it explicitly ruled out these addicting substances for alcoholics. When I diplomatically brought up the subject, he left and never came back.

In his particular case, taking Valium may or may not have been the right thing to do, but he hid his use from his AA colleagues, who believed he was drug and alcohol free. In thinking about him, I recognized that he'd been functioning well for many years, so it's possible this treatment may have been right for *him*. For example, dosing with a tranquilizer may have kept his anxiety manageable, allowing him to resist using alcohol, his drug of choice, to get high.

For many other addicts of all types, substituting one addicting substance for another will only get them back into a downward cycle again. Nonetheless, I suspect that my patient's request is a far more common situation than many in the addiction field realize.

What does Drug Treatment Cost?

The costs of addiction treatment vary greatly. For example, free AA meetings are found in virtually every community in this country (and in numerous other countries). At the other end of the spectrum, some individuals spend many weeks in an in-patient facility. Inpatient treatment costs range from a few thousand dollars to well over $30,000, depending on the socioeconomic status of the patients. Though some insurance policies "cover" treatment, the coverage may be well below the actual cost. Since addicts often go back to using after treatment, they may need several admissions before sustained recovery can begin. So, to understand the real cost, pick the treatment you'd choose and multiply it three to five times. Then you may come closer to the real cost.

The Need for Realism

In order to honestly examine addiction, it's necessary to pass on the bad news of its poor prognosis, even with treatment. However, I don't intend to discourage addicts or their family members and I certainly don't want to quash hope. There is hope for addiction, and I personally know several recovering drug addicts who have lived accomplished lives and have functioned well for many years. Unfortunately, they remain a small percentage of the addiction universe.

Unbeknownst to their parents, kids in large numbers are beginning their first stages of the addiction process at this very moment. This is why it's so important that you know what you are up against if you fail to take action now. Don't wait until your youngster has a so-called drug "problem," only to learn he or she has a lifelong, incurable disease. Act now and prevent it!

Points to Remember

• Parents appear to underestimate the risk of addiction and the early onset of addiction in kids.

• Drug addiction is a chronic, incurable disease.

• Addiction treatment can be costly, especially inpatient treatment.

• Treatment is largely ineffective if the goal is to stop drug use completely.

• There is still hope for addicts who wish to recover and a small percentage function very well with treatment.

7

We're Failing to Protect Our Children

We all hear about it, the "War on Drugs," I mean. I can't point to an exact date we declared this war and media coverage of it waxes and wanes, depending on what other news takes center stage. Yet, we all know there's some kind of struggle going on, although what this actually means baffles me. We can certainly agree that this war on drugs takes place on more than one front. For example, all of us agree that law enforcement is primarily responsible for efforts to stop drug trafficking. The DEA (Drug Enforcement Agency) also has a role in this war because it is responsible for regulating the lawful distribution of certain drugs through prescription as well as enforcing laws against illegal drugs and their distribution. On the public relations front, in the 1980s, former first lady Nancy Reagan initiated the "just say no" campaign targeted to children.

We need to look at what is being done about drug addiction on several levels in this country and analyze what works and what doesn't. We also need to examine attitudes about drug use in our society, which from what I can see range across a wide spectrum. On one end, a few hold accepting and relaxed attitudes about drug use, and on the other end, some hold strict, punitive opinions. I imagine that the majority have ideas that settle somewhere in the middle.

A "Victimless" Crime?

In both this country and Europe, some groups argue that although selling drugs may be a crime, using them should not be. This is part of a libertarian viewpoint, which in essence suggests that citizens be allowed to do anything as long as it doesn't hurt somebody else. So, if I want to participate in dangerous behavior, society shouldn't stand in my way, as long as what I do doesn't harm others. Debates over seat belt use and wearing helmets on motorcycles arise from a libertarian orientation.

When it comes to drugs, the "individual rights" approach is dumb. Anybody who has dealt with the problems of addiction knows that using addictive substances is not an individual act, a *victimless* crime. Children born with fetal alcohol syndrome (FAS) because their mothers drank throughout pregnancy are most certainly victims. What about sexual partners of IV drug users who acquire HIV or hepatitis? Ask a member of MADD (Mothers Against Drunk Driving) whether they consider themselves and their dead children to be victims. And these are only obvious and direct victims.

Think about the cost of disease, injuries, and other medical problems that addictions cause. Drug treatment costs alone are astounding—and growing. Furthermore, we all pay for it, one way or another. As taxpayers and private insurance subscribers we pay this cost, too. Most addicts who reach the point when treatment is needed don't have jobs and thus, they don't have health insurance. We also must include our shared cost of drug abuse because of the link between addiction and crime. Today, the vast majority of inmates in our prisons landed there in the first place, either directly or indirectly as a result of drug addiction.

We need to face the reality that we're all victims of drug use and addiction. If nothing else, our public health costs and ever-increasing insurance premiums affect everyone. Maybe you've been robbed or otherwise attacked in a criminal act; maybe you've felt forced to buy an expensive security system for your home or business. Or, if you've sought treatment for addiction yourself, then drugs have made *you* a victim.

As you can see, we all suffer because of drugs. However, some of us suffer much more than others. I mean, of course, the addicts themselves and the family, friends, and co-workers who love them.

Can We Win the "War on Drugs?"

Ostensibly, after all the effort and money spent to bring down drug kingpins and drug dealers, we should be winning this drug war. Logically, the solution would seem as simple as putting in jail those who will stop at nothing to get our kids addicted to their products. After all, these are very bad people. So, once we rid the streets of them, everything should be okay. Right?

Some years ago, Hugh O'Conner, the son of the famous actor, Carroll O'Conner, was found dead in his apartment, a clear case of suicide related to his worsening addiction problems. O'Connor bitterly and publicly condemned the man who supplied Hugh with drugs. While I understand his bitterness, the drug supplier was just the middleman, not Hugh's problem.

For the O'Conner family, and millions of others in our country, it doesn't look as if we're winning the war on drugs. And others ask why, if we're winning this war, our prisons filled with men and women convicted of drug-related crimes, yet we have more addiction than ever? I urge you not to forget that as long as there is money to be made by selling something in this country, somebody will fill the role of providing it, *no matter the risk.* And, there will always be money to be made selling things as long as there is a demand for that product or service.

In the 1980s and 1990s we built more prisons to house more criminals, and this action looked like one of the fronts of this war on drugs. However, we could double the number of prison beds in this country and fill them all and we will not see a decline in drug crimes or drug addiction. Every time we sentence a drug criminal to prison, his competitor will fill his vacancy. This business is just too lucrative for us to run out of drug "entrepreneurs" in this capitalistic society. If alcohol prohibition in the early twentieth century taught us anything, it was that when significant demand for a product or service exists, those who provide the product or service will overcome all legal barriers to meet customer demand. Prostitution gives us another example of this phenomenon.

It may sound as if I'm arguing against laws prohibiting the sale of illegal drugs. But that's not true. In fact, I'm glad our country takes a stand and fights drug trafficking. If we didn't set these limits, we'd soon find ourselves in the same shape as many other counties in which society has literally deteriorated due to rampant addiction.

In reality, however, we aren't winning or losing our fight against drugs. Rather, it's being fought to a stalemate. So, accept the fact that no matter what we spend or what we demand of law enforcement, we will *never* win the war on drugs unless we do something else along with those actions. The one thing we can do is *remove the demand* for drugs.

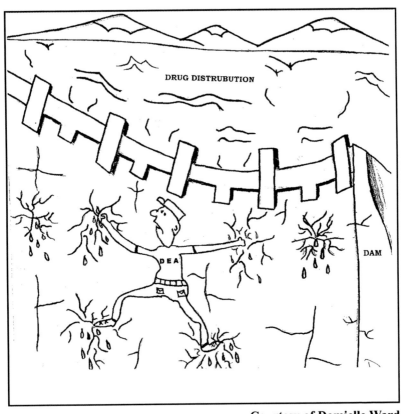

Courtesy of Damielle Ward

Should we Outlaw Alcohol, and even Tobacco, Altogether?

Given what you've read thus far, your knee-jerk reaction to this question about alcohol and tobacco might be yes! But as we think through this issue, we can see that outlawing alcohol and tobacco for adults would be a setup for disaster. Just look at the joke of Prohibition. For thirteen years, from 1920-33, it was illegal to sell and use alcohol. Once the laws regulating alcohol were removed, it became a commodity on the black market and overall, consumption rates probably never went down. And what a black market it was. Crime and corruption spiked, and Prohibition led to the creation of organized crime.

Can you imagine what kind of market we'd create if we tried this experiment again, but added tobacco, too?

Prohibition failed for cultural reasons. Alcohol and tobacco had been widely accepted substances, and not only in our country. Given the centuries long history of alcohol in most cultures, our society made accommodations to it, that is, we recognized its dangers, but maintained that the majority of people could consume alcohol without becoming addicted.

This accommodation makes sense. Today, we know that alcohol is a relatively weak addicting substance and 90% of people can consume it without becoming addicted. Prohibition ended in 1933, and while alcohol remains and always will be a problem for some individuals and families, at least our government regained some control of its sale and use.

The issue with tobacco is similar to alcohol in some ways, but important differences exist, too. Like alcohol, tobacco was a culturally acceptable substance among the indigenous peoples of the American continent. Later, it was introduced to the Europeans who settled here—and it certainly caught on. I can't help but snicker when I think that introducing Europeans to tobacco was an unintentional payback for the disease and deprivation that my ancestors introduced against them.

In the past, even many of the most conservative groups in our society accepted tobacco as the commonly used substance it was. Even today, some Amish communities grow and use tobacco, and these conservative religious people would never find drugs and alcohol acceptable. However, they think of tobacco as just another crop.

Throughout the world, the idea that tobacco is harmful didn't emerge until the 1960s and the notion of it being an addictive substance has been around only since the 1970s. Once information began emerging, it accumulated quickly, and we now recognize that tobacco is highly addictive and extremely dangerous. Given the harsh facts about tobacco, conventional wisdom would suggest that it should be completely outlawed. But again, that would be another disaster like Prohibition. Picture the tobacco mafias and cigarettes as a product on the black market. Currently, we have regulations on tobacco that can track its production, promotion, and sale. If we outlawed it, those regulations would disappear. And, finally, would you really want to draw important and limited law enforcement resources away from busting meth labs and crack dealers in order to pursue cigarette "criminals"?

Lessons Learned

Our experience with tobacco, from its wide acceptance to the bleak facts we now have, has taught us something we can apply elsewhere. For example, how have we achieved the progressive drop in smoking rates among adults since the 1970s? First, everyone in this country has become well educated about the dangers of tobacco use and the reality of nicotine addiction. Second, we've made great efforts to protect youngsters from access to tobacco, and more than ever, laws against selling tobacco products are enforced and cigarette vending machines are a thing of the past. Third, smoking is no longer "cool."

In 1976, I was invited to another doctor's home for a party. When I approached the front door of the home, I saw something very odd. He'd posted a sign on the door with the diplomatic request: "No smoking in our home, please." Wow, that was really stepping over the line, I thought, even for a doctor from California!

I wasn't a smoker and I appreciated this doctor's thinking, but the sign struck me as a big insult to smokers—a social faux pas. When I went inside though, I was relieved to see so many relaxed people, all socializing with each other, and of course, no smoke permeating the air. A week later, I tried a similar strategy with a smoker friend of mine, but I can't say his response was as positive. Today, smokers don't expect to smoke in a non-smoker's home.

Over the years we've seen the momentum tipping toward designated non-smoking areas. First, the smoke-free territory was noticeable by its demarcation, but now, in most of the country, we can enjoy museums, banks, many malls, virtually all public buildings, commercial aircraft, and most any restaurant without fear of breathing cigarette smoke.

When you think about it, within three decades or so our society went from considering smoking sexy and glamorous to thinking of it as an unhealthy addiction, which it is. Smokers find themselves gently (or not so gently) ostracized in social and work situations, which has been incentive enough for some to quit. Since they can't smoke at work and they can't smoke with friends in public spaces, the only place left is their homes. This atmosphere has definitively robbed smoking of its cool image.

Intensifying social pressure against smoking benefits all of us, but especially our children. Because a social taboo exists against tobacco use, fewer people try it at a young age and, therefore, fewer become addicted. We can't be overly encouraged, however. For example, some recent data on adolescent smoking indicates that these downward trends not only can change for the worse, but may already have.

Still, the dramatic shift in public attitudes about smoking, along with strict enforcement of underage use, gives us a model to embrace to prevent drug addiction. It's true that most Americans think that a taboo already exists against drugs, and they're right to an extent. However, as I'll explain later, our taboo against drugs is somewhat misplaced when it comes to young people.

Drug Prevention Programs are not Working

We've seen several school-based drug prevention programs used in various areas of the country. DARE (drug abuse resistance education) is the most notable. Unfortunately, the programs have shown disappointing results. In fact, one study suggested that more children used drugs *after* attending a DARE program! Criticisms of the program focused on the way in which it appeared to educate the kids to the "benefits" of drug use, that is, getting high. Of course, the participants learned the negative things too, but kids tend to retain certain information while conveniently forgetting the rest, especially if it spells out risks.

I think we can point to other reasons why drug prevention programs fail. First, if you consider that the imprinting effect of drugs such as alcohol and marijuana occurs so early, then children sometimes "choose" to use drugs without really being conscious of it. In particular, we see this with alcohol because kids and many adults don't think of it as a drug or even an addicting substance. Many people of all ages don't consider inhalants and marijuana as addicting.

Second, studies of child seductions by sexual predators shed light on early substance abuse. Although it's been tried many times, it's difficult to arm children with defenses that effectively protect them against predators. Research shows that sexual predators are simply too smart and will overcome the limited reasoning powers of children. This is why younger children must be supervised constantly against possible abuse, and we can apply the same idea to children immersed in a world filled with sophisticated, seductive media, along with peer persuasion. No amount of education alone can resist these forces.

Even though I just argued that these efforts haven't worked very well, I believe we should continue to enforce drug laws and educate children to resist drug use. But the evil power we are up against is too strong for education and law enforcement to fight alone.

Can we Allow Children to Make their own Decisions?

It amazes me to even think we would abdicate parental decisions to our children in such critical area as using various substances. It's silly to think that we can give our kids all the facts and then allow them to make up their own minds, and suggest, even believe, they will make the right decisions. However, this is a common assumption among many parents today.

The reason this argument for supplying information and trusting that kids will act responsibly is so wrong goes back to the facts about brain development in children. Remember that the adolescent brain more closely resembles a child's brain than that of an adult. Teenagers really are kids in adult bodies, and brain development is what makes the difference in maturity.

It stands to reason that if we turn over critical decisions to children they are more likely than not to make the wrong one. Beyond that, in terms of addiction, the consequences for a 12-year old becoming intoxicated for the first time, as compared to a 21-year old, are profoundly different. Therefore, parents who choose not to prevent drug and alcohol use in their children are, in essence, making an affirmative decision for their children to use, abuse, and become addicted. The influence of evil waits and watches, always ready for a vacuum.

Do Children have a Right to Privacy?

We Americans put great value on the right to privacy, and we go to great lengths to protect it. But I am perplexed that some argue that children have a right of privacy protection from their parents. With the exception of some crazy state laws that prevent parents from controlling a teenager's abortion, or even being notified about it, I'm unaware of any such legal protection for youngsters. The U.S. Constitution certainly makes no mention of minor children's privacy rights.

As a parent, you not only have a right to know what your child does, you have an obligation. When it comes to your kids, you need to know where they are, who they are with, what is on their computer, what is in their room, and anything else you deem important.

Yes, this attitude and practice creates tension between parents and children. But, if they have no choice but to communicate with you honestly and openly, you will be able to accommodate, at least to an extent, some of their desire for privacy. This parental policy is flexible. If you're satisfied with your child's level of honesty and openness, then you're free to relax the monitoring to whatever degree you're comfortable. Remember, however, that if they fail to provide adequate details about their activities or you know they're being deceptive, then you can escalate your monitoring, limit their freedom—or both.

When my kids were adolescents they protested this lack of privacy. However, my wife and I came back with a response based on the old Cold War adage, "trust but verify." Beyond that, we have always stressed the need to earn trust. To simply trust a human controlled by a juvenile mind is asking for trouble and disappointment, at least until such time they have proven their trustworthiness and reasonably good judgment. Both my experience and published statistics bear out the fact that kids know more and do more than their parents think they do.

A word of caution: when it comes to monitoring teenagers' correspondence and activities, don't *overreact* to what you may see or hear. Kids use language and engage in discussions that are coarser and more adult-like than you probably expect. I advise keeping quiet about those things and instead look for only the most serious and imminent threats. If you react to small issues, you will drive communication underground and you may miss chances to uncover the serious problems brewing. These would include potential sexual predators in some degree of contact with your child, your child's potential sexual activities, suicidal thoughts, or drug abuse. I provide information about ways to gather this information in a later chapter.

Points to Remember

• As parents we are failing to protect our children against drug addiction.

• Drug use is *not* a victimless crime.

• Enforcement of drug laws is helpful but not a solution.

• Drug prevention education is helpful but not a solution.

• It is up to you, the parent, to make the final decisions on serious matters regarding your kids.

• You have a right and an obligation to know everything in your child's life that may be potentially harmful.

8

Moral Character

As you may have noticed, in the realm of addiction prevention, we rarely hear discussions about the concept of moral character. Instead, education tends to command the lion's share of attention. However, I believe character is critically important in this discussion. After all, if learning about the dangers of drugs and alcohol were enough, the addiction problems we have today wouldn't exist.

Perhaps the varied voices discussing addiction today steer away from the concept of character because it is difficult to define, primarily because individual and even group value systems differ greatly. For example, some parents might think it's a good idea to put their 15-year-old daughters on birth control pills because they anticipate that these girls are likely to engage in premarital sex. According to my value system, though, this would be a bad idea. Still, despite disagreements, we must find ways to discuss moral character development and apply the concept to drug abuse and preventing addiction.

A Working Definition

The best definition of character that I've come across was a line in a speech delivered by former Congressman J.C. Watts: *"Character is doing the right thing when nobody's looking."* I realize Watts was paraphrasing any number of people who have expressed this idea in one way or another.

But to me, the phrase shows tremendous insight and provides a quick and clear image of the way we can make decisions that reflect on our moral character. Further, in order to understand what constitutes character in decision making, we must understand the motivation behind our life decisions.

Motivation: What Drives our Decisions?

For purposes of this discussion, I'll break down decision making into three motivational processes. First, we can make a decision based on a reward. If you take advantage of a sale to buy a table at 30% off the regular price, your decision is *reward driven*. Second, if you decide to drive within the speed limits because you don't want a speeding ticket, your decision is *punishment avoidance driven*. Third, if your decision involves neither reward nor punishment avoidance, but rather, is based on what is right or better; that is, what is moral, then your decision is considered *character driven*.

A business associate once told me a story about a large sum of money that had been erroneously deposited into her bank account. She boasted about "playing it smart," which she defined as not withdrawing the money, but at the same time, not notifying the bank about the error either. She chose to wait, and if after an extended period of time the error went undiscovered, she would withdraw the money. She rationalized that since the bank made the mistake, she couldn't be prosecuted. Unfortunately, at least from her point of view, the bank discovered the error and removed the money.

Still, this woman seemed quite pleased with herself for "almost" getting away with keeping money that didn't belong to her. Clearly, she was driven to make decisions based on reward and punishment avoidance, not character. It also became apparent that we shared totally different value systems. She put value on being "clever" and keeping something that wasn't hers, as long as punishment wasn't involved. Given the same situation, my values would lead me to report the error and return the money to its rightful owner. Needless to say, I didn't do business with this woman again.

I'm not suggesting there's anything necessarily wrong with making decisions motivated by reward or avoiding punishment. We all make everyday, mundane choices based on those motivations. The issue arises when such considerations conflict with and win out over character-driven motivations. If I were to spend $50 so my wife and I can attend a symphony concert, my reward-driven decision doesn't conflict with any moral concerns. On the other hand, if I were to spend the $50 to buy illegal drugs to get high, my motivation for reward would conflict with my value system, which holds that such behavior is immoral and doesn't reflect good character. It goes without saying that when these conflicts occur, character-driven decisions should win the day.

The Source of Moral Authority

In recent decades, it's been trendy or "fashionable" for people to define their own morality. Superficially anyway, the 1960s brought us the notion that if something feels right or feels good, then it must be morally good. Of course, most people understand that this attitude has failed our society in the past, and common sense tells us that without laws or social norms we can expect only chaos. Many cite the decade of 1960s, which, among other things, included rapidly evolving drug use and the so-called sexual "revolution," as what drive many moral problems we face in our society today. It is clear that morality must be based on something other than our individual whims.

Since we know that "making it up as we go along" doesn't work, then clearly we all need some type of authority from which we can derive our sense of morality. For thousands of years that moral authority for Jews and Christians has centered around the Ten Commandments. In fact, laws in most countries today are either derived from or are similar to The Ten Commandments. For me, I choose the teachings of the Holy Bible, especially those of my Lord, Jesus Christ. If you want to make moral character-driven decisions, you need an authority; just "doing your own thing" doesn't cut it, because without an authority to draw from, your decision making will inevitably be driven only by reward or punishment avoidance.

For those without religious beliefs, as well as for those who do, we can look to another moral authority of a sort. We call that authority the morality of mutual consideration, or what we normally think of as the Golden Rule: "Do unto others as you would have them do unto you." Atheists, agnostics, and believers alike should know that the golden rule is addressed in the Bible. Matthew 7:12 quotes Jesus as saying, "Therefore, whatever you want others to do for you, do also the same for them—this is the Law and the Prophets."

So, if you are ever unsure that a decision is moral and character driven, ask yourself how you would feel if another person made the same decision and it might affect you. The golden rule represents an important "litmus test," as the saying goes, and my—former—business associate failed it.

And Then We have a Conscience . . .

We can consider moral character an attitude, a set of beliefs, or a state of mind. But, what good is moral character if there is nothing to propel it into action? However, God instilled in us the *potential* to act, and when we fulfill this capacity we call it a *conscience.*

Of course, not everyone has a conscience, and we have a term for them, *sociopath*. Ted Bundy, the infamous serial killer, is a classic example of a sociopath. Bundy and others like him lack care or concern for the feelings of others. Sociopaths are unable to empathize with others, and even lack the ability to feel sympathy for animals or humans. Though every sociopath is not a murderer, most "cold blooded" murders are sociopaths, especially serial killers. Needless to say, our prisons are full of sociopaths. Since sociopaths have no conscience, they certainly have no moral character either.

I'm not suggesting that all drug addicts are sociopaths; in fact, most are not. But I am suggesting that strength of character and the conscience within it functions as a powerful resistance against addiction and the crimes that seem to go with it.

A Closer Look at Conscience

Character-driven decision making is nothing without a conscience and a conscience is nothing without a moral compass, that is, the moral character to direct it. Because it's an abstract concept, it can be difficult to find the right words to define a conscience. I prefer to define conscience as that "inner voice" that speaks to us when you consider stepping outside of our personally defined, moral boundaries. Another definition is our moral-centering process.

In chapter 4 I discussed the conscious and unconscious brain, and with regard to drug addiction, we know that *conscious will* is often trumped by *unconscious* brain functions, because it is our nature to be motivated by reward or avoidance of punishment. This becomes important for youngsters who begin to experiment with drugs. As the drugs begin to reprogram the pleasure center of the brain, their lives become seriously *reward driven*, meaning that they are driven to seek the reward of euphoria (getting high). They also must avoid being caught because of family, school or job, and legal repercussions, which means they are driven by their desire to avoid punishment. However, if they've developed moral character and a conscience is activated, then we hope these adolescents will respond to that inner voice, the conscience, and stop using addicting substances before it's too late.

Character and Walls of Protection Against Addiction

Earlier information presented showed that the "first wall" of protection in preventing drug addiction is *delay of first use of a drug (or first intoxication with alcohol)*, ideally until age 21, but at least to age 18. When this occurs, you and your children have a good statistical chance of escaping the hell of drug addiction.

As described earlier, the "second wall" of protection is *social awareness and societal taboo.* Through a combination of social standards and education our children come to the realization that, like smoking, underage drinking and drug use are bad for them.

Character development is the "third wall" of protection. Social awareness, societal taboo, and character development serve to augment the first wall of protection by helping youngsters to avoid first use. Also, if they begin experimenting with alcohol, tobacco or drugs at a later age, character will help increase their resistance to the psychological addiction that may occur.

Facing Facts

How many adolescents leave home, either to attend college or to otherwise begin an adult lifestyle, without experimenting with alcohol? By my estimate, more than 95% will experiment with alcohol as part of their transition to adult life, and some will try tobacco and pot, too. I know that this sounds like an astounding percentage, but it is not an exaggeration. I even hear reports that very conservative, religious colleges see use of alcohol and tobacco among students. I advise parents who feel sure that their youngster is not among them to think again. When it comes to alcohol, the prevalence, social pressure and allure are far too strong for all but the most resistant kids, and the same is true, at least to some extent for tobacco and pot. So, as a parent, don't feel like a failure if your adolescent experiments at this stage. Nonetheless, I maintain that of those who delay drinking to age 18-21, who consider drugs to be a social taboo, and who have good character, relatively few will ever become alcoholics or drug addicts.

Character: The Gift that Keeps on Giving

If you can accept my contention that your "angels" are likely to experiment with alcohol when they reach college, enter the military, or otherwise live independently (around 18 or so), then you must share my anxiety about other things they are likely to do once out of your control. However, if you have done your job to build character and conscience in your children, then as older teens and young adults they are more likely to choose less addicting substances like alcohol over more addicting substances. It follows, too, that they will use these substances less frequently and will tend to choose to avoid intoxication, which may lead to dangerous or unacceptable behavior. As adolescents continue to mature they will pass through the experimentation stage and grow into adulthood as no more than occasional, social users of alcohol—at most. This should be *your* goal as a parent in raising your children.

How to Build Character in Your Child

My initial advice to those who are thinking about having children is straightforward: Don't have children unless you're prepared for the long and daily commitment to raising them.

This includes maintaining a loving, stable marriage as well as spending plenty of time with your spouse and children. Don't ever forget that parents are made for children, not children for parents.

We've already discussed the immature, undeveloped newborn brain. The newborn's "world view" is limited, too. As babies we have no direct control over our environment. However, we quickly discover that our every need can be easily met through communicating our pleasure and displeasure to our parents. Newborns have the perspective that they are the "center of the universe," which at this stage is as it should be.

As young children mature and develop, it's important that they learn that while they're loved and important, they are no longer the center of the universe and that others have needs and priorities too. Sometimes others' needs or desires have a higher priority than theirs. Many parents find this transition difficult. In fact, I've seen (and you may have, too) parents who continue to consider the needs and desires of their children above their own and all others—and even after their kids reach adulthood.

More than that, parents often insulate children from the consequences of their (negative) actions. You know what I mean. They may believe that classroom problems are the teacher's fault and later, they go to any length to keep their kids out of legal trouble. At home, they may brush off bad conduct and fail to punish the behavior. As a result, these children may never learn self-discipline or respect for authority.

So, as children mature they must be taught to respect the needs and desires of other individuals, and children should *expect* to be punished for bad behavior. This is the first step toward character development.

Discipline is Essential

To understand discipline in the context of preventing addiction, we need to again consider the pleasure center of the brain, the Ventral Tegmental Area (VTA) (discussed in chapter 4). Specifically, our Creator designed us with a built-in learning system to ensure that we will both behave in ways that promote survival and avoid behavior that could cause harm. In general, behavior that is good for survival stimulates the VTA, which makes us want to repeat the behavior. These behaviors could include eating, play activities, giving or receiving praise, the simple act of taking a warm bath, and so forth. Conversely, actions that don't promote survival tend to make us uncomfortable or may even cause pain. These include things like skipping meals, not wearing a coat in cold weather, picking up a hot cooking pot with bare hands, or being spanked.

Addicting drugs stimulate the VTA to extreme and artificial pleasure levels, so extreme that we can fall into a vicious feedback cycle through which our brain drives us to pursue pleasure from drugs above all other behaviors. Once the feedback cycle is established, the addict is driven to use drugs repetitively and at higher and higher doses, while at the same time ignoring the survival mechanism of the VTA. Therefore, when the pleasure center interacts with addicting drugs, its ultimate purpose is distorted, and rather than working for our betterment, the VTA can destroy us. It all depends on how we use it.

As a parent I chose to use or even exploit VTA properties to teach my children to behave well, have good self-discipline, and good character. It is my contention, and there is research to support it, that parental failure in this area will lead young people to early drug experimentation and ultimately to addiction.

Let's get Psychological

In psychological terms, we experience *positive reinforcement* when environmental stimuli affect the VTA and cause pleasure. When stimuli make us uncomfortable or cause pain, we experience *negative reinforcement.* These results are also referred to as reward and punishment.

Earlier, I said that decision-making is driven by either reward, avoidance of pain or good moral character. However, young children have immature brains and thus lack the intellect to have developed character, so they can't use good moral character to guide their choices. Therefore, at young ages, children can only respond to reward and punishment.

As they mature, it's important to work through reward and punishment to properly shape the behavior of your children. I see many parents try to appeal to their very young children's rationale intellect or even character for proper behavior. These parents may lecture, convince, appeal to, or otherwise beg the young child to "act" right. These "strategies" fail in young children for the simple reason that their immature brains can't function through intellect, much less any aspect of character.

Consequently, young children (even under 2-years old) must be taught good behavior (discipline) through clear, concrete instructions and boundaries oriented toward their level of maturity. Just as concretely, young children should know exactly what punishment they will receive if they do not comply. By the same token, they should receive reward for delivering the acceptable behavior you have clearly defined.

As children mature to early school age, it becomes increasingly important to teach values and associate them with reward and punishment. For example, you can reward children for good academic performance or punish them when they fail to complete important school tasks like homework. In the process of rewarding or punishing, it makes sense to teach your youngster the importance of a good education (according to your value system), and, therefore, the need to study and perform well in academics.

You can teach other important values such as honesty, courtesy, respect and similar values that children in this age group can understand. Begin discussions about proper sexual behavior and the need to avoid alcohol, drugs, and tobacco on this basic level, with the emphasis on values. In addition, I recommend that you avoid detailed explanations about what drugs do or even why people use them. Simply make it clear how bad, dangerous, and "uncool" they are.

When my eldest daughter was quite young, about age four, we worked hard on the tobacco issue. Consequently, we encountered a few embarrassing public situations in which she would point to an adult who was smoking and say, "Yuck, he's smoking!" Nevertheless, the embarrassment was worth it because today she's an adult who does not use tobacco.

When children reach adolescence, your emphasis should transition from reward and punishment to moral character, based on values as well as rational decision making. This is the time that children are much better prepared neurologically to digest and understand why drugs and other poor decisions like premarital sex are bad ideas. First, they should be taught how it violates your family's value system. Second, they should be taught the "whys" and "hows" of certain bad behaviors and instructed about the likely bad outcomes. You can provide real life examples of others who have suffered such bad outcomes from bad decisions.

How do I Invoke Reward and Punishment?

We all like to be rewarded for our behavior. In an ideal world we could simply reward good behavior and our children would never do anything wrong. But, kids are humans, too. Like you and me, they want to work as little as possible, be rewarded as much as possible, and do what they want when they want. So, no matter how you try to motivate your kids with reward, they will either test your limits or simply cut corners in what is expected of them. This means that to be effective parents, we must be able to use punishment as well as reward. Because a purely punishment-oriented system works no better than a purely reward-oriented system, a balance of the two is necessary.

The following represents the most effective approach, adjusting for age and maturity:

• Remove all unnecessary pleasures, i.e., games, electronics, transportation.

• Tell your children exactly what your expectations are with regard to behavior, school work and performance, chores, and anything else you think is important.

• Clearly define both rewards and punishments. The rewards should include foregoing the nonessential pleasures listed above, which to them is like giving certain privileges back to you. The punishments should be severe enough and long enough that your children will be unlikely to violate your "agreement." They need to know that they will pay a significant price for noncompliance.

• The rewards should be given *only* after the desired behavior has been completed.

• Other conditions established to receive rewards and avoid punishment should involve character issues, such as honesty, integrity, fairness, and so forth.

• Kids should have the burden of proof for everything. This stance tends to extinguish any thoughts of "gaming" the system and making you defensive about your reward and punishment decisions and judgments.

The Protest I've Heard so Many Times

"I have tried reward and punishment but it doesn't work on my child." I can't count the number of times I've heard this from frustrated and failing parents, and I've come up with four common reasons that parents fail.

• Parents fail to remove the unnecessary pleasures first, so the kids still get everything they want without good behavior. Their unnecessary pleasure items and privileges are then removed only after the frustrated parents get angry and decide to punish.

• Parents fail to show self-discipline. Typically, the children are given access to their unnecessary pleasures because parents lack the will and self-discipline to resist their kids' nagging.

• Parents become too sympathetic to their children and give in to their requests or demands even though they don't deserve these rewards or pleasures.

• Parents have been unable or unwilling to require that their kids respect their parental authority.

It's been my experience that the more consistently you use this system, the sooner your youngster will begin to comply. If you persist, maintain the system, and you stay patient, it becomes easier to sustain these practices. After the kids learn the system, they usually become comfortable with it and it becomes like a game to them—and kids love games. If you play it right, you *all* win.

What about Spanking?

Spanking children is a controversial issue, with studies showing conflicting results. I was spanked as a child and believe it was done with love. I credit spanking with having helped protect me, instill self-discipline, and helped to build my character. I have also occasionally spanked all four of my kids when they were younger. As adults, my wife and I enjoy a close, loving relationship with them. We're very proud of all four of them, and none have addiction problems.

Studies show that despite what some "experts" say against spanking, most parents spank their kids from time to time. However, a full discussion of the pros and cons and techniques of spanking are outside the scope of this book, but a number of books on raising children do discuss the subject.

Parents must have Character and Self Respect, Too

Today, it's a commonly held view that children are more influenced by their peers than their parents. This is true when it comes to momentary decisions. Peers greatly influence sudden decisions to take risks and even such short-term decisions as "what to wear." However, studies also show that parents have far more influence on long-term social, religious, political, and character attitudes of kids than peers or teachers. Studies show something even more important. Children are more influenced by their parents' *behavior* than what their parents teach them. In other words, parents must "walk the walk, not just talk the talk."

I know firsthand that this can be difficult at times. My mother preached to me about not smoking, although she smoked heavily. That looked like an obvious contradiction, and I didn't understand until I could grasp that she was addicted to tobacco.

Most young people have similar trouble understanding certain things. How can you expect your teenager to avoid drinking or becoming intoxicated if you do? How can you expect your child to attend church if you don't? If you deal with people dishonestly, don't be surprised if your children do the same. Finally, if you treat your own parents or other family members badly, don't be surprised if your kids follow suit.

Remember that some day you may look forward to your children's visits when you're in a retirement center or a nursing home. So, live your life today as you would have your children live theirs now and in the future. Chances are, they will do as you do.

Conscience Development

Recently, my 24-year old daughter made a comment about her "inner voice." She said that whenever she considers doing something that her mother wouldn't approve of, she can hear her mother's voice saying, "don't do it," or "be careful," and so forth. Far more verbal than I, my wife took every opportunity over the years to teach our kids about good character. She considered every problem, disappointment, or question as an opportunity for moral teaching. Sure, these impromptu sessions often were met with rolled eyes, inpatient "yes, moms," or outright indignation. At the time it seemed that just about everything either of us said "went in one ear and out the other," as the saying goes. However, we've been surprised that as our children have reached adulthood and are successful in their lives, we hear our words spoken back to us like a delayed echo. My wife and I marvel that some of our character-related statements come back to us in the exact phrases we used when the kids were growing up. We suspect they can't remember where they even heard many of these "pearls of wisdom" that seem to guide their lives today.

What we know is that our children remember well the lessons we taught them daily, and beyond that, they have incorporated these moral teachings into their lives. Often my college-student son will say, "Dad, remember when you told me about ___? Now I see what you meant." That blank could be filled in with any number of issues.

Lately, as friend after friend show signs of addiction, my

son points out that he can now see the things that I had warned him about. Some of his friends now have DUI citations, or have been admitted to drug treatment centers, and some have overdosed. Thankfully, all those years of conscience and character development are paying off for him and our other kids. *The inner voice—the conscience—is so important.*

Points to Remember
- Moral character is doing the right thing for the right reasons.
- Character is one of the three important walls of protection against addiction.
- A conscience, respect for others and self, and discipline are important in character development.
- Spanking is a legitimate part of disciplining children.
- Parents will fail to teach character if they do not live in moral character.

9

Parental Practices
and Preventing Addiction

Nothing is more misunderstood today than the concept of self-esteem and ways to build it in children. "Wikipedia" aptly defines *self-esteem* (self-worth, ego strength) as a person's subjective appraisal of himself or herself as intrinsically positive or negative to some degree. As the common myth goes, parents have an obligation to constantly shower their children with all kinds of praise, deserved or not. By extension, it's somehow considered good to indoctrinate kids with the idea that they are equal to all people in all things—or perhaps even better.

The preoccupation with self-esteem appears to have begun in the 1960s, along with many other changes in our society. I can speculate that misinterpreting the phrase "all men are created equal," which Thomas Jefferson included in the Declaration of Independence, may have contributed to the problem, especially when combined with other thoughts about equality. However, Jefferson intended this statement to be interpreted figuratively, not literally. He meant that citizens in this country should be given an *equal* opportunity to succeed, not a guarantee that all actually would succeed in equal measure.

Though this idea of Jefferson's was a great platitude, we know today, that Jefferson and other patriarchs had "built in" exceptions to this idea. For example, certain groups, i.e. African-Americans and women, have not enjoyed this status of equality until recent years. We hope that through the laws and social changes that have taken place since the 1960s we can edit Jefferson and say today that truly, all men and women are created equal.

As a practical matter, equality of opportunity works differently. For example, as I'm sure we all agree, children who compete for a position on a baseball team or enter a science fair should have an equal chance to win. Logically, we know that some kids have more natural intelligence than others and some are more athletic than others. We also know that some kids are more motivated and some are better prepared than others among their peers. If the contest or test is judged fairly, the child with the best results will win, no matter the level of ability going in or the degree of effort. The same principle applies to adults in work situations. When conditions are fair, the person with the better resume or work history will likely get the job or promotion.

When it comes to the worthy things in life that must be earned, we are anything but equal in our abilities or even potential. Furthermore, there is no guarantee that the person who tries the hardest will win. We are all born with certain abilities or potential—and lack of abilities, too—that may either help or prevent us from successfully competing against others in various areas. So, while we don't have equal ability, motivation, or work ethic, in this country we're born with the expectation of equal *opportunity* to be successful. It is what we do with this opportunity that sets us apart from one another. Most of us logically conclude that we gain our competitive edge when we exploit our personal abilities and assets.

So, given the reality that we're not guaranteed equal success, our challenge as parents involves helping our children grow into adulthood with good self-esteem (ego strength). Children who are told they are "no good" or "not good enough to succeed" will begin to believe it. Furthermore, even without being told, if children continuously experience failure in their pursuits, they will believe that they as individuals are failures. Eventually, they probably stop trying, which leads to judging themselves as "losers," or as having low self-esteem.

It's critical that parents assist their children to build self-esteem as they grow and develop. However, it's ineffective to simply convince kids that they are just as good in all things as their peers, coaches, teachers, and others. For example, I knew of a boy on a local Little League team, who wanted to pitch (the position players most admire), but he had very little pitching ability. The coach observed that the boy ran fast and could catch the ball quite well, so well that he saw his potential to be an all-star outfielder some day. Therefore, the coach played him at center field to take advantage of his abilities.

This should have turned out well for everyone involved, but the father convinced the boy that he was as good, if not better, than any pitcher on the team, so the kid insisted on pitching periodically. Predictably, tension developed between the coach, the player, and the dad over this issue. Over time, the child refused to develop his center field skills but continued to "cop an attitude" about the coach's unwillingness to allow him to pitch.

During one game the coach reluctantly put the boy in to pitch, with embarrassing results all around because the boy performed very poorly. More than that, these distractions and his bad attitude meant that he never really developed as a center fielder—he just didn't try. Whenever he played poorly or made a mistake, he and his father blamed the coach or other team members. Of course, the boy's self-esteem plummeted because he didn't live up to his father's unrealistic expectations, plus he believed his father's love was conditioned upon his playing ability.

Eventually, this boy quit playing baseball and later became involved in drug use. This is sad because he had such potential as a ballplayer. Had his father raised him properly, he probably would have excelled as a center fielder and thus, developed good self-esteem.

Good Self-Esteem is a Product of Success

When you tell children they are good or successful at something when they're not, one of two things will happen. On one hand, they won't believe you, and they discount what you say because they know otherwise, or they will believe you and become delusional about their capabilities in that area. The delusional response is the worst outcome because kids will keep attempting to perform or boast that they can do things they aren't capable of.

As an owner of a medical practice and several businesses, I have seen this phenomenon a number of times. For example, job applicants will sometimes make various claims of abilities that they sincerely believe they have. However, once they have the job, their inability to perform the job they were hired for is revealed. At that point, these employees will either be offered a lesser position or be terminated. This unfortunate situation doesn't benefit anyone. Eventually, these employees may conclude that they aren't capable of performing well in any position, so they don't pursue other jobs that do match their skills. Naturally, these individuals suffer from low self-esteem.

So, when raising your children, it's not important what *you say* they can do, it is important what *they know* they can do.

What You Can do to Build your Children's Self-Esteem

What I said above helps clarify important things you can say to your children to begin the process of building their self-esteem. First, and most important, tell them and show them constantly that you *love and value* them greatly. It's essential that they know this love is based on nothing but the fact that they are your kids. Children need to know that your love *cannot and need not be earned*, and that they can't do anything to lose it. In other words, they have your *unconditional* love.

The way kids feel about themselves begins with their perception of the way their parents value them. As discussed in chapter 8, proper ego development requires a balanced perspective of kids' importance relative to their peers, adults, and other authority figures.

Next, youngsters need guidance in their journey toward finding the things they can do well. Help them identify these abilities and encourage them to develop them further. If they appear good at certain sports, encourage them to excel in this area. If they show potential in music, encourage them to develop it. If they're good at spelling, encourage them to enter spelling bees. Emphasize and cultivate the things they do well and give them recognition for what they do. Don't mislead them to think that they excel in things they really don't.

In addition, it's just as important that you identify children's *weaknesses* as their strengths. Kids, being very perceptive, know what they are "dumb" at. If they can't identify it themselves, their peers will do an excellent job of pointing it out. Besides, what good is it to emphasize things they do well when the other things they do poorly already negatively affect their self-esteem? This is why weaknesses also need attention. Identifying weaknesses is most important in academic areas, because parents can intervene and work with their children directly or bring in a tutor to help bring about improvement. Give your kids praise for any small academic accomplishments in these weak areas.

While it's true that your children may never excel in weak areas, they will probably improve enough to at least be competitive. Furthermore, I recall a number of instances in which kids worked on their weak academic subjects, only to find themselves, surprisingly, beginning to excel in these classes.

One of my daughters struggled during her pre-adolescent and adolescent school years because of ADD (Attention Deficit Disorder). Her situation affected her self-esteem so much that she began to show behavior problems, and some of her peers took every opportunity to point out her weaknesses, both real and manufactured. My wife and I became discouraged, too, and began to give up expectations that she'd ever go to college, much less earn a degree. However, we tried to encourage her and we made arrangements to get her special counseling and tutoring.

Over a period of weeks and months we began to see small slivers of progress. We felt very encouraged and gave her plenty of praise for this progress. As months extended into years, her progress and academic performance began to accelerate, and she was even given the opportunity to mentor younger children. This lifted her self-esteem considerably, and as a dividend to all her progress, her behavior began to improve, too. Today, not only is she a college graduate and a statuesque beauty, but she's working on her doctorate in clinical psychology. And she plans to counsel children who experience the same trials she went through.

To be effective, the important process of building self-esteem in children must be done appropriately and with the knowledge that it requires a constant show of unconditional love, as well as enhancing strengths and shoring up weaknesses. In addition, to be effective, this process must be carried out in small steps. A child's self-esteem builds gradually and over time with small, genuine successes. Finally, it's important to praise children for all their large and small accomplishments. Don't offer underserved praise, but always show them love without reservation.

Money is Dangerous for Young People

Today, money appears to have important influence on drug experimentation, and ultimately, addiction. First of all, when kids have money, it's easier to buy alcohol, tobacco, and later on, drugs; second, money gives youngsters a false sense of empowerment and entitlement.

As I interact with families in my medical practice, I am amazed at the attitudes some adolescents maintain about what they think their parents owe them in term of material things. Even among lower income families, many kids feel entitled to cars, designer clothes, cell phones, and cash—and some think the top-of-line makes and brands of these things are their due as well. These expectations are usually driven by a "keeping up with the Jones'" mentality, not necessarily a true desire for these things.

Based on my observation, the more parents respond to these demands, the more kids escalate their demands and the worse their attitudes become. As they accumulate stuff, their attitudes reflect an increasing sense of snobbery, self-importance, and false empowerment. In most cases, the parents are barely getting by, yet they respond by complying with these outlandish requests, all as part of an effort to prove their love. I've seen parents go to great lengths to provide these material things, including sinking further into debt and taking on second and even third jobs. The kids end up with more stuff, but less and less time with their parents.

As a consequence of this cycle that characterizes a materialistic upbringing, kids begin to love things instead of people. They may lose any sense of a family bond and love, and this leads to extreme self-centeredness. This cycle is costly in several ways. For one thing, some adolescents become bored with the way material things make them feel. Since their family relationships have broken down, they can't turn to parents and other family members, but these teenagers still want other things that make them feel good. This is what leads directly to experimentation with addicting chemicals. Initially, they may turn to alcohol and perhaps marijuana, but eventually tolerance and boredom develop with these introductory chemicals, so then, at least in some cases, they move on to crack, heroin, or crystal meth. The cycle of materialism can result in this sad outcome.

On the other Hand . . . Money can be Good, Too

Zig Ziglar, the famous humorist, salesman, and Christian speaker once said, "I have had money, and I have not had money, and I like having money better." Many others have expressed the same idea, and there is no question that life is easier in our society if you have enough money to enjoy basic pleasures. Remember, though, that money is merely a medium by which we exchange goods and services. Money itself is neutral, neither good nor bad; only attitudes and the way we use money can be judged as good or bad.

The Bible expresses concern about our attitudes toward money. For example, 1 Timothy 6:10 states: *"For the love of money is a root of all kinds of evil."* On the other hand, Christians willingly give money to their churches, foreign mission work, and various charities. So we can use money for good or evil. Since you must have money to live in our society, nothing is wrong with earning and accumulating it, as long as you maintain a wise attitude about it and use it accordingly. It's particularly unwise to give money to youngsters to spend on substances that can lead to their destruction.

As a parent, you have an obligation to provide your children with the material things necessary for daily living—basic nutritious food, clothing, school, and transportation. To the extent you can afford them, these should be good quality things and not just the bare minimum. In today's society, transportation may include a car at the proper age. However, the car and other items don't need to be "fancy" and the kids don't need all the upgrades. Those are the things that foster a materialistic attitude.

Teenagers who want "more and better" can earn these desired things either by work you give them or through a job. In addition, once kids buy an item it should be their responsibility to maintain and repair it, at least to the extent possible. These are important guidelines for both poor and wealthy families.

As a physician and business owner I've been able to increase my earning power over the years. Like Zig, I know what it's like to be poor, but I also know the benefits of increasing my income. Because of my range of experiences, I believe that my attitude toward money is both balanced and respectful. It's my responsibility to impart this attitude to my children rather than giving them the frivolous things that kids like to have. So, although my wife and I can afford to give our kids nice material things like boats, fancy ATVs, motorcycles, and sports cars, we would never buy them.

Because we can provide certain things, our kids have basic, late model cars, nice clothes, and fully-funded educations. However, they all had to earn spending money, either through chores at home or from outside jobs. We have found that when kids earn money rather than having it handed to them, they respect it more and spend it wisely.

This arrangement works very well within my family. I don't feel pressured to buy unreasonable things and my kids are eager to earn their own money. They also appreciate what they have and they know their mother and I love them—and we feel their love for us as well. Finally, my kids respect money and what is required to acquire it far too much to go out and waste it on drugs or tobacco, at least so far.

Kids and True Compassion

It's my contention that parents often do certain things for their kids based on what they think of as compassion, yet these are not really compassionate acts at all. Conversely, some things that truly are compassionate may be viewed as mean and "heartless" by others.

To illustrate, we can look at addicts' families, many of whom have had to learn the lessons of compassion in painful ways. Their experiences with the addict, along with their involvement with treatment centers and Al-Anon, have taught them that "helping" addicts is often hurting them. A wife who covers for her alcoholic husband by calling in sick to his job is a classic example, as are parents who manipulate the legal system to avoid punishment for their drug-using teenager. Sometimes bosses think they're being compassionate by cutting their poor-performing addicted employees some slack. In each case the family or boss is trying to help, but these actions hurt addicts by insulating them from the things that may provide motivation to get help and stop using.

As an addiction continues its downward spiral, the progression of the disease accelerates unless something interrupts it. That something usually comes in the form of being fired after showing up late for work yet again, or getting another DUI or other legal citation. Any number of problems can befall addicts. As bad as these consequences seem at the time, they may be the only hope families have that their addicted loved ones will be motivated or even forced to accept help.

If a family member, boss, or friend deflects or blunts the impact of these consequences, this not only often delays an addict's willingness to accept treatment and possible redemption, but may contribute to delaying help so long that the person will be past help and die.

Too often, the idea of compassion is defined as how you feel when you do something for somebody. In other words, if *you* feel good when you do something you perceive as good for another person, then you are being compassionate. However, when dealing with addicts, what feels good to you may actually contribute to worsening their condition. Addiction treatment experts call this behavior *enabling*, and a person who engages in the behavior is called an *enabler.*

Experience has shown that we learn to enable the addictions of our friends, families, and co-workers gradually over time. This process appears to result from an evolving dynamic between the addict's unconscious mind, which seeks to deceive him and those around him, and the natural desire of other people to be helpful and caring. A vicious cycle emerges, and addicts unconsciously and subtly train enablers in how to enable. In turn, the enablers make addicts sicker by tacitly or actively insulating them from the negative consequences of their addiction.

So, does making the addict worse sound like a compassionate act? You might agree that it doesn't, but millions of friends, family, and co-workers engage in enabling behavior that brings downward spiraling results. However, many change their behavior once they learn that they actually harm the addict. Sadly, many enablers, especially close family members, will continue to enable behavior until their loved ones die from their addictions.

Enabling may Begin Before the Addiction

Understanding enabling is a critical step in preventing addiction because enabling dynamics between parents and children may begin well before the kids use any addicting substances. For this reason, you must analyze your relationships with your children to see if enabling already takes place in your home. This is a serious examination, too, because enabling increases the chances of early drug use and, therefore, addiction. Perhaps you don't think you're an enabler, but on the other hand, given what you've read so far, you may question some of your actions. The questions below will help you determine if you're engaging in enabling behavior right now.

• When your children get in trouble in school, do you believe them when they tell you that the reports are false, that all those other people are telling lies?

• When you receive reports that your children are behaving badly, do you believe them when they claim other kids led them into it?

• When your children talk about conflicts with teachers, do you take their side?

• When your children perform poorly on a test, do you believe their story that somehow or another it was the teacher's fault?

• When you receive a report that your child attacked another child or damaged property, do you believe his or her denials?

• When your children are arrested for DUI, do you believe them when they say it isn't their fault?

• When your children fail a drug test, do you believe them when they tell you that there was a mistake—that the test is wrong?

If your answer was yes to any of the above questions, chances are you're enabling your kids, at least to some degree.

Yes, of course it's possible that your youngster is telling the truth in a particular situation. However, the point is that you should investigate the situation, but be skeptical of your child's claims. Always remember that children have great motivation to deceive parents.

Of the seven questions above, I have dealt with the first five on more than one occasion. Each time, the burden was on the kids to prove the allegations wrong. In every case, I discovered that the kids were at least partly responsible for the situation in which they were accused of some wrongdoing. Even more importantly, however, I credit my skepticism as responsible, at least in part, for never having received reports on the last two questions. If you asked my kids about this, they'd tell you that they knew punishment would be swift and severe, and only hard proof would convince me of their innocence.

My experience with other families dealing with these situation leads me to believe that almost without question, parents usually believe their children. It baffles me that parents can be so naïve. Doesn't healthy skepticism seem more reasonable? Yet, because they want to believe their children are honest, they prefer to stay in this state of parental naiveté. In addition, parents may feel disloyal if they suspect their kids are lying. Unfortunately, this begins the enabling cycle because kids are assured of parental protection, and they don't experience the consequences of their actions. Meanwhile, the parents stay deluded about their youngsters' behavior.

As my sons transitioned from middle school through high school, I was able to witness this phenomenon up close. My boys were involved in several minor incidents involving other kids. Once we were notified, we immediately grounded the boys and monitored them closely for a significant period of time after the punishment ended. Their cohorts in "crime" often received little or no punishment and some parents thought the whole thing was humorous or of little consequence. In some cases my wife and I were criticized for being too strict.

Today, some of these parents are struggling with severe behavior problems involving their adult offspring. These problems include DUIs, alcohol-related car accidents, and even prison sentences. I can assure you that these parents now find nothing about their current situation comical or inconsequential. Despite all that has happened, most of these parents continue to enable their drug-addicted children.

Trust me, covering for your kids, lying for them, or running interference to get them out of trouble is only going to enable them to get into bigger trouble later. When that happens, you will be much less able to help them.

Protecting your Children from the Wrong Crowd

The idea of the "wrong crowd" has been with us for many years. I usually chuckle when I hear parents refer to their kids' problems as related to hanging out with the wrong crowd. I may have used the phrase myself. Don't forget that while you're claiming that other kids negatively influence your children, other parents are probably saying the same thing about your kids!

In all seriousness, though, from the standpoint of behavior and addiction, negative peer influence is a real problem. The difficulty is that we tend to under-appreciate the role that our kids play in this problem and over-appreciate the role of their friends. Beyond that, we tend to ignore our contribution as parents altogether. For instance, do you serve alcohol to minors in your home? Many parents think this is an innocent action, but I think it's a travesty. How well do you control access to alcohol, tobacco, or even adult-themed media (pornography on TV and the internet) in your home or in the home of neighbors? Bear in mind that even young children can be very clever about getting into these things and deceiving you about it. It is quite alluring to them and don't think that because it is for adults, they won't attempt to gain access.

I think the best way to handle the "wrong crowd" issue is to talk with the parents of your kids' friends and through conversation share your value system and learn about theirs. Even if they don't agree with your concerns about underage drinking and pot use, you can hope that they will respect your stance. As a practical matter, it may be difficult to limit your kids' exposure to the so-called wrong crowd. On the other hand, it makes sense to encourage activities that involve kids and families with whom you're comfortable. In addition, another practical solution is for you and your kids to create a list of places and events that you consider safe.

Believe it or not, kids usually accept reasonable parental stances, and they'll find it comforting as well. On several occasions, I've been surprised when my kids responded with relief when I've made certain friends, places, or events off limits. Although I didn't know it at the time, the kids were stressed about these situations, too.

Intelligence is Valuable

The type of *intelligence* I'm talking about is the kind of information you both overtly and secretly gather about your child's activities. This is another important reason to communicate with the parents of your children's friends. Kids love to talk when they're in a setting that makes them feel comfortable, and if your kids aren't talking to you about something that's going on, their friends may be talking with their parents. Therefore, if you want to know what your kids and their friends are up to, talk with other parents. Before you open these conversations, you must be willing to listen to negative information about your kids. If you quickly become defensive and claim your children would never do such things or take the attitude that people are lying about your kids, the other parents will shut down the pipeline of valuable intelligence.

You can also gather intelligence through dialogues with your own kids. Naturally, they will gloss over their involvement in any unacceptable activity, but often you can calibrate their likely involvement by listening to their responses to your gentle questioning. Later, you can verify your concerns through other means. Remember that your kids will more freely and accurately report on what other kids are up to than on their own actions. Once you have checked out your concerns you can let other parents in on what you've learned.

Technological advances have provided other information-gathering tools and options. For example, you can buy inexpensive, undetectable computer monitoring software that can save and replay screen information on your child's PC. (The resource list includes the website for relevant software.) You can also place GPS (Global Positioning System) on autos, and location-finder cell phones are now being marketed which use GPS location finding technology as well. While technology continues to add options, I still believe that nothing beats plain, old-fashioned dialogue with your kids and their friends' parents.

I realize that some parents find it distasteful and discomfiting to talk about "cloak and dagger" intelligence gathering. But keep in mind what's at stake here. The intelligence work you do now is critical, but only temporary. When your child reaches ages 18-21, the time of independence, your work should be done. On the other hand, failure to prevent your children from becoming addicted represents a permanent failure and troubles will follow the addict and the entire family for the rest of your lives.

Being Your Child's Friend

Absolutely nothing is wrong with being a companion to your kids, but the way you do that is important. For example, some parents try to engender a co-equal friendship with their adolescents. So, while many mothers and daughters and fathers and sons often do something fun together, it's critical that the parents avoid adult-like activities. You probably know what I mean. In this role of "pal," some parents essentially set up their adolescents in early sexual experiences, alcohol or drug use, or gambling. But this kind of "companionship" does their kids a great disservice. I've even seen role reversal, a situation in which the parent takes the role of the child and the child becomes the parent. This is common with an addicted parent.

To be an effective companion-parent, you must firmly establish that you are a parent first and a friend second. In addition, it's a bad idea to burden your kids with your own personal problems or baggage. While it's certainly okay to talk about the type of struggles you have, never enlist your kids' help to solve your personal problems, especially when they involve your spouse or ex-spouse. Above all, you must continue to behave as a responsible adult.

Recently, I counseled a teenager with anxiety problems. She was particularly stressed about the fact that while she lived with her father, she couldn't seem to get along with her father's new wife. Apparently, she didn't like the way her step-mother treated her father, and in particular, she commented that her father didn't "take up" for himself.

This girl's mother was in the exam room, and I asked this teenager why she didn't choose to live with her mother. I learned from her answer that the judge officiating in the parents' divorce case wouldn't allow this, because the mother had a live-in boyfriend. As the girl explained all this, it became clear that I was seeing a case of child-parent role reversal. Many of the girl's problems resulted from parents' inability to deal with their own problems in an adult, responsible way. In other words, my adolescent patient was forced to deal with her parents' problems as well as her own. The parents weren't raising her; she was "raising" them. In this case, who is looking out for and protecting the adolescent? Certainly these problems and lack of parenting increase her risk for drug experimentation.

As you can see, the way you raise your kids has tremendous impact on their likelihood to turn to drugs. They need three key things: the protection of a healthy ego, a respect for money and how it is earned, and a good and proper relationship with their parents.

Points to Remember
- Unconditional love from their parents is the foundation of self-esteem development in children.
- Self-esteem in children derives from successes small and large and the recognition. of these successes from others, especially their parents.
- Kids need to learn respect for money and how to responsibly use it.
- Avoid being an enabling parent to your youngster.
- Network with other parents and talk with your kids frequently.
- Be a friend to your child if you want to, but be a parent first.

10

Addiction and the Family

Volumes have been written about the profound effect of addiction on the family. But what about the reverse? How does the family influence addiction? In terms of parenting, this in an important area, particularly the ways in which parents unintentionally *facilitate* addiction in their youngsters. Thus far, I've described several problems, including that of allowing early exposure to addicting chemicals, lack of character development, misunderstanding self-esteem and discipline, and so forth. However, other dynamics and issues may also facilitate addiction in young people.

Keep Secrets Together, Get Sick Together

In the addiction field, it's well known that unhealthy dynamics develop in families in which at least one member is an addict. You will recall that enabling contains two main components, the first of which is "protecting" or insulating the addict from the consequences of his or her behavior. Secrecy is the second major component.

Within the addict's family, secrecy fulfills one purpose, which is to prevent anyone (including friends, colleagues, and the community at large) from finding out about the family's problems. *Family secrecy*, a common phenomenon in addicted families, also is a defense mechanism that occurs with other pathologies, such as sexual abuse. For obvious reasons, sexual abuse and domestic violence are almost always shrouded in extreme secrecy.

Family secrecy usually evolves and takes on a life of its own. It's motivated by both the desire to protect the addict from detection and possible punishment and to avoid family embarrassment. Secrecy can be subtle. For example, family members may avoid telling law enforcement, teachers, counselors, pastors, or even extended family about what's going on in their homes. Secrecy may also involve telling small lies that evolve into a complex web of not-so-subtle deceit. Those involved in addiction treatment have a saying about this: "You're only as sick as the secrets you keep."

At first, secrecy seems harmless. Not going to work or missing an appointment is explained as being down with the "flu." Or, a woman may say that a swinging door gave her a black eye, when in reality, her drunken husband punched her. Most of us can understand why people tell these little lies. After all, what wife (in this case) wants to admit that her husband is too hung-over to go to work or even worse, is capable of physical abuse.

Spouses are not the only beneficiaries of family secrecy. Increasingly, I see kids' misdeeds occurring from about middle school all the way into young adulthood receive "protection" by the family, mainly parents. Alcohol abuse, pot use, violence, vandalism, and school problems are swept under the rug. Even when these problems elevate to the level of criminal behavior, the parents quickly respond by trying to get charges reduced or "fixed." They use court connections if they have them, or lacking that, they promise the family court judge that they will handle their kids' problems at home.

However, experience shows us that each time the early and minor offenses are quickly dispatched the stage is set for similar but much worse problems later on. If the behavioral offenses go unexposed, then addicts (or pre-addicts in some cases) lack motivation to change, which allows them to continue their downward spiral of addiction.

What's both interesting and important about this phenomenon is that it's ultimately futile to try to hide the problems. Secrecy simply doesn't work. Through the ever-present grapevine, friends, extended family, and other acquaintances observe or otherwise find out what's going on. But families entwined with addiction lose a sense of perspective and they usually work even harder and go to even greater lengths to cover for the addict. New and more intense efforts don't accomplish their purpose, but they do accomplish something else, namely what is known as the "elephant in the living room" effect. In essence, this means that a code of silence develops by which those outside the family accept that certain topics are off limits. An implied agreement exists within and outside the family. The result is collective denial. The family and all associated with it enter an implicit agreement not to discuss or even acknowledge certain problems. The problem can be likened to an elephant in the living room that everyone pretends isn't there.

So, in the end, addicts have recruited their families into their denial system, and in turn the families recruit friends, extended family, and the community at large into a collective denial system. What everyone involved in addiction, including addicts, knows is that denial serves only to delay addicts' (or pre-addicts in some cases) confrontation and ultimate treatment of their problems.

Like addiction, family secrecy begins with small steps. At first it's informal and unspoken, but over time, as the addiction worsens and the addict becomes sicker, the behaviors worsen, too. For example, with more missed work, more family arguments, including possible violence, family members are forced to talk among themselves about their perceived need to "not tell" anyone about what's happening. This is how family secrets begin. The stakes can become higher, too. The parent-addict may lose a job, or the young adult addict goes to jail, and with these events, the family is usually well instructed and indoctrinated on how, when, and why to keep secrets.

Ultimately, the non-addicted adult in the family usually takes on the role of educator and facilitator of secrecy and, therefore, chief enabler. Over time the family secrecy becomes strongly institutionalized.

As discussed earlier, additional issues (referred to as *co-morbidities*) such as physical abuse, eating disorders, and other mental illnesses may emerge in an addicted family. These severe problems may be hidden for many years due to the institutionalized secrecy. Unfortunately, this form of family secrecy may become multigenerational. In other words, family secrecy, and the techniques and behaviors that keep it going, begin to be the norm, and may feel normal, which is why this system can so easily be passed on to successive generations.

What does this Teach us About Addiction Prevention?

Because of its institutionalization, family secrecy may begin *prior* to the onset of addiction. For example, one family, whom we'll call the Simpsons, was infamous for alcoholism that ran through their extended family. The husband, Bill, a young executive, was married with three kids. Though he never drank or used drugs himself, his father was a notorious alcoholic and his brothers were well-known drug users and dealers. His wife, Sandy, also had been raised in an alcoholic home characterized by secrecy. Both Bill and Sandy knew that the wider community held negative views about their families, and they despised that situation. However, when they married they made a pact to never drink or use drugs and they followed through on this agreement.

When their oldest child was about age 12, Bill and Sandy discovered that he often drank alcohol with a neighborhood friend, and then over time he began smoking pot, too. Bill and Sandy spoke to their son about his behavior and punished him several times, but they never communicated with the parents of the other child, nor did they take *effective* actions to prevent his access to drugs. They didn't seek help or outside counseling either, preferring instead to keep the problem "in-house," primarily because of their embarrassment. Meanwhile, however, their son was rapidly developing a serious drug addiction. Other concerns revolved around the way in which their "secret" information would affect their son's chances for a scholarship to a prestigious college. "Coincidentally," the younger daughter developed an eating disorder, which went unaddressed, again, because they feared embarrassment.

Conventional wisdom suggests that the family should have sought drug treatment for their son and counseling for their daughter. However, because Bill and Sandy had a lifetime of intense training about family secrecy, combined with strong motivation to build a good image and reputation for their family, they couldn't bring themselves to seek help for their ailing kids. Consequently, the family secrecy policy they held resulted in neglecting their problems, which then smoldered and worsened over time. As you can see, once a family institutionalizes secrecy, it's passed down to new generations, and then it has the chance to facilitate more addiction and other unrelated problems as well. In this case the family secrecy defense was put in place *prior* to the addiction problem.

Should I Really Air my "Dirty Laundry"?

Just to clarify, it isn't necessary to tell everyone in your church or neighborhood or office about your problems. Individual and family health isn't dependent on talking openly about every issue. But rather than retreating into a state of denial, it's important to seek treatment or counseling when a problem exists. It's appropriate to ask for help when we need it, and it's certainly not a sign of weakness. Sadly, some people harbor a fear of looking weak and being unable to solve their own problems.

It is important to understand that giving up the unhealthy practice of secrecy does not mean that you give up your privacy. *Privacy* means limiting the amount and kind of information you share. For example, if you seek outside professional help, then you would openly discuss your problem in an atmosphere of confidentiality. Both professionals and those involved in lay assistance (such as parents' support groups) understand privacy as an important legal and ethical concept. Alcoholics Anonymous (AA) takes the issue of anonymity seriously and has traditionally protected the privacy of its members. Likewise, other 12-step programs such as Narcotics Anonymous (NA) for drug addicts and Al-Anon for families of addicts and alcoholics use this term in order to indicate their privacy policy. In addition, crisis centers exist to help individuals with any acute emotional problem and they, too, must respect the callers' privacy.

Based on both ethics and relevant law, doctors and all allied healthcare providers including lab technicians and secretaries must maintain patients' privacy, too. The Health Insurance Portability and Accountability Act (HIPAA) is the most current federal law governing healthcare personnel and it carries stiff penalties against healthcare providers who fail to maintain your privacy.

Practically speaking, fewer people will ever be aware of potential addiction problems in your family if you seek help early. Keep in mind that once addiction reaches a "full blown" stage, much of the community at large already knows about it. It makes much more sense from the standpoint of privacy and effective intervention to seek help as soon as *you* recognize an addiction or, better yet, a pre-addiction problem in your family.

In addition, if you truly love your addicted or pre-addicted family member, then lying for or making excuses about his or her behavior makes no sense, either. In other words, if your son gets a DUI, a sign of addiction, then talk to the judge about the best options to get help for him, rather than denying the problem altogether and trying to get him out of—or minimizing—punishment. If your kids or spouse don't show up for work or an important appointment, don't make excuses. Covering up and protecting are not your responsibility, so don't accept that role.

In practical situations you may be asked to explain your child's failure to turn in a school project or show up for class. In this situation, don't invent an excuse, but simply suggest that all involved ask the teenager why he or she failed to meet an obligation. In this case, you are neither covering up for the addict or "blabbing." In other words, you're letting the addict or pre-addict handle the situation. This forces the individual to deal with reality and become motivated to handle the problem in a healthy way, rather than relying on parents to provide an escape hatch.

The Rapidly Changing Family Unit

Today, the classic American family unit, known as *traditional* family and made up of two heterosexual parents with only their biological children, is the exception rather than the rule. Nowadays, two other significant family units are increasing in number. One is the *single parent* family, typically headed by a single woman with kids from one or more biological fathers, and usually living near or below poverty level. The other is the *blended* family, typically a middle-class patchwork group that includes heterosexual men and women who have been married before, have divorced, and have now remarried. Their kids are usually "his" and "hers," and possibly "theirs." Many combinations are possible in blended families. A third and lesser known trend is the *same sex* family, but since we have little data about same-sex families, I'm unable to address its impact on addiction.

We usually think of the traditional family as ideal, and in terms of stability, financial health, and addiction prevention, statistically this is the case. However, non-traditional families are part of the modern family landscape and are definitely here to stay. Non-traditional families have unique parenting challenges, especially in preventing addiction.

Single-adult families, notably those headed by women, tend to be low income and problematic when it comes to discipline. This combination of low income and poor discipline definitely translates into higher rates of addiction among the children. Furthermore, statistically, these families tend to continue in intergenerational poverty and unwed pregnancies, both of which serve to continue the poverty and addiction cycle. Parenthetically, most of our current prison inmates come from single-parent, low-income families.

Blended families also face several challenges. First, the dynamics among family members can be difficult and complex and individual members often carry more than the typical amount of emotional baggage. Second, discipline often becomes difficult, because children can be manipulative and cleverly pit one parent against another. They quickly figure out which parent is more permissive, which parent suffers guilt, and what emotional "buttons" to push to achieve their goals, which may include material things and premature freedom from parental control. For these and other reasons, the children may become self-centered and materialistic. Three characteristics—self-centeredness, materialism, and freedom from parental control—make alcohol and drug experimentation and ultimately, addiction, much more likely.

I would like to say that traditional families are all like "Leave it To Beaver," and therefore, protected from addiction. This wouldn't be an accurate characterization, however. The traditional family may not be handicapped by the problems that burden single-parent and blended families, but they have the many challenges I've already discussed. So, it's fair to say that addicts can emerge from any family, no matter the structure or composition. On the optimistic side, parents in even the most difficult family situations can apply the principles presented in this book and substantially protect their children from addiction.

Church and Family

As a Christian, I have observed that addiction problems seem to develop more often in families that are not *churched*. In the U.S. today, surveys report that most adults claim a Christian affiliation, and most of that group attend church, at least to some extent. But, if you look deeper, you'll find that a much smaller percentage of people who claim to be Christians actually attend church regularly. I consider only the regular attenders to be truly churched.

From what I can tell, the lives and lifestyles of the sometime church-goers differ little from those who don't attend church at all. Conversely, among those who are churched, that is, the family attends church and Bible study regularly, a greater degree of agreement on family value systems and lifestyles tends to exist. Overall, it appears that those who embrace the churched family value system have fewer addiction problems.

There are several theological and spiritual reasons why this may be the case though not necessarily accepted by non-

Christians. However, we can point to other attitudes and lifestyle characteristics that both Christians and non-Christians can accept.

Here are a few:

• Churched families value an intact family unit.

• Churched families condemn alcohol abuse, and the use of drugs and tobacco.

• Churched families subscribe to a single, higher moral authority (God).

• Churched families believe in a moral code based on the Bible's teachings.

Other religious groups, such as Judaism, the LDS Church, and Islam, to name only a few, have similar value systems. While I don't agree with their spiritual or theological teachings, these groups show lower addiction rates among members who regularly participate in the religion.

Change is Here to Stay

Today's families are undergoing enormous changes, especially in the way they're structured. These changes create additional opportunities for addiction to attack family members. If you're starting a family or planning one in the future, consider the qualities and steps that can help prevent addiction, including active participation in church and Bible study. If you already have children, then consider what you can do to maintain its stability, and consider the benefits of active church participation as well.

Points to Remember

• Keeping problems secret within the family only allows them to fester and worsen.

• Secrecy promotes denial of addiction within the family.

• Modern families are undergoing unprecedented challenges that put children at even greater risk for addiction.

• Though not always possible, setting a goal to make your family a traditional one will lower the risk of addiction and other societal problems.

• Active family involvement in a church reduces the risk of addiction.

11

High Risk Activities
That Can Lead to Addiction

As both a parent and a physician, I've observed that parents generally underestimate dangerous situations in our society that can lead kids into addiction and other problems. For example, when my sons were in high school, they went out with girls as young as 15, yet most of the time the parents of these girls never contacted us in order to coordinate the protection and safe return of their daughters. Most of the time, we didn't know if these girls had a curfew, but we offered our protection to them anyway.

Considering the dangerous times we live in, how can any parent automatically assume that other kids or even other parents will look after the safety of their vulnerable child? How did parents of these young, teenage girls know to trust my sons or us, their parents, when it came to the availability of alcohol or drugs? Did they know our values? How did they know that we would be present when their daughter came to our home to watch TV? Obviously, if the kids were unsupervised, they'd have had the opportunity for inappropriate behavior involving drinking and/or sex.

When my daughters were dating, we carefully scrutinized each dating situation. We wanted to know who they would be with, where they would be at all times, plus they had a strict curfew. We did the same with our sons. However, we were less concerned for their welfare since they tended to be older and controlled the transportation. The boys were stronger as well, so we weren't as concerned about their physical wellbeing. By the same token, though, we made sure that our boys were concerned with the safety of the girls they dated.

However, regardless of the sex of your child, exposure to alcohol, drugs, and tobacco is a risk. My kids have been to several homes in our community where adults offered them alcohol with full awareness that the kids were underage. We also noted that some of our kids' friends were allowed to bring alcohol into their homes, which meant that our kids had access to it during visits. In our small town, we have become aware of parents who are drug addicts and whose kids were friends of our kids. Though I know of no specific circumstance in which drugs were offered to my kids, obviously a risk is present in such situations. In addition, it's possible that the kids in those homes use drugs and could offer them to their friends.

So, given the risks, why allow the kids to visit these other homes at all? It's a logical question. However, we didn't learn about the addiction problems until my kids visited these home several times and our kids talked to us about what they'd seen and heard. You see, these families look very normal from the outside. They live in "good" neighborhoods and in nice homes, so superficially they have the things that make them appear normal, even though they are deep into major drugs— methamphetamine and crack. While it's true that these parents often end up in financial ruin or even eventually spend time in prison, they can keep up the appearance of normal life for quite some time.

You can't assume that other adults, other parents, or older kids will look out for the safety of your children. The families that live in your community and in many ways look similar to

164

your family may be very dissimilar. Their kids may look and act like your kids, but the value system in their homes relative to underage drinking, sex, and even drugs may be vastly different. You will have no way of knowing the general atmosphere and value system unless you are watching and listening, and talking with your kids and with other parents.

Living Vicariously

I don't think a substantial study has been done on parental attitudes about potentially dangerous teen behaviors, so I can only speculate about the mixture of behaviors I've observed and draw some conclusions. First, I've noticed that some parents live vicariously through their children. In fact this occurs to such an extent that the parents seem to "cheer" their kids on to participate in activities that may lead to drinking, smoking, and even sexual experiences.

I've speculated that these are things that the parents did or wish they could have done as kids. In some cases they reason that since these activities didn't hurt them, they should be okay for their youngsters, too. Or, perhaps they had strict parents who put certain activities off-limits and these parents may still feel deprived of some valuable experiences. So now, as adults, they allow or even urge their kids to do the things they were never allowed to do, thereby indirectly having the "fun" they missed out on as youngsters.

You, too, may have noticed that certain mothers, for example, are overly involved in their kids' popularity. They seem to identify with the kids more than with other adults. They dress like their daughters and may even act flirtatious around the teenage boys that visit. They take up their daughter's ambitions and try to make sure their daughters win at all times, whether it's winning a position on the cheerleading squad or winning the right boyfriend. In this situation, I believe social climbing is at work and these mothers will encourage behavior they believe will help their kids, even if it means exposure to alcohol and drugs, buying their daughters faddish, sexy clothing, and even early sexual behavior. To young teenage girls who are unable to see the superficial values on display, these women may seem like the "fun" moms in the neighborhood.

I'm not letting fathers off the hook here. I tend to see less overt behavior because fathers tend to be less involved in the first place. However, some dads try to be their sons' pals, sharing alcohol or smoking because these things seem "manly." Other boys might think of these men as the "fun" dads. And we've all seen fathers who encourage their sons to excel in a sport to the point that one wonders who really wants to be the star.

Second, there seems to be a sense of entitlement and even rebellion on the part of parents as well as kids. The attitude goes something like this: "Other kids get to be popular and have fun. So nobody is going to prevent my kid from having the same fun and enjoying their popularity." For the kids, an added bonus in this attitude manifests in the form of the parents' willingness to provide what they perceive as "the best of everything." Unfortunately, this means that kids with undeveloped value systems are riding around in sports cars or wearing very expensive watches or other jewelry. The kids may ask for and get expensive recreational equipment, like ATVs, boats, jet skis, and so forth that in reality the parents may not be able to afford.

As I said before, in some communities, it's reasonable for kids to have transportation, but I don't believe it's wise to provide the "ultimate" car, so to speak. Let the kids grow up and work for those "upgrades." Unfortunately, the parents may view these material things as necessary to enhance their kids' popularity and increase their own social status. In essence, the parents use the kids to "keep up with the Joneses."

The third explanation involves fatalism or a sense of defeat. We hear this logic applied to birth control for youngsters. Parents have brought girls as young as 13 to my office to get birth control methods. Sometimes the girls are not considering having sex and really don't want to, nor do they want the birth control. Parents don't bring their sons to the doctor for birth control, but they may encourage their sons to have and use condoms. The values involved in sexuality, not to mention the negative consequences of early sexual behavior, may not be part of the discussion between parents and kids. Rather, the conversation is all about and limited to "birth control."

Many parents have a fatalistic attitude about alcohol and marijuana. That is, they assume that kids are going use these substances, so they shouldn't concern themselves with the "if" but rather, the "where and when" of drinking or smoking pot. These are often the same parents that help plan the parties and provide the booze. Their logic is that because the kids will drink anyway, it's their "responsibility" as parents to provide a safe location and safe travel home.

The fourth and most cynical explanation is that some addicted parents apparently hold the sincere belief that because drinking alcohol is "good" for them, drinking is also good for everybody else, including adolescents. I know this sounds crazy and I have been reluctant to believe it myself. But among adult alcoholics, some are so enamored with drinking that they think everybody should daily experience its "wonderful" effects. My kids have mentioned several adults, known to be heavy drinkers, who not only offered them alcohol, but even seemed to push it on them.

My first exposure to someone like this was in 1978 when I was part of a group of Navy doctors who traveled to the Republic of Panama to study tropical medicine for six weeks. A naval officer greeted us at the Panama City airport and took us on a tour of the city. As this was my first trip outside the

U.S., I was interested in seeing the sights. He showed us important landmarks in the city, but he made it clear that the really important landmarks were the liquor stores! After years of being stationed in Panama, he'd memorized a network of stores and all the easy and convenient routes to them. This officer spent the better part of two hours endlessly extolling the virtues of booze, but he knew little about the culture of Panama. This guy made it clear that most of his free time was spent drinking, and he showered us with offers to buy booze for us so that we could do the same.

Even looking back, I can see that even though we were an adult group, he would have easily transferred his enthusiasm about alcohol to adolescents and probably thought nothing about offering it to them. I never met his children, but unfortunately, I'm sure they witnessed the same enthusiasm about drinking that we did.

The following day we met with the physician who headed the program, and coincidentally he spoke about the worsening alcoholism of the same naval officer who'd given us the tour. The doctor mentioned that the officer was being relieved of his position and sent back to the states for alcoholism recovery treatment, although the officer didn't know this yet. Apparently others in the Navy didn't share this guy's opinion about the benefits of alcohol.

I mention this officer in part as a warning not to underestimate how enthusiastic some alcoholics can be about their drinking. Because of their disease, some truly do think it's the answer to all problems. Therefore, when it comes to your youngsters, these adults represent potential exposure to addicting substances.

Your Kids are Already Drinking and Smoking

Well, don't panic yet. I mean this rhetorically. It's just that kids are drinking alcohol and using tobacco and pot far earlier than their parents think possible. Nowadays, it's not unusual for kids to begin experimenting with alcohol as early as age *eight*. By age 12 many have not only had at least one drink of alcohol, they have experienced intoxication. Many current reports indicate that kids as young as 12 are smoking marijuana.

How are they getting these substances? The short answer is, "very easily," at least in the case of alcohol and tobacco— one or both substances may be right in your home. You might declare that these are for adult consumption only, but do you think that kids won't try them? Remember, your kids want to be an adult just like you.

If kids can't get alcohol or tobacco in your home, their friends have homes, too, and these substances may be available there. Their friends may have willing older siblings or even parents who will accommodate your kids' desire to try these forbidden things. In the case of marijuana, their friends, or friends of friends, have it ready to buy "twenty-four, seven," as the saying goes. But you're the adult and the parent, so it's up to you and only you to protect them from these introductory addicting substances.

Now, Swing into Action

I know that some parents have a problem accepting that their innocent "baby" would have any interest in addicting substances. Trust me, when they reach a certain age, certainly by puberty (and possibly before), they will be curious, if not actively interested. So, don't wait until they reach puberty. Act now! I recommend the following:

• Closely control all tobacco and alcoholic beverages in your home. *

• Closely control all abusable prescription and nonprescription drugs in your home.*

- Closely control all abusable inhalants in your home.*
- Consider changing your lifestyle if you're using or even abusing some of these substances. Stop using for your kids, if not for yourself.
- If you are unable or unwilling to stop using addicting substances, then use them in private so that your children do not observe your use. Even better, seek treatment!
- Or, if you are unwilling to get treatment, explain and reinforce the fact that alcohol and tobacco are designed for adults and are only legal for adults. In the case of my parents, they indoctrinated me to avoid tobacco, although they smoked. But they were honest in telling me that they wished they could stop, but they were unable to. So, tell your kids that you're addicted and give them sage advice on your addiction problem, specifically by urging them not to begin and by explaining the problems it has caused you.
- Discuss the fact that although other kids and adults use these substances, they can be harmful and inappropriate at any age, but especially for young people. In addition, explain that addicts usually claim to have control over the use of substances when they really don't. Acknowledge that it may appear, at least at first, that these substances have not harmed these other individuals, but point out real life examples where these substances have been harmful over time.
- Monitor your kids for use of addicting substances. Don't convince yourself that what you detect is just "in your mind," and a product of your active imagination. (Chapter 13 covers examination and detection methods.)
- Be a healthy skeptic. If something doesn't look right or "add up," check it out. Don't be satisfied until you have proof one way or the other.
- Question and examine your kids with special care at certain times, i.e. your child's visit to a neighbor's home, prolonged time spent with friends, and during weekends.

• Avoid defensiveness if your children get angry. Their anger is often a just a defense mechanism that could mean your suspicions are correct. And if you are correct, then the kids are busted. If you're wrong, then the kids are put on notice that you're watching them closely. It is a win-win situation as long as you reinforce that you're acting from your love for them. In addition, establish that your actions are not about distrusting them, but based on your distrust of the alluring, addicting substances.

• Mentally prepare yourself to test for drugs, alcohol, or tobacco should your suspicion justify it. Remember, it is better to test too early or too often than too late or too little. Testing is simple and well worth the low cost.

• When dealing with other parents, make your feelings and attitudes about alcohol, tobacco, and drugs very clear. Try to recruit them to be on the lookout for information that your child may be experimenting. This also serves to clarify *your* boundaries for your kids while under the supervision of other adults. You hope, of course, that they will respect those boundaries.

The Threat of Boredom

My grandmother often said: "An idle mind is the devil's workshop." How true this is today, and busy parents have trouble appreciating how quickly children can become bored. Be advised, though, if your kids don't have activities to fill their time, they will go looking for them. In other words, immature, active brains will drive them to find activities to fill a vacuum, and a greater than 50-50 chance exists that they will choose activities that don't meet with your approval—like experimenting with addicting substances.

Consequently, keep your kids busy. Summers and prolonged holiday breaks can present challenges, but most communities offer numerous choices of year-round organized activities for kids of all ages. These year-round activities are beneficial, but the months and weeks of school breaks are especially important. I suggest choosing activities based on a number of criteria. In general, the activity should be:

- Something your child enjoys.
- A good match with your child's abilities, so it will enhance self esteem.
- Safely supervised to avoid sexual abuse from adults or even older kids.
- Something that builds skills in a particular area.
- Physically active—providing the exercise that helps control weight.
- An area of interest that could lead to a healthy adult hobby.
- Something that includes the possibility to learn how to earn and manage money.
- A vehicle that allows the child to enjoy helping or caring for people or animals.

Remember, though, that it isn't necessary or even possible for a single activity to meet all of these criteria, but try to include as many as possible, recognizing that most kids are involved in more than one activity at a time. My children usually played a sport, held a part time job, volunteered for organizations, and had a hobby, but usually at different times.

Now that I've offered a list of beneficial activities, I must also caution against the growing trend of involving kids in too many activities, because being too busy can lead to intense stress. Let kids be kids. They need to relax, listen to music, play games, and watch television—just like adults. Allow the kids their downtime, too, knowing that their brains need opportunities to recharge.

Media and the Internet

Children's internet use stirs up plenty of controversy, not unlike the debate over TV that went on while I was growing up. At that time, many parents feared that television would replace reading and turn our minds to mush. And we saw a collective anxiety over the "shocking" sexually-oriented material in movies shown on television; by today's standards, however, those movies and other programming were very tame. If you're over age 50, you may recall that through the 1960s, fictional married couples climbed into their twin beds—no double beds on TV shows back then! This stands in contrast to the far more sexually explicit material and coarse language seen today. Current programming is far more cutting edge than anyone could have predicted. The development of cable TV, with its vast array of channels has stretched the boundaries and will probably continue to do so. In addition, the collective anxiety of yesterday's parents was not only justified, but underestimated at least in one area; for the most part, today's kids choose TV, radio, and the internet over books.

In the 1960s, a futurist predicted that humans would eventually evolve into beings with large brains and heads and small bodies with atrophic muscles, all because watching television became the chief human activity. Little did this futurist know that we'd see just the opposite situation instead. Today, we tend to have larger bodies because watching television is a sedentary activity that leads to weight gain.

I don't have the knee-jerk reaction that various media are bad for us, end of story. Certainly well-documented dangers exist, but the internet, music, TV, and even newer developments in media are here to stay. As parents, it makes sense for us to exploit the media that benefit our children, while working hard to protect them from the problems. This debate is analogous to the debate over money, in that like money, media including the internet, are neither good nor bad. Media are neutral, but our attitudes about them and the way we use them give them value.

Specifically, the internet is proving its usefulness, and our access to all types of information is amazing. I recently used the internet to do deep and detailed genealogical research, and what I accomplished in only a few months would have taken many years and extensive travel before the availability of online research. At an accelerating rate, high school and college students are taking complete courses online. All in all, the list of advantages is long and increasing.

As we all know, the internet has a dark side, and the explosion of online pornography viewing is one example. The ability to buy illegal or abusable drugs is growing exponentially through the internet, and journalists have chronicled child abuse and exploitation by online sexual predators. At the same time, it's likely that in the coming years your children won't be able to complete some homework assignments or consult certain reference texts without access to the internet. For these reasons, I recommend that you embrace the positive features of the internet and protect your children from the bad. The same advice applies to television and music. Here are my recommendations:

• Keep your child's personal computer in a central place in the house where you can monitor it, or install stealth monitoring software—or take both actions, and monitor, monitor, and monitor your child's internet activity.

• Don't rely on filtering software to prevent your child's access to inappropriate websites or information. It's not effective.

• Read, take courses, and use consultants to learn about computers, email, and the internet. Most parents know less than their kids and this puts them at a distinct disadvantage when it comes to monitoring their children's online activities.

• Participate in appropriate internet activities with your kids. For example, computer gaming can be great fun and you can use the opportunity to find a common activity that enables you to spend time and talk with your kids as you learn more about computers and the internet. A number of PC computer and Nintendo-like games can be played between two people at home or online against other players around the world. These include war games, sports, and martial arts.

• A number of educational opportunities are available on the internet. You and/or your kids can study foreign languages, take college courses, and compile family genealogy, and so forth.

• Beware of computer accessories like camera and microphone attachments through which others can view or hear children in real time in the internet world. Many cases of child abuse from outside predators have resulted from these computer accessories.

• Beware of computer chat rooms and the use of websites in which kids can chat with strangers or post personal information. These also represent opportunities for contact with predators and drug dealers.

• Even in this era, television has redeeming value. For all the unsuitable programming, the cable networks have given us channels that my family and I enjoy, including discussions of history, politics, science, other cultures, and appealing areas such as shows about nature and wild animals, along with home remodeling and related programs.

• Because it's such a varied mix, you need to monitor and control television programming, always keeping in mind that certain pay channels on cable and satellite viewing offer particular dangers.

• It's difficult to control your children's access to music. Not only can anyone buy music, but without your knowledge, your kids can download it for free through the internet. Music with rebellious, sexual, and violent themes is alluring to youngsters, but obviously, I believe you should discourage them from listening to it. One way to do that is by providing them with alternative kinds of music. You may be surprised that your kids find classical music appealing, and they even like the music we enjoyed as kids. I chuckle when my eldest son discovers a song that he really likes—only to find out that it was popular when I was his age.

• Consider that media and the internet are forms of entertainment, and in general, you must control and limit their access to them, and that includes time as well as content. The fact that your kids love these forms of entertainment actually gives you added power. For example, allow access to the internet or television *only* after they complete their obligations, such as homework and chores. Beyond that, make access to entertainment contingent on consistently showing acceptable attitudes, respectfulness, and compliance with other disciplinary guidelines in your home. Remember, *you* have the leverage, so use it!

Media and Addiction—What's the Connection?

Considerable *indirect* connections exist between media (including the internet) and addiction. First, we have constant commercial signals coming our way. For decades now, tobacco and beer producers have used TV, radio, and magazines to lure young people into consuming their products. Fortunately, our society has done much in recent years to curtail this advertising, and concerned citizens, including parents, have brought about these changes.

Second, for many decades, the movie industry has suggested that smoking and drinking are sexy and glamorous and by extension will make us sexy and glamorous, too, just like the characters on the screen. Youngsters are particularly responsive to this message. Third, music with its associated visual images, suggests that young people who use addicting substances of all types are rebellious and independent. Even media personalities, the "bad boy" rockers and waif-figured supermodels, suggest that rebellious behaviors like smoking, drinking, and using drugs are cool.

The internet, specifically, now plays a key role in legal and illegal drug distribution. Even brief web-browsing stints will lead you to a number of pop-up advertisements for mail order prescriptions. These prescription drugs can often be purchased without a legitimate visit to a doctor. There have been documented cases of severe addiction problems in people who have been able to purchase large amounts of addicting prescription medications exclusively through the internet. Even scarier, these drugs are usually sent from a foreign country and they may be counterfeit, which means that what is sent may or may not contain the expected drugs and, even when they are, the drugs may be impure and unsafe.

Unaccounted Time

I believe that unaccounted for time is the least understood and least appreciated component of high risk activities. If you protest and say you trust your children to be where they say they'll be and doing what they say they're doing at all times, then think about your childhood. Were you always exactly where your parents thought you were? Did your parents know exactly what you were doing? Troubling thought, isn't it? And why would your kids be any different?

Your kids, and my kids, and the neighbor's kids, too, know consciously and intuitively what activities adults approve and disapprove of. However, because they are youngsters, they are by nature curious about many things, and they also are influenced by their friends and will seek adult activities to the extent they can. Consequently, they will participate in forbidden activities *if* they calculate that their parents will not discover it. On the other hand, if they know that you keep close track of them and are willing to apply quick and decisive discipline when deserved, they will likely avoid such activities.

Children usually test parents when it comes to tracking their activities and location. They will try deception, or they'll put you on the defensive in an effort to discourage you. Kids are clever and can really make *you* feel paranoid and way outside the norm among parents. But don't fall for that ploy! As my children have reached adulthood, they have reassured us that we did the right things, but they also admit they didn't like our monitoring at the time.

It's effective to always put the burden of proof on the youngsters. They must prove or at least be reliable about what they tell you. In addition, expect them to tell you that no one else's parents are like you. It's an age-old tactic. You may have heard this complaint numerous times already, and sadly, they are probably right, at least some of the time and about certain issues. Some parents are lax in monitoring and they trust their kids too much. But, that doesn't matter, because you are responsible for them and they must be responsive to you. As kids, many of us heard another age-old statement: "I don't care what so and so's parents allow, in this house we . . .."

I recommend being strong in making your kids account for their time, but also be balanced. As the kids prove themselves reliable, give them more freedom. Reward trust as it is proven, but only one careful step at a time. Freedom should also be given relative to age. For example, until they went to college, our children always had a curfew, an early hour at young ages, and we gradually extended it as they became older and showed responsibility, trustworthiness, and the maturity to deserve it. If at any point they betrayed that trust, we started all over.

By the time your youngsters reach age 18, the age of independence, your goal should be that they no longer require a curfew or any significant time accountability. Why age 18? This is the age most kids leave for college, enlist in the military, or begin fulltime work. It no longer makes sense to closely monitor their activities at home when you can't do this after they leave home, at least for any extended period of time. Bear in mind, however, that situations and maturity vary. For a variety of reasons, some kids need to stay home and perhaps go to a local community college or take other post-high school training for another year or two. In that case it may make sense to continue some accountability, albeit limited.

Making the Transition to an Independent Life

All parents worry that their children will "go wild" when they leave home. And they don't like to hear that yes, the kids probably will go wild. This scares most parents, and my wife and I were no different. But, almost all kids go through this stage on the way to their fully independent lives. It's part of their natural transition to adulthood. Even the very conservative Amish society recognizes this phenomenon. The Amish call it *rumspringa*, which is a formal rite of passage, a time that adolescents are allowed to leave home and live hedonistically, or in other words, "sow wild oats." The young people may participate in activities considered sinful by their religion, even drunkenness. However, upon returning to their communities, they must live a plain, sober, and simple life again.

I'm not suggesting that you approve or encourage this behavior. But I am saying that once your kids are out of your complete control, this wild period is likely to occur, so don't be surprised or discouraged. If you have used the principles of this book and parented well, then your children have a good chance of surviving this period without harming themselves. Your kids have waited to begin experimenting with addicting substances to a more mature age, and you have helped them develop good character and a conscience, along with self-discipline. Finally, because you've also raised them in a churched environment, they should be able to quickly and safely pass through this stage.

Once they identify themselves as independent adults, with no need to be rebellious, the party lifestyle will usually be much less attractive. When she reached this point in life, one of my daughters commented that being rebellious wasn't fun anymore because there was no longer anything to rebel against. As your adult children begin their work and professional lives and take on adult responsibilities, such as marrying and planning a family, they will find that using addictive substances takes a backseat to the other joys and responsibilities in life. Your kids will have much more important priorities.

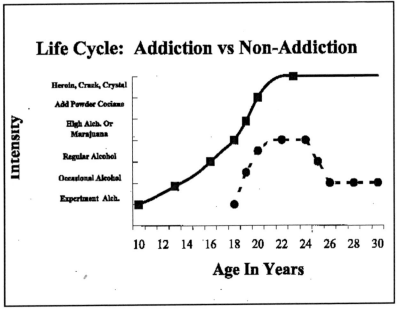

Courtesy of Susan Shaw

When the Kids Become Visitors

Other issues emerge when older adolescents and young adults reach independence and return home for visits. They usually expect to be able to live the same way they do in their new homes, an attitude that can lead to conflict. Specifically, parents and young adult kids may experience tension over sleeping arrangements with a sexual partner, or the issues may involve smoking, drinking, or drugs.

Two important considerations arise when parents and their adult or near-adult children run into conflict over lifestyles. The first is the question of allowing behaviors you find unacceptable to take place in your home. The answer is that you're under no obligation to allow anything you consider inappropriate to happen under your roof. Remember that you're an independent adult, too, and it's your home. If your son chooses to drink alcohol and you don't normally allow alcohol in your home, you have the right to make it clear that he can't drink in your home, nor can he come home drunk.

The other consideration involves financial support. When kids leave home, especially for college, they usually are somewhat independent in their campus town, but they still depend on you for financial support. Therefore, you have some say about how *your* money is spent. If you believe your child is spending your money unwisely, i.e., on alcohol, drugs, tobacco, or gambling, then remove some or all of your financial support. You have financial responsibilities to the rest of the family, and besides, if you don't withdraw the funding, you're a tacit enabler of behavior you don't like.

If your children are older and mature enough, and sufficiently independent and rich, to participate in activities reserved for adults, then they're old enough to support themselves. Kids with this mindset often learn to make the right decisions about these activities only after dealing with the day-to-day priorities you cope with. Put this "pay your own way" action into effect from the beginning, because the longer you wait, the poorer the result.

Too Much Money

As I said before, money is either good or bad, depending on your attitude and how you use it. In terms of the risk for addiction, most kids from middle class and above middle class homes have too much money. By this I mean they generally have more cash than they need or they can easily account for to their parents. This is not a value judgment, just an observation.

If kids want to buy alcohol, drugs, and tobacco they need cash, or lacking that, they steal these things from their homes. If you've taken my advice and have closely controlled access to these substances, your children will be forced to buy them, and from a kid's point of view, that means parting with money. If your children are not yet addicted but merely experimenting, they have to decide if further experimentation with drugs is worth the cost. Is it worth buying booze with the money they were saving for a bike, a video game, fishing gear, or any number of things young people want? If money is limited, they'll likely choose the item they've saved their money to get.

These are healthy dilemmas, and you want your children to experience them. But if you wait to monitor your children's money and spending until they become addicted, they are far more likely to spend their money on their drug of choice rather than on things that used to mean more.

I recommend giving your kids earned allowances, meaning that they must do chores to get it. Provide opportunities to make more money by doing additional chores or holding part-time jobs. The work they do for the family or their outside job not only helps build character and self-esteem, but it leads kids to understand the true value of money. Having a limited amount of money at their disposal and requiring them to work for what they have, leads to a correct and balanced view of money. That is to say, while kids may not hesitate to waste your money on addicting substances, they are much less likely to spend *their* hard earned money on such things.

Too Much Mobility and Independence

Most adolescents want greater freedom and independence, and children usually believe they know more and have greater ability to deal with the world than they really do. Their immature brains lead them to this erroneous conclusion. In addition, they often act on "reliable" but totally incorrect information their peers feed them. Ultimately, this mindset is likely to result in experimenting with addicting substances.

Some children are at greater risk than others for acting on immature assumptions For example, some children arrive home from school before their parents come home from work. These children, often referred to as latchkey kids, exemplify the problem of excessive or premature independence. Children, often surprisingly young, may be unsupervised in that one to four hour gap between the end of their school day and their parents' return home. Some of the earliest exposures to sex and addicting substances occur during these parental absences.

If this situation exists in your home, you must put a stop to it, even if it costs you financially. In two-parent homes this may mean that one parent needs to stop working for a period of time, or shift to part-time work. Obviously, in single-parent homes this is more problematic, and the best solution may be to network with neighbors and extended family members and pool resources to help each other cover these hours.

Beyond the latchkey phenomenon, there are plenty of ways that children slip away from their homes and get into trouble.

Often their absence is not noticed or the parents are relieved that the kids are entertaining themselves. However, when your kids are not under your direct supervision, it's imperative that you know where they are and can account for their activities during their time away.

The problem of mobility and addiction is similar to time accountability and addiction and usually arises around the time kids get their drivers licenses. I don't need to tell you what a watershed event this is for teenagers. However, for obvious reasons, the mobility they gain, and the sense of freedom, may begin as much as a year or two earlier if your child has an older friend with a license.

When kids become mobile, the "fun" really begins. The opportunities to get their hands on addicting substances increase, while accountability becomes more difficult. Of course, the high rate of traffic accidents and even deaths of young people represents an even more worrisome problem. These accidents may occur while driving under the influence of alcohol or other substances, lack of driving experience, thrill seeking, or a combination of factors. Therefore I have several recommendations to you when it comes to protecting your kids as they begin to drive.

First, I recommend adopting the safety policy that your newly licensed driver is prohibited from having any non-adult passengers for six months. Studies show a very high accident and injury rate among newly licensed youths with young passengers. Obviously, they are too inexperienced to drive the way they often do to impress their friends. They need an adult to keep them in check.

Second, I always emphasize the need to *buckle seat belts*. This can't be stressed too much. Many mistakes drivers make (including while under the influence) that lead to crashes have been "forgiven" because a driver or passenger or even riders in another vehicle have survived because they used their seat belts. In fact, seat belts are an excellent back up plan to avoid injuries and death.

Seat belt use is part of my family's indoctrination routine, and it began when we took our newborns home from the hospital. Never in their lives were our kids allowed to ride in a vehicle without being restrained. As parents, we buckled up, too, thereby showing our concern for our own safety and to model the behavior for our kids. By ages 2 or 3 our kids were so indoctrinated to use seat belts that they reminded others in the car if they didn't immediately buckle up. As obvious as this seems, I still find myself reminding kids from other families to buckle up when they are my passengers.

As a physician who has worked in a number of emergency rooms over the years, I have seen many car-crash victims, some of whom have been seriously or even mortally injured and some who were barely scratched. I have *never* seen a serious injury to a victim who was properly restrained by a seat belt, no matter how serious the crash. I realize that this is based only on my experience, and I know traffic deaths can occur even when every passenger used the seat belt. Nonetheless, my personal experience has strongly convinced me of their value.

In addition, I stress to my kids that they should never drive under the influence, or get into a car with a driver who has been drinking or using drugs. As experienced adults, we know that alcohol and drugs impair coordination, reaction time, and judgment. Kids greatly overestimate their own ability and the ability of others to drive under the influence. It has always been our policy to emphasize that if they are left with the choice of driving under the influence (or being a passenger in a car with a driver under the influence) or having no transportation home, then call home! Naturally, we will later ask questions about the situation, but facing us is nothing compared to dying in an accident.

Sleepovers and Campouts

For those of us who work hard to monitor our children's activities, account for their time, and examine them for evidence of use, still more dangers present themselves in the form of sleepovers and campouts. These typically begin just before adolescence, and while not all kids think of these sometimes unsupervised events as opportunities for drug experimentation, some certainly do. So, children naïve to addicting substances will often get their first exposure at one of these parties, even though that might not have been their intention.

For example, kids plan an overnight party for a small group of friends, and one or more have access to alcohol, usually stolen from their homes or purchased through a connection. They may plan this party when parents will either be home later or not at all, but even if the parents are around, the kids may drink outside or in some other "safe" location. The home they select for this party is usually the one in which the parents are the least likely to either discover the drinking or care all that much if it is uncovered. These gatherings are also prime opportunities to smoke cigarettes and use marijuana.

The campout is a variation on the same theme, and the kids may head off to a remote spot, although a backyard may be suitable for a campout. To uninitiated parents, this may seem like innocent fun, but I guarantee that one or more of the kids will bring some type of abusable substance along. Beer seems to be the drug of choice for most campouts.

Body Piercing and Tattooing

In recent years, these forms of body art have become much more popular among kids, and it amazes me how much body piercing adolescents participate in. For the most part, piercing is generally not dangerous to one's health, although minor skin reactions and infections occasionally develop.

Tattooing, on the other hand, is definitely *not* advisable, despite the faddish and flashy display of tattoos among athletes and movie stars. First, a tattoo is permanent and becomes faded and distorted over the years. Second, potentially deadly hepatitis types B and C can be acquired through tattoos. Third, as a person's values and lifestyles change, those tattoos that reflect the old values and lifestyles don't change at all. For instance, many people have needed to modify tattoos that included the name of a former lover or spouse, but attempts to remove tattoos result in large, unattractive scars.

Body art comes into play in drug addiction as well, although obviously, not all who have a tattoo are addicts. A sailor who gets a single tattoo on his arm or an adult woman who has a small butterfly tattooed on her lower abdomen are not necessarily drug addicts or even rebellious—just dumb, at least temporarily!

On the other hand, kids who seek a more substantial expression through body art do tend to get involved in drugs. The most likely connection between body art and drug use involves rebellion or the subcultures within what we can generalize and call the counterculture. The "Goth" or "punk" movements are specific counterculture groups. In both groups, the kids often dress in black, wear heavy white makeup, paint their hair bright colors and use fairly intense body art and piercing. Goths usually smoke cigarettes and many practice an odd sort of devil worship, although the kids involved in "punk" culture may not have any interest in those non-mainstream beliefs. Not all Goths are drug addicts, but a high percentage experiment with all types of drugs, including hallucinogens. Not all kids who acquire extensive body art are into the Goth subculture, and may be part of the more "colorful" fringe of punk culture. However, most kids within the Goth and punk groups probably use body art because their existence revolves around rebellion.

Parents should be aware of body art and its subcultures, because your child's interest in it is an important signal. While the vast majority of kids outgrow this youthful indiscretion, the damage caused by it could last a lifetime. This is why I recommend being very careful if this type of culture begins to influence your child. It's about a lot more than the way these kids dress, and their value system dictates that they push boundaries to the limit. And that definitely includes the use of tobacco, alcohol, and drugs.

When you see that your child has become interested in body art or has a fascination with the Goth or other subculture, then be on alert, because your child is likely headed into rebellion and possible drug experimentation. However, this can be a tricky situation because you don't want to create more rebellion or add to the danger that your child could run away from home. If you overreact and cut your child off from these other friends, the reaction could be serious and dangerous. But on the other hand, you must lovingly resist your teenager's attempts to pursue body art and that form of rebellious lifestyle.

I recommend that you ask your child what's pushing the rebellion. When you explore what's going on with your child in this situation, you often discover that the issues are peers not parents. You may need to consider venue or environmental changes, such as changing schools. Counseling may be in order, especially if the rebellion is directed against you. If that's the case, don't take it personally because rebellion often is simply a product of adolescence. In most cases, if parents don't overreact, but seek counseling instead, the adolescent will outgrow or work through the rebellion with time.

Eventually, most kids who seek even this flamboyant type of rebellion will reach the other side and pass into adulthood, and they will seem like themselves again, only much more mature. However, your highest priority is to prevent permanent damage to their lives and health through body art or the drug addiction that may result from this temporary period of rebellion.

Other Parents' Attitudes about Addicting Substances

When it comes to your children's exposure to addicting substances, other parents could be the most insidious danger of all. As my kids have reached adulthood, I've asked them about their attitudes about and exposure to alcohol, drugs, and tobacco. The most surprising thing I've learned is that many parents, even in our small community, made alcohol available to my kids, and even offered it to them when the kids were still legally underage. This is extremely frustrating since my wife and I have never minced words and have openly condemned any alcohol use by our kids.

What's more, some of these adults have been close friends of ours, but apparently they substituted their parental judgment for ours. I mention this because you can't take for granted that other parents will respect your wishes and attitudes. One of the reasons I wrote this book was to reach parents who may be ignorant to the array of dangers that exist. At the very least, I hope you're sensitized to the vast number of situations in which your kids can be introduced to addicting substances, and you may not suspect that this could happen.

Points to Remember

• Dangers to your kids may come in the form of boredom, the internet, unaccounted for time, mobility, independence, too much money, and even other parents.

• Such seemingly innocent activities as unsupervised sleep-overs and camp outs are notoriously dangerous.

• Prepare yourself to be pressured by your kids and even other adults when it comes to monitoring risky activities.

• Your kids will experiment with addicting substances much earlier than you think.

• Read this book and take action now!

---

* By "closely control" I mean the following: purchase a minimum of these substances for your home, making it easier for you to account for their use. Keep them in a place that you can monitor easily. Various kinds of glue should be given to kids for only for brief periods, during which you can supervise their use. If you suspect any abuse at all, throw away what you don't need and lock up the rest.

12

Don't Act too Late or too Slowly

No matter how I emphasize the importance of preventing addiction in youngsters, I can't rid myself of the nagging concern that too many parents will absorb the information in this book, yet still delay early detection or not take quick action. Unfortunately, this reluctance to act is already prevalent in homes across this country. The other concern I have is that when parents finally react, will their response be forceful and complete enough to be effective?

My concerns are grounded in reality, because I know that although much has been written about addiction, information about prevention is far more limited. One area where significant limitations exist is in the area of detecting early drug use in kids. Typically some feature story appears in print or on radio or television that gives parents instruction about being on the lookout for classic signs of drug use in kids, such as tiny pupils or needle tracks on their arms. But I contend that by the time parents begin their attempts to detect such obvious signs of drug use, their kids are probably past the experimentation and transition stages. It's likely the youngsters are already fully addicted.

This is why it's critical to detect early and address aggressively the transition period in addiction. Better yet, work to prevent your kids from experimenting with addicting substances at least until they reach the age of independence.

This will serve to stop the addiction cycle before it really begins. But there is another important reason to stop experimentation early. Every year we see tragic deaths directly related to alcohol and drug experimentation—sometimes with their very first use.

Deaths in kids from drug and alcohol related traffic accidents, boating accidents, hunting accidents, and the irresponsible use of ATVs are reported in the newspapers constantly. Acute alcohol poisoning and even drug overdoses are seen in hospitals (and morgues) more frequently nowadays in first-time users. Most of these ER visits and deaths are due to a combination of youthful misjudgment and a mind-altering substance and occur long before the child ever had a chance to transition into addiction.

Remember the six classic steps of addiction:
1. Drug (and alcohol) experimentation
2. Increasingly regular use (or abuse)
3. Tolerance
4. Physical dependence
5. Psychological dependence
6. Addiction

These stages are important because some type of transition period characterizes most, if not all chronic diseases. This period represents the time between the disease-free state and the point that chronic disease is fully and irreversibly established. For example, we've recently discovered that patients may live for years in a pre-diabetic or transition period before developing full-blown adult onset (Type II) diabetes. In addition, if we detect this transition period of diabetes and intervene with a program of diet, exercise, and medication, then it's possible to delay the onset of symptomatic diabetes. So, timely actions are critical to delaying the full expression of this chronic disorder for many years—perhaps even for a lifetime.

When we achieve this delay we may be able to prevent the deadly complications of diabetes.

With some chronic diseases the transition period may be too short to detect or unresponsive altogether to early intervention. An example of the former is a hemorrhagic stroke, a sudden rupture of a blood vessel in the brain causing sudden damage and a lifetime of disability or death. An example of the latter is rheumatoid arthritis whose clinical course can hardly be affected even with the earliest of intervention. It too, leads to a lifetime of disability. In other chronic diseases, such as coronary artery disease, the transition period may be quite prolonged but silent. Therefore, if we evaluate adults at risk before they experience advanced symptoms, and detect the disease within the transition period, we may be able to prevent a heart attack. And we all know that heart disease is a common cause of disability as well as sudden death. Ultimately, working with many chronic diseases in the transition period may save lives.

While we need more research on the subject, it appears that drug addiction (including alcoholism and nicotine addiction) also is a chronic disorder with a transition period. Some substances, such as the highly addicting drugs like heroin, crack, crystal meth, and nicotine appear to have short transition periods. Within weeks or even days of first use, signs of full-blown addiction may appear. Alcohol and some other depressants are examples of drugs with a lower addiction potential and which may have a long or even indefinite transition period.

The Implications of Chronic Disease

A *chronic disease* is a progressive medical condition that has reached an irreversible stage, and, therefore, it can't be cured. With the chronic disease of addiction a *transition period* is defined as the time between the beginning of the experimentation stage and the beginning of the *irreversible point of addiction*, which occurs at the point within the progressive addiction cycle at which the addict can never return to a non-addicted state. That is, the individual can never use any addicting substances, including alcohol, without likely returning to the compulsive and excessive use of his addictive drug of choice. As explained in chapters 4 and 5, early drug use and subsequent addiction causes this irreversibility because it creates permanent changes in the brain.

Within the classic steps of addiction, exactly where do we find this *irreversible point*? Unfortunately, we don't know the answer to that question. Needless to say, the sooner we intervene or interrupt the use, the less likely it is that the person will finish the transition to full addiction. While we don't know exactly where the transition period ends (and full addiction begins), we do know that it varies according to the age of the user and the addiction potential of the drug used. It is the imprinting and priming processes in immature brains that facilitate the transition from experimentation to frequent use and then irreversible addiction.

Because of the effect of drug imprinting and priming, the younger the person and the more addicting the drug when first used, the shorter the transition period to full addiction. Conversely, the older the person and the less addicting the drug when first used, then the longer the transition period to full addiction. It may be so long in many cases that addiction will never occur at all. Those who drink alcohol on occasion or only in a social setting illustrate the latter group. We also know that there are ethnic and genetic differences among people that may affect the transition period, but currently it's not possible to effectively measure these differences.

So, when dealing with young drug users, the sooner we

detect and intervene, the more likely we will catch the condition in time. As a parent, if you manage to intervene early enough in the process, you may spare the child a lifetime of suffering from the deadly, chronic disease of addiction. And as the parents of addicts will tell you, it's worth doing anything possible to prevent this frustrating and deadly disease.

Phase Lag of Drug Use and Recognition

Phase lag is a technical term that we can apply to almost any mathematical or scientific comparison of two actions in which there is a time difference or delay in response. In this context, I'm using this term to describe the delay between kids' drug use and parents' recognition (and therefore, their response). This concept is critical because as a physician I often deal with young people who are currently fully addicted to drugs and can only be helped (but not cured) through prolonged and repeated rehabilitation. Then, when I look at the natural history of their disease, I see common trends. Put simply, it seems that parents are always "zigging" when they should be "zagging." They detect and recognize the problem late and act even later. Too often, they stay stuck in outright denial.

I recall several situations in my community in which parents told other parents that they had seen their son or daughter intoxicated. In each case the parent denied it was even possible. A typical response is: "My Jimmy [or Joanie] would *never* drink alcohol." They deny the fact that several witnesses saw the obviously intoxicated teenager.

Then, late in the illness, when parents finally begin to intervene, they use methods appropriate only for earlier stages in the addiction process. In other words, they underestimate how far the youngster has progressed toward addiction and what it will take to change the course of the disease. This is what I call the *phase lag of drug use and recognition.*

Another concept, the *addiction track*, refers to the history or course kids are on as they move toward full-blown addiction. As you will see, we can mark addiction-track kids through ages or stages of growth and development.

Birth-10 Years, the Childhood Phase

In this phase, addiction track children tend to be directly protected from addiction, at least at first. They have little interest in adult activities and only a weak network of friends. In addition, they haven't yet acquired effective deceptive behaviors and are generally receptive to guidance from their parents. Nonetheless, the stage is set for them to become addicted later. These children may observe addictive parental behaviors and attitudes, and they lack consistent moral and religious training. These children may also have weak self-esteem and equally weak moral character development. They usually lack indoctrination and education about avoiding addicting substances. These deficiencies will prove to be critical failures in their later development of addiction.

Ages 10-12, the Preadolescence Phase

During preadolescence, addiction track kids begin to discover the fascinating attributes of adult behaviors, such as the use of tobacco and alcohol (and sex, too). They usually understand that marijuana and worse drugs are "bad" and their parents strongly disapprove of them. They begin to develop social networks, which are now greatly enhanced through the internet. Within minutes peers can distribute important but secretive information about activities they value, including those that their parents would not approve. This is the time when they begin to experiment with tobacco and alcohol.

I have seen a number of examples of this new, *digital grapevine* in my community. I noticed in recent years with the

196

advent of *instant messenger* over the internet and *text messaging* via cell phones that kids schedule impromptu parties very rapidly, often in minutes. These parties usually occur in homes that are unsupervised by adults. In a couple of cases my wife and I left our teenage son at home alone when going briefly out of town. Just the mere mention of our being out of town to one of his friends led to problems. We can cite at least six occasions when between half a dozen to about 15 adolescents suddenly showed up at our home with beer and tobacco. My son didn't even know some of these kids. In each case a simple invitation by my son to one friend led to visits and activities by other kids that my son didn't intend to invite and didn't consider welcome. We know of other parents who tell similar experiences.

During this phase, parents often greatly underestimate the availability of and familiarity with a variety of substances and activities. Parents also may be blind about the kind of access kids in this age group have to acquire, use, and hide what they have and do. Parents are usually very naïve to adult-like activities that kids consider doing or are already doing at this age. They are also very naïve to the willingness and ability of children to be deceptive about things they know parents will disapprove of.

I can only speculate about the reasons that parents are so out of touch. Maybe they didn't have an interest in these things when they were kids, so they assume the same is true for their kids. Or the parents may believe that they were very precocious pre-adolescents, but because of their influence as parents themselves now, their kids are innocent and would never think of doing the things they did at their age. For one reason or another some parents are blind to what their kids know about and/or are willing to engage in.

In reality, preadolescent kids across the country experiment opportunistically with tobacco and alcohol and their parents have little or no knowledge of it. Often the information is available, just as it is in my community, but parents choose to remain in a state of denial. Therefore, parents do nothing about it. They don't attempt to indoctrinate or educate kids about addiction, or have frank discussions about risky behavior, and they may not hold their kids accountable for this behavior. Within this age group, some kids experiment with marijuana and other drugs, but in terms of numbers, it's a relatively small minority.

Ages 13-16, Early Adolescence Phase

In terms of addiction track kids, this group has already experimented with tobacco and alcohol and by early adolescence these experiences hold little novelty. While they still enjoy those substances, they just don't consider them "cutting edge" when it comes to participating in adult-like activities. They begin to establish regular alcohol and tobacco use, but in order to break up the monotony that has set in and to experience more thrills, too, kids often play drinking games that encourage binge drinking.

By this stage, respect for dangers involved with alcohol has dissipated, and they believe they can handle it just fine. Existing taboos about drugs begin to diminish as well, and they begin contact with older kids who are marijuana users and dealers. The pot smokers indoctrinate them to hold in contempt any idea that marijuana could be addicting.

Therefore, to be even more daring and to seek an even better euphoria, kids begin adding marijuana to their mix of substances, and by that point they increase their use of alcohol and tobacco and pot use becomes a weekly event. Substance abuse is usually associated with both planned and impromptu parties, and most of these gatherings have plenty of booze and pot. Newer and even more thrilling substances, such as hallucinogens, also may appear at these parties.

Parents of adolescents may finally begin to break out of their denial and show some concern. They may witness or hear things that trigger questions about their children's possible involvement in drinking or smoking. However, kids from this group may have been briefed by their friends about the right things to say that deflect parental suspicions, or they figure these deceptive strategies out for themselves.

Even after parents discover the alcohol, pot, or tobacco use, they tend to deliver only a brief sermon, but take no further action. In this phase, parents think their kids are merely experimenting, but as you can see it's likely they have already passed through experimentation. But the misinformed parents tend to dismiss the entire issue by considering the behavior to be typical teenage drug experimentation.

Ages 16-18, Late Adolescence Phase

Once addiction track kids progress through each of these phases and have reached late adolescence, then in many cases they're heading rapidly toward the final stages of addiction. When it comes to alcohol abuse, these older teens tend to be divided into two groups. Either they will begin drinking several times per week at lower levels of intensity or they begin the early stages of less frequent but more intense drinking—the *binge drinking* we hear about.

At this age the frequent and low intensity drinkers may drink alone. The binge drinkers prefer to drink with friends and may go a week or two without drinking, but when they drink they show no restraint in their drinking or behavior. Binge drinkers are more likely to get into fights or drive after they've been drinking and end up with DUIs. Typically, they also begin to have blackouts (episodes of temporary amnesia with intoxication) and drink themselves into unconsciousness. Within this phase group, it's common to see them rushed to the emergency room with a diagnosis of acute alcohol intoxication.

Further differentiation of substance abuse may occur. Some adolescents prefer marijuana instead of alcohol as their drug of choice and use it regularly. Some stay with alcohol and use it frequently. Kids who smoked cigarettes only at parties or chewed tobacco only when out with his friends are fully addicted at this point. They can't go a few hours without nicotine, much less a full day. Marijuana users, not only smoke pot to get high, but they use it to "unwind" (relieve anxiety) at the end of the school day.

Parents of this phase group usually come to the realization that their kids are drinking alcohol and using tobacco regularly. Meanwhile, this is the period when problem drinking usually occurs; they get a DUI or they're arrested for theft, violence, or vandalism. In this situation, the parents usually respond with a combination of embarrassment, disbelief, and defensiveness. They may begin talking with their kids and even invoke some temporary punishment. On the other hand, they will work through the legal system to lighten or deflect punishment as much as possible. Within weeks, if not days, these adolescents have their driving and other privileges fully restored. At this point, we see the start of the stages of serious parental enabling.

Ages 18-21, Onset of Independence Phase

As discussed earlier, I consider age 18 the age of independence because this is usually when adolescents leave home. However, most who go to college or trade school are not fully financially independent until they finish their education and find a job. Twenty-one is usually the upper limit age of this group. So independence begins with leaving home but does not come to completion, fully, until young adults begin to support themselves financially.

When adolescents leave for college or otherwise move away from home for any reason, they often feel a great burden lifted. They are free! For the adolescents who have *not* been on the addiction track, this marks the beginning of experimentation, their *rumspringa*. Like the addiction track group, they probably drank a lot of alcohol as seniors at the high school prom. But unlike them, this was possibly the first time they were ever intoxicated. They view drinking alcohol as being novel, daring, fun, and adult-like—somewhat the way the addiction track kids felt during the preadolescent phase. More progressive substance abuse such as smoking marijuana and trying worse drugs is generally still taboo for this group and will probably remain so their entire lives.

Conversely, the addiction track kids "hit the floor running" when it comes to the age of independence phase. As soon as they get to college (or move away from home), they quickly locate the other "party" kids. This triggers accelerated use of alcohol and marijuana. If they have not already begun experimenting with cocaine—and worse drugs—they will shortly do so. They do this because if they haven't become addicted to alcohol or marijuana (which they really have, even though they deny it), they can "handle" any drugs.

This is the point that parents of addiction track kids finally become concerned. Legal problems like second or third DUIs and drug possession charges begin to emerge in this phase group. Parents begin to bargain or plead with, or threaten their kids. Instead of suggesting or forcing treatment for addiction, they try to offer logical suggestions, such as not drinking too much at one time! Or, they may "concede" that getting drunk is okay, but smoking pot isn't. At the same time, college grades probably begin to decline, and in some cases kids stop going to class altogether. After all, no parent is around, so accountability is on the back burner, and besides, by this stage, every night represents another opportunity for a party.

Ages 21-29, Onset of Adulthood Phase

Normally, this age group represents the time in which kids generally finish college or other vocational training and begin a career. However, many addiction track kids have quit school or flunked out of whatever educational situations they were in. If their family has connections, they may have had a job arranged for them. Otherwise, they may move from one job to another because they cannot get or hold a good, steady job with promotion opportunities.

Social activities become the center of life for these adults, and this means a life centered on drugs and alcohol and others who live the same way. All other young adult activities, recreational and otherwise, drop in priority. Several times a week, this phase group "parties" into the late hours of the night. Eventually, they stop seeing and associating with friends and family who don't see drug use or alcohol abuse as an essential part of their lives.

Romantic relationships are problematic too. Often these adults have a string of relationships that falter, but one or even several unwed pregnancies result. If a couple marries, both may be addicts, or one is an addict and the other is an enabler. Because of tolerance to the substances, alcohol and marijuana probably no longer provide an adequate euphoria, at which point the addict graduates to crack, heroin, or crystal meth. Addicted adults are likely to continue to rack up DUIs or drug possession charges and may begin dealing drugs or stealing. In order to survive and continue using without having a job, they must steal or deal drugs. Eventually, they end up serving time in prison.

Often, parents and spouses continue to enable, usually by providing money to live on and to finance legal expenses. Finally, the family or the court considers an intervention for drug treatment. If someone can pay or the addict has insurance, then treatment is the likely result. In these situations, addicts tend to go to treatment willingly because if they don't, they'll end up in jail for their crimes.

I wish I could say that after finishing a course of drug treatment that the addict gets well and the family is restored. However, statistics tell a different story. Only a very low chance exists that addicts stay on the path of recovery. More likely, they return to drugs and the cycle continues for many years. Addicts can't hold steady jobs, have repeated legal problems, they marry and divorce and marry again, they agree to therapy, but then go back to drugs again.

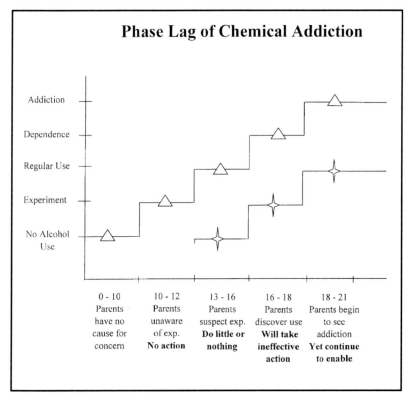

Courtesy of Susan Shaw

In this phase, adults eventually begin to use when alone instead of with small groups. As this happens more and more, it finally all comes down to one "friend" and only one friend—their drugs.

What does life usually look like in the non-addicted group? In general, and there are many variations on this theme, these young adults complete college or vocational training, enter the military, find a career path, pursue further education, or start working in their field. They may marry, too. Remember that most of these adults were "getting drunk" like everybody else at the high school prom and during their college days. But, once beginning a career and forming a family, drinking to the point of intoxication or getting high loses its appeal. *Rumspringa* is over!

For example, as the non-addicted mature, drinking too much may mean an unpleasant hangover, so they make a different choice. Or, taking an extra drink may mean risking a DUI. Pot is illegal, so they won't risk using that either. When this group has children, they may need to drive the babysitter home, or they hang out with other young parents and their children. As non-addicted persons, they will settle into a life of fulfillment and probably drink alcohol only socially, if at all. They will begin to concentrate on advancing their careers and raising a family, and their recreation involves activities that they can enjoy without getting high.

As you can see by this description, the progression of drug use of the addicted person diverges significantly from the non-addicted person during early adulthood. This divergence continues to widen throughout life. Addicted adults move from one job to another, but never get ahead financially. They move from one relationship to another, often having children through various sexual relationships. They also begin to develop health problems and often look old for their age, but all the while they increase and intensify their drug use.

Non-addicted adults usually maintain a successful career path and likely become financially successful in varying degrees, while often maintaining stable marriages and intact families. These men and women usually value their health, out of concern both for their spouses and children and for their own well being. In general, their use of substances is limited to alcohol, often used with diminishing frequency and intensity over time. (These individuals may also be addicted to tobacco, but as discussed earlier, nicotine addiction does not cause behavioral problems, although we know it's detrimental to health.)

Needless to say parents of fully addicted adults become helpless to "save" their adult children. Because of their love and out of an intense sense of guilt and a feeling of failure as parents, they will continue to try to help these addicted young adults. And the addicted kids will use their parents' guilt to continue to manipulate them for financial handouts and other financial resources, such as a place to live. Young adult addicts will also manipulate parents (and others) to come to their aid and rescue them when they run into the nearly inevitable legal, marital, or health problems. These individuals may seek periodic drug treatment and may sincerely try to change their lives. Sadly, altered brain chemistry, anatomy, and brain circuitry will stand in their way. The desire to get high "just one more time" will be a constant companion in their thoughts and will *never* go away.

Get in Sync

I hope you now realize that children have knowledge, networking capabilities, and cunning that sometimes far exceed our expectations. What I hope is that this information opens your eyes to what goes on with your kids when it comes to addicting substances.

Many years ago, as a physician and young father, I noticed that even toddlers are usually more capable in their physical and cognitive abilities than parents realize. When I expected my kids to be able to only walk, they were already beginning to run. When I expected they couldn't open a door, they were already unlocking it and exploring the back yard! Take those events as a prelude of what's to come. As kids grow older, the gap between what you think they can do and what they are really capable of only grows larger.

This parental expectation-child capability gap comes into play big time when it comes to drug experimentation. Children are vulnerable to addiction by virtue of their continuous growth and development, their tendency toward deceptive behavior, their curiosity, and the allure of addicting substances. This is why parents must shift their expectations forward to take into account this extremely important gap.

What Interventions would have Worked?

Here is a review of what should be done during the various phases in order to stop the progressive addiction cycle.

• **Childhood phase**: Prevention is the correct intervention. Begin religious and moral training very early. Indoctrinate your child to view alcohol as bad for kids (if you believe alcohol to be acceptable for adults) and drug abuse and tobacco as bad for everybody. Consider changing any of your lifestyle behaviors that may cause confusion as you indoctrinate your kids. Begin a culture of maintaining close contact, affection, and communication between you and your kids.

• **Early adolescence phase**: Don't be naïve! Expect that your kids will have opportunities to experiment with tobacco, alcohol, and possibly pot, and also expect them to be deceptive about drug experimentation. Control and monitor their locations and activities closely. Consider using detection methods and technologies (discussed later) well before you think you need them. Begin networking with parents and determine those whom you can trust to help protect your kids from experimentation.

• **Late adolescence phase**: You should have detection and monitoring methods and/or technologies in place. You should have a network of like-minded parents who will watch your kids while you watch theirs. Closely monitoring locations and activities is not as practical as during early adolescence. Nonetheless, try to prevent prolonged periods of unaccountable time and require your kids to notify you of their location at all times. If you detect any use of addicting substances, you should address them swiftly and substantially restrict the child's freedom. If a question of detection arises, the burden of proof should be on the child. You should end restrictions gradually and only after trust has been earned.

• **Age of independence phase**: Assuming that your children are away at college, in the military, or have otherwise moved away from home, they will no longer be under your direct control and monitoring. Most of your parenting is completed by this phase. Accountability should shift from monitoring and detection to performance, meaning that your focus should be on grades, class attendance, staying out of trouble, and other indirect parameters. If your youngster begins to falter in these areas, especially if you suspect alcohol or drugs are involved, then you have some important decisions to make. If the problems seem minor, then a heart-to-heart discussion with a warning may be sufficient. If these problems continue or become more significant, such as falling grades or legal problems, I recommend a more substantial approach. Unless your child is in the military and living in an environment entirely beyond your control, you should require the child to return home to live and to attend a local community college, while also being involved in some sort of drug rehab therapy. This may seem severe, but it can have a very important role in turning your child's life around. Besides, "overkill" does no damage, but if you do too little, you may never get another chance to stop this transition to addiction. If your child complies and does well, then provide one more chance to go back to an out-of-town college, but with continued accountability, such as periodic drug testing if appropriate.

• **Onset of adulthood phase**: If you have done your job during the previous phases, you should never have to face this phase of addiction development. Unfortunately if your child is part of a blended family where you could not invoke all the discussed protections, or you intervened too late or failed in some other way to protect your child, he or she may have reached this phase. Therefore, if your child has reached the onset of adulthood phase, you need to assume that he or she is *already* addicted.

Only two things can be done at this point. First, you must get involved in Al-Anon, because you will learn how to help your youngster without enabling the addiction. Second, you must do whatever you can to get your young adult child into addiction treatment. It is likely you will need to remove financial and legal support. You should reassure your child of your love and that you will do anything for him or her as long as it advances the cause of getting well. (See chart next page.)

Points to Remember
• Parents typically do no planning to prevent addiction in their children.
• Parents are slow to recognize emerging drug experimentation in their children.
• Parents react slowly and weakly when drug use among their children is discovered.
• The addiction process has a point of irreversibility that when reached, no return to a non-addiction state is possible.

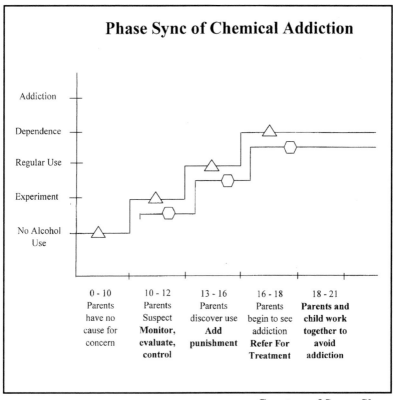

Phase Sync of Chemical Addiction

	0 - 10	10 - 12	13 - 16	16 - 18	18 - 21
	Parents have no cause for concern	Parents Suspect **Monitor, evaluate, control**	Parents discover use **Add punishment**	Parents begin to see addiction **Refer For Treatment**	**Parents and child work together to avoid addiction**

Courtesy of Susan Shaw

• If drug use is stopped during experimentation or transition, addiction will fail to occur.

• As the addiction cycle in youngsters progresses, the parental expectation-child capability gap appears to hamper attempts to prevent drug use and addiction.

13

How to Detect, Deter, and Monitor for Addicting Drugs and Why you Should!

Given the world we live in today, I see no way to raise non-addicted children without being fully knowledgeable about alcohol, drugs, and tobacco, along with ways to detect their use. Now that you have essential information about these chemicals, you need to learn how to detect, deter, and monitor for their use in your kids.

When Two Forces Clash, Deception is Likely

I've spoken before about the deceptive behavior that almost all kids engage in. When my wife and I were young parents we got an education about this kind of behavior. Our first child seemed honest and her behavior was always good. In fact she tried very hard to please us, which may have been the cause for a temporary downfall.

Like many elementary school kids, each week she was required to bring home a stack of graded papers for us to sign. During one school year, she began systematically removing the papers with low grades and then replaced them after the remaining papers in the stack were signed. Had we been even slightly suspicious, we would have checked to see if the papers had been re-stapled. Our daughter still had to figure out how to change the grades on her report card to reflect what we saw on her papers, and when she attempted to use a pen to change printed Ds to Bs on her report card, we discovered the deception.

Today our lovely and very honest daughter is an elementary school teacher with a master's degree. She's always been a good person and a high achiever, and I know the steps we took to correct her deceptive behavior worked well. The point is that kids are human, too, and humans often will try to deceive others in certain circumstances. In her case, she wasn't willing to do the work to please her parents, but at the same time, her desire to please us drove her to alter her report card.

My son was the "player" in a more relevant example. As we did with all of our children, we made it clear to him from a young age that the use of drugs, alcohol, or tobacco was strictly forbidden. Prior to getting his driver's license, we saw no indication that this rule was violated. One night, not long after getting his license, he missed his curfew for the first time. I called his cell phone to find out why, and during the course of our conversation I noticed a slight slur in his speech. In addition, the excuses he came up with to explain why he was late simply didn't add up. To get to the bottom of things, I drove to his supposed location, but when I arrived, no one was home. He and his friends were actually off drinking beer in a remote area, and he obviously lied to keep from getting into trouble and to avoid disappointing us.

As I drove home I spotted his pickup truck pulling in front of me onto the street leading home. I also noticed his vehicle weaving a bit. Luckily, he made it home safely because when he stepped out of his truck, he showed signs that he'd been drinking. Following the same advice I've recommended to you, his mother and I lowered the boom and he was punished for his deception and for drinking. We also began more intense monitoring and raised the accountability standards that applied to him. Over time and in stages, he was able to earn back our trust.

What happened with both kids illustrates a typical dilemma. As they mature, children want to remain in the favor of their parents, and other adults, too, such as teachers and coaches. At the same time, they have an intense attraction toward thrills, euphoria, risk taking, and adult-like activities. When these two natural drives clash, kids are often pushed to deceive.

Experimenting with addicting substances brings the drives together in a big way. The kids inherently know that their parents disapprove of drinking and smoking cigarettes or using drugs. Some kids will resist these temptations at first, but if given the opportunity, *almost all* will succumb to the temptation to experiment with some of these things. Kids don't want to disappoint their parents, so they will usually do almost anything to make them happy. But since the forces that push kids toward experimentation are very strong, then for many kids the only way to reconcile these opposing drives is to deceive their parents. They want their parents to believe that they are not involved with alcohol, tobacco, drugs, or sex; likewise, the parents want to believe this, too. Nonetheless, the behavior often happens.

Once kids choose to try the forbidden behaviors, they look for ways to avoid detection. Unfortunately a third common force enters into the equation, namely, parental denial. Many parents will go along with their kids' deceptive behavior to the point of full denial, and they refuse to believe their child would ever deceive them in any way, despite evidence to the contrary.

When I spoke to my son on the phone the night he'd been

drinking, my first response was to tell myself that my suspicion was wrong. Of course I didn't want to believe the truth. But my better judgment took over when I realized how important it was to be honest about the situation, so I was able to overcome my moment of denial and begin investigating. Had I chosen to deny or ignore the situation, my son might have continued to drink *and* drive—with unthinkable results.

I trust that by reading this book you are prepared not to buy into your child's deception and trap yourself in a complex system of denial. So, armed with an appropriately skeptical attitude, here is vital information you need to overcome deception.

Substance Detection and Monitoring

It's generally easy to monitor your children in order to detect addicting substances. It's done by evaluating physical signs along with testing. For the sake of simplicity, I've grouped the information by substance type:

Alcohol: As far as future drug addiction is concerned, alcohol represents the biggest danger for young children, because it's well established as an introductory or gateway drug. Therefore, it is *critical* that you detect and deter its use early. Here are some of the ways to detect its use.

• *Physical signs*: Alcohol will typically cause euphoria, giddiness, and increased energy at first. After about an hour it begins to cause relaxation. By the third hour of use it causes sedation and often sleep. An observer might notice slurred speech, poor coordination (staggering gait), and glazed and red eyes. The distinct odor of alcohol is detectable, depending on the amount and type of alcoholic beverage used. In heavy drinkers the odor of alcohol may persist for a number of hours after drinking stops, which means the odor may be obvious the morning after a night of heavy drinking. You can detect this physical sign of intake by requiring your child to blow a breath directly into your face. In most cases you will easily smell the alcohol odor on your child's breath.

• *Testing*: The *breathalyzer* is the most commonly used method of testing for alcohol intake. Alcohol is metabolized in the liver and eliminated as waste; however, a small amount is excreted unmetabolized through the lungs, the kidneys, and sweat. When one blows into the breathalyzer, it detects the small but reliably measured part that is excreted through the lung. At this time, a home breathalyzer costs under $100. If you believe you might have difficulty detecting your kids' alcohol use, then I recommend getting one. I also believe you should use it in any situation that you think your child may have an opportunity and inclination to drink. In addition, breathalyzers can be installed into vehicles, which means that the driver can't operate the car without passing the breathalyzer test. Obviously, that system can be defeated if your kid gets a friend to blow into the breathalyzer in the car.

A less practical method involves blood and urine testing. Your family doctor can perform this test if you have suspicions but have not purchased a breathalyzer. However, alcohol is excreted quickly, so 12-24 hours following the last use, it is unlikely you can detect it.

Tobacco: Boys often first begin using smokeless forms of tobacco, mainly snuff and chewing tobacco. Sadly, this practice often begins with their involvement in athletics, because kids see coaches using these products; thus, using snuff and chewing tobacco become "acceptable" for an athlete to begin his nicotine experimentation. Later, he likely will try cigarettes or cigars at parties. Girls tend to follow the more typical women's smoking patterns and use cigarettes almost exclusively. It's just as important to detect and deter your kids' early use of tobacco products, as it is to prevent any use of alcohol or other drugs, but not for the same reasons.

Never forget that tobacco products alone kill more people in this country than any other single substance. While it may have some introductory or gateway effect, thereby leading to other drugs, in itself it's dangerous enough to be avoided. In addition, tobacco is highly addicting, perhaps as addicting as heroin. In addition, take no solace in the fact that your youngster uses smokeless tobacco verses smoking cigarettes or cigars. Once addicted, kids will often use different forms of tobacco interchangeably. Therefore, when it comes to all tobacco products, your very best chance to avoid addiction in your kids is to prevent, detect, and deter any use.

• *Physical signs:* Young cigarette smokers may not be easy to detect. The characteristic odor is usually detected only by non-smokers and is directly proportionate to the amount of smoking. So, those kids who are smoking only at parties or in secret may be well addicted before you are able to detect any physical signs. If they choose to deceive you, smokeless tobacco use is difficult to detect. You have to see them cough up dark spittle, or spot traces of tobacco on their gums at the base of the teeth, or examine the inner surface of the lower lip. Those are about the only ways to detect its use. If you do examine your child's mouth, a characteristic white patch, *leukoplakia*, caused by snuff is often seen under the lower lip. This is significant because it's the forerunner of mouth cancer.

• **Testing**: Nicotine urine testing is quite easy and accurate. It can be done at your family doctor's office or you can order an inexpensive kit and perform it at home. Nicotine can be detected for up to four days after last use.

Marijuana: Though pot can be ingested when added to food, it produces euphoria more effectively when smoked (inhaled). Although its use is against the law, the drug is plentiful in the U.S because it can be locally grown anywhere—and is. I've known about pot grown in backyards, abandoned fields, gardens, and even hydroponically in a closet. The live plant is green with long, pointed leaves, but when it's processed for consumption, it's dark, much like tobacco. People usually roll it in a cigarette or cigar paper to smoke it, generally sharing it with other kids as part of the ritual involved with its use. When kids cross the line into pot use, they are crossing the line, figuratively and literally, toward a life of illegal drug use and probable addiction. Along with alcohol and possibly tobacco, it is an introductory or gateway drug.

• *Physical signs:* Marijuana has a characteristic semi-sweet but pungent odor. Like tobacco smoke, it can adhere to one's clothing, skin, and hair. If you smell it on your children, it doesn't necessarily mean they're using, but it may mean they're hanging out with kids who do. I recommend further testing to determine if they're using the drug. When intoxicated or "high," users can look much like alcohol users. Giddiness, slowed and slurred speech, and lack of coordination (staggering gait) are typical signs.

• *Testing:* Marijuana is stored in the body fat. Therefore, after last use it will be excreted for a longer period than most drugs. Often when marijuana is detected in the urine, kids claim that it was passive inhalation (inhaling smoke from other users). However, don't accept this excuse. First, when measuring levels in the urine, a "cutoff" point exists to eliminate detection of low level, accidental inhalation of particles. Second, if your children are passively inhaling that much marijuana because of close proximity to friends, they might as well be smoking it. Besides, if they're spending that much time with marijuana users, they'll eventually use it anyway. Your family doctor can perform urine testing or you can purchase a home testing kit. It can be detected up to 2-3 weeks after last use. Hair can be tested as well, and pot is detectable for up to 3 months.

Cocaine: Cocaine is made from the *coca* plant, which is indigenous to South America. Because it must be imported, drug cartels from Mexico and Columbia sprang up in the 1980s. Because of this drug interdiction in the sea and air became a primary mission for the Coast Guard. When processed it is made into a white powder that is ingested by "snorting" (inhaling into the nostrils). It is absorbed directly into the mucous membranes. Once tolerance develops the user often goes on to the purified "crack" form which is smoked through a glass pipe. Typically, the user begins snorting it at parties along with drinking alcohol and or smoking pot. Upon converting to crack use, users become solidly addicted.

• *Physical signs:* Because cocaine is a type of stimulant, the usual signs of stimulation will be observed. The user will typically have euphoria, super alertness, jitteriness, red eyes, and dilated pupils. The drug is metabolized quickly, so this effect is short lasting. As a result, it is unlikely you will see these signs because cocaine users typically get high late at night and in privacy. More likely, you will notice them appearing drowsy and tired during the day after the drug has worn off. Over the longer term, the signs may include weight loss because the drug causes appetite suppression. In addition, cocaine users may show signs of paranoid thoughts or outright psychotic behavior.

• *Testing:* Testing is typically done on urine. It will be detectable in urine for up 3-4 days after last use. It is also detectable in hair for as long as 3 months after last use.

Heroin (and other opiates): Natural opiates are derived from the *opium poppy plant* grown mainly in Afghanistan. It is

217

processed into the weaker opium form used around the world for centuries. It is also made into heroin (a much stronger form for abuse only) through illegal labs, and into morphine, which is commonly used for medical purposes. In recent years synthetic opiates have been produced by pharmaceutical companies for medical use, although they are highly abusable too. Heroin and most natural and synthetic opiates are not only highly addicting, but *very* easy to overdose with (and die), because the dose that stops breathing is not much higher than the dose needed to get high. Heroin, morphine, and Demerol are not absorbed in the stomach, so addicts inject them into their veins. Nowadays, there are synthetic forms of potent opiates that are also highly addicting, even orally. These include Oxycontin and methadone. Oxycontin has become so sought after by addicts that there have been a number of cases of addicts who rob pharmacies for this drug and ignore all other drugs including other opiates.

• *Physical signs:* The classic sign of heroin use is needle tracks on the arms, resulting from frequent self-injections. However, since potent oral forms of opiates exist, needle tracks may not be evident. While under the influence, users will show signs of euphoria, sedation, and very small (pinpoint) pupils. Chronic opiate addicts will usually become very thin and appear malnourished.

• *Testing:* Most standard home testing kits can test for traditional opiates, such as codeine, heroin, and morphine. If you suspect newer, atypical opiate use like Fentanyl, known by the street names "china white" and "percopop," you can ask your doctor to perform the necessary special tests. Urine tests will be positive for 2-4 days, and hair for up to 3 months.

Methamphetamines (and other stimulants): Although you may have heard much about this drug in recent years, it is relatively new to the illegal drug market. Its use is spreading rapidly and it may ultimately prove to be more addicting than any substance we have seen thus far. It can be taken by any route, including orally, intravenously, snorting, and smoking. Because the ingredients are inexpensive and easy to find, it can be "homemade" in the so-called "meth labs," which are really nothing more than hidden places in private homes. Nothing has to be grown as in the case of cocaine, marijuana, and heroin.

Meth, as it is called, causes severe crime and social problems in any community in which it becomes plentiful and available, and that includes my small town and many others in every state in the country. When children are removed from homes because their parents are addicted and involved in illegal activity involving meth, these adults will sometimes refuse to stop using or accept treatment, even to get their children back. According to current trends, we may begin to see a whole new crime wave due to this drug alone.

• *Physical signs:* Because this drug is chemically related to cocaine, its effects on the body are similar. Users show signs of euphoria, super alertness and irritability, and red eyes. Chronic users also appear thin and unhealthy and show dramatic signs of premature facial aging.

• *Testing:* Methamphetamine as well as prescription amphetamines show up in urine drug testing for about 3-5 days after last use. It also is detectable in hair for up to 3 months.

Monitoring Communication

Kids experiment with substances almost exclusively in groups, which is why it's vital that they communicate with each other and make their plans to "party." By party, I am not talking about balloons and birthday cakes. When drug users use this term, they are referring to a gathering of friends for the primary purpose of using drugs and alcohol. Today, computers and cell phones represent the two major tools for communication. Both provide opportunities for parents to discover what their kids are thinking and, more importantly, what they're doing.

Personal Computers: Kids use computers to communicate through email and instant messenger. By using monitoring software programs, you can become aware of everything your kids type into their computers and everything they view on their screens. You can buy this software through a computer professional or through the internet, and you'll find that it's inexpensive and easy to set up. The software "resides" on the child's computer, but it is not evident to him or her when placed into "stealth" mode. It records every keystroke and image that appears on the computer, and you can view this activity later through a specific combination of keys and a password. If your home computers are networked, you can look up the information on another workstation if properly configured.

This kind of software has other advantages, too, including your ability to find out if your kids are viewing pornography, are in contact with potential sexual predators, and other dangerous activities. I recommend not telling your kids that you intend to use or are using this software, which means that you need to avoid becoming upset about little things—coarse language or mindless conversations between kids that seem inane to you or that may be unkind or otherwise bothersome. Once your youngsters suspect that you are spying on or monitoring their computer, they will change their mode of communication. If you learn something through monitoring the computer (or any other means) that demands further investigation, find some excuse for how you obtained the information.

You want to be sure that you can avoid disclosing your monitoring methods or other sources of information.

I've found that the best method of hiding your source of information is to tell your children that you have received information from a source who requested confidentiality. Parenthetically, most information I have learned was from an older sibling to whom they confided. Wouldn't you think they would have figured this out? Besides, where the information came from isn't important; the only important issue is that your child was doing something you don't approve of. Don't be reluctant to express this to your child. Remember, you are the parent!

At first, teenagers often resent this intrusion into their lives, but I have always found that once you explain that you are really not interested in their personal "business" and you simply want to keep them safe, they understand your motivation. The first time I was confronted by one of my kids over this, I felt tremendous guilt. I was surprised and relieved that he not only understood, but seemed to appreciate my explanation that my motivation was rooted in my desire to keep him safe.

When you confront your kids, don't disclose exactly what you learned. Typically I address the issue by asking a general question, such as, "Tell me what happened last night?" Or, I might ask an even more pointed question, "Tell me about the alcohol you drank last night?"

It is evident to kids from these general and open-ended questions that you know something. Once on the defensive, it is amazing what they will tell you or how easily they will confess. Every single time I've questioned my kids in this manner I've learned several important things unrelated to the information I already had. In other words, you never know what will come up when kids sense that you already know things they thought they'd managed to hide.

The filtering software for computers that allows you to block certain websites you believe are bad for your kids is ineffective in preventing your child from seeing pornography and being vulnerable to sexual predators. Kids are very smart with computers and they know how to defeat or work around these filters, which can be very annoying, as well, because they sometimes filter out legitimate information your kids need, such as access to scientific and health information.

Cell Phones and GPS

Kids frequently use cell phones to communicate and are especially enamored with their text messaging capabilities. At the present time, I'm unaware of any way parents can monitor this form of communication, but GPS (global positioning system) technology has been added to some of the new cell phones on the market. Therefore, this may be of some help to parents in monitoring their kids' locations and activities.

Increasingly, GPS systems are used to track vehicle movement. For example, many trucking companies use GPS systems for tracking purposes, as well as to monitor speeds and stopovers. You can outfit your child's car with such a system. You can order a GPS system through the internet, have it installed, and sign up for a monthly subscription. Then you'll go to the appropriate website to learn where the car is and how fast it's been traveling—valuable pieces of information, to be sure. It's possible to achieve these steps and track your child using stealth techniques, meaning that you can hide this system, but it's more difficult to accomplish than concealing computer monitoring software. Obviously, if kids know they're being tracked, then they'll begin traveling to all their social events in a friend's car.

The "Old-fashioned" Curfew

It's important that kids have curfews until they leave home

for college or the military or to otherwise live on their own. Over the years, I've seen kids, even elementary school kids, who essentially had no curfew. Allowing children to run free without proper supervision is very high risk for both drug use and sexual activity.

The later the hour, the worse the behavior should be your rule of thumb. So, when you settle on a curfew, consider what time the acceptable activities typically end. You're asking for trouble if the curfew limit is significantly beyond the time the activity is over for the night.

We based the curfew policy in our home on two basic guidelines. School nights usually demand an early curfew, i.e., 8:00-10:00 pm, depending on the age. Of course, regardless of the curfew time, school work or chores must be completed. Weekend or holiday curfews are more relaxed. You can use an easy formula that sets the curfew an hour later than the grade. So, ninth grade equaled 10:00 pm, tenth grade equaled 11:00, eleventh grade equaled midnight, and twelfth grade equaled 1:00 am.

We also adjusted curfew times according to special activities, so that formal occasions such as prom night merited a later curfew. On the other hand, if the kids fell short of our behavior or attitude standards, we sharply reduced curfews and when the appropriate behavior and attitudes came back, we returned to the previous curfew in steps.

Home Alone

I have touched on this issue earlier, but it is so important I'll mention it again. Allowing kids, even older teenagers, to go unsupervised in yours or neighbors' homes, even during the daytime, is a bad idea. First, studies show that most underage sex is conducted in a home while parents are away, even for brief periods. Second, a home without a responsible adult is an open invitation to an impromptu party that can be organized in minutes, usually at night and especially during the weekend.

If you or another adult can't be in the home at all times when your child is there, I suggest a specific back-up plan. Either you or another responsible adult should "drop in" unannounced and at unpredictable times. This provides possible detection and definite deterrence. Out of fear of detection, your kids will probably calculate that it is too risky to do things at home. Another idea is to have neighbors contact you if "too many" cars appear in your driveway.

Education and Indoctrination

As I've said, I'm not a big fan of education designed to prevent or deter alcohol or drug experimentation. I have this attitude because the evidence is strong that education alone or as a *primary* strategy is ineffective. However, education has a definite place in our fight against addiction.

Young children have somewhat limited ability to assimilate information that they can then apply to everyday situations. To cite one example, it surprises most adults, but it's been well demonstrated that when it comes to repulsing sexual predators, kids don't have the ability to judge who is dangerous or even who is a stranger. Because of this, young children must be indoctrinated against dangers. This means that we need to teach them imperatives such as "Kids never drink alcohol!" or "Smoking makes you sick!" or "Never let anybody touch your private areas unless your mom or dad says it's okay!"

As children mature, they are ready for more nuanced education about the ways of the world, including more in-depth education about drugs. However, as I mentioned, the drug prevention programs that set out the evidence and then encourage the child to make a decision are not useful. In other words, it doesn't make sense to go on about the "pros" and "cons" of drugs, a strategy that by its nature discusses the "fun factor" involved with their use. To be effective, education must focus on the harmful short-term and long-term effects, and if we leave the decision to children, we may have made the decision for them—to use.

On balance, I believe it's a good idea to teach your youngsters about the dangers of alcohol, tobacco, and drugs, as long as you don't exclude the other prevention measures discussed in this book. As you know by now, addiction is a multifaceted problem that can't be dealt with only through education.

Planning Your Strategy

Information and technology are of no help unless you have a strategy to use them. The way you apply information and technology depends on many variables, including the specific dangers present in your neighborhood and your children's schools, coupled with your child's personality. Keep in mind the three principles of using these methods effectively to create a powerful strategy: *detection, deterrence, and monitoring*.

We've discussed some detection methods, but deterrence is important, too, and depends on several things. First, your kids need to know that you strongly disapprove of experimentation with *any* addicting substance. Second, make sure they understand that you take this issue very seriously and you will not tolerate any violation of the rules in this area. Third, let them know you trust them (if you really do), but you don't trust their immaturity, peer pressure, and drugs themselves. If you have reason not to trust your kids, then explain why.

Deterrence also depends on effective detection, monitoring, and taking action when needed. Failure to detect, monitor, or to follow through with appropriate action will lead to defeat. In this case, defeat means that your children will begin to experiment, and continue to experiment, without your knowledge. This defeat is significant because it may lead to addiction. At the very least, it creates conditions ripe for your kids to travel the path toward addiction.

Your specific strategies must match the age group. For example, most kids start using computers in elementary school, so that's when you should begin using monitoring software for their home computers, which I realize may or may not be shared with others in the family. Regardless, I recommend keeping the computer in an open location, making it is easy for you to pass by and look over your child's shoulder. These steps should help protect against predators, and allow you to assess your child's level of sophistication about drugs and sex. In general, kids who hang out together have about the same level of knowledge and savvy, so the computer provides valuable clues about what they're up to.

With this age group, make sure you're in tune with what happens at overnight parties, more for potential sexual molestation than drugs. Know where your kids are staying and with whom, make sure you are comfortable with the adults in that setting, and carefully discuss the event once they're back home.

By the time your kids reach pre-adolescence (ages 10-12), alcohol and tobacco are their likely experimental substances, but watch out for marijuana, too, no matter where you live. In neighborhoods with a prevalence of street gangs and drugs, consider detecting and monitoring for even stronger and more dangerous substances.

During pre-adolescence your alcohol, tobacco, and drug detection, deterrence, and monitoring should be in full swing. Make sure you know where your kids are at all times. If you allow your child to go to an overnight party or campout, prepare the same way you would for younger children. In

226

addition, the following morning when your kids are back home, give them a hug as you inconspicuously examine their appearance. Look into their eyes and smell their breath. If you detect or suspect something, question them, but if you are not fully satisfied, *test*!

During early adolescence (13-15) the risks of experimentation multiply because peer pressure increases and children are becoming more independent. This means you need to increase communication as opportunities grow. Parties take place in private homes and word quickly spreads that parents are away, because that's where the party will be! Remember, too, some parents condone or even facilitate drinking. Be prepared to examine and test your teenager during risky periods such as weekend nights and after sleepovers.

Believe it or not, learning that teenagers have drunk alcohol may be a good thing. Once "busted" they have no argument against intensified monitoring. I was caught by surprise when I found out that my 16-year-old son had been drinking beer, but this experience was quite "sobering" for my wife and me. I didn't perform a breathalyzer test on him because he admitted to it when confronted. After a lengthy discussion with him, during which I expressed my disappointment and my concerns about potential addiction and driving under the influence, there was no doubt in his mind that I would be watching him closely—and rightfully so.

For the two remaining years my son has been living at home, he has undergone close monitoring for further alcohol use. He has been compliant with our requirement that he let us know where he is at all times. When he comes home during the day, he finds one or both of us so that we can greet him and see how he's doing. More importantly, when he returns home at night, he undergoes the same ritual required by all our kids. He must come to our bedroom (we always wait up for him), hug and kiss us goodnight, and allow us to check his breath. He has had a strict curfew, and he's accountable for his time and movements, especially at night.

Over time, he's gained back some privileges and is under less scrutiny because he has proven his trustworthiness. Since we intensified detection and monitoring, we've had no problems with him. Once he reaches age 18 and goes off to college, we will feel comfortable that he does not have a latent addiction waiting to rear its ugly head. As you can see, we turned this disappointing episode of underage drinking into an opportunity to watch him closely. We would have done it anyway, to some degree, even if he had not been caught drinking with his friends; however, because he was caught, he was in no position to make the claim that such monitoring was unjust.

This is not to suggest, however, that you should allow your kids to drink in order to set a trap. I still recommend that you prevent use as much as possible. But if prevention fails and your kids drink, smoke, or use drugs in any form, you'll be well positioned to turn this failure into an opportunity to help prevent them from entering the addiction cycle.

The late adolescent period (16-18) can be the most trying. First of all, high school proms are thought of by kids as "slam dunk" times to get drunk. Therefore, the peer pressure to drink moves from individual social groups to a somewhat institutionalized ritual. Kids are ready to begin *rumspringa*! For many parents, unfortunately, this is the time to look the other way when it comes to teenaged drinking. As mentioned before, parents will often provide alcohol and a post-prom place to drink, under the misguided belief that this act will protect the kids. Given the age, level of mobility and independence, and ease of getting fake IDs, it's almost impossible to stop all opportunities or pressures to experiment with addicting substances, especially alcohol and tobacco.

All four of my teenagers drank some alcohol during this phase, but their use was infrequent, intake was moderate, and we eventually found out about it through some source or detection method. In each case we took action appropriate to the circumstances. Your kids will likely use during this phase, too, but work very hard to keep it limited to alcohol. Make a big deal out of any discovered use and adjust your strategy to prevent more use in the future.

During "onset of independence" age (18-21), detection, deterrence, and monitoring must substantially change. Your youngsters have probably left home, so curfews and kisses aren't much help anymore. You hope you've trained your kids well and they will make you proud as they begin independence. However, there are still opportunities to dampen or prevent unwise, risky, and unacceptable behavior.

At this age, money might speak loudly, and it's more than likely your independent children are still at least partially dependent on you for financial support, particularly if they're in college. So, use the leverage you have left. For example, if you're paying your child's college fees, or some portion of them, make it clear from the beginning that they have opportunity to get an education or training with your help that will lead the way to complete independence. Therefore, anything other than a full, earnest effort in school is unacceptable.

In other words, you'll support (to the extent you can) the first trip to school, but if they fail to study and show up for class, then they will bear the entire financial burden of the next one. Today, most colleges don't disclose grades or class attendance directly to parents, but you can make it clear that a condition of continued support is openness about grades and any other academic information.

It's also important to monitor your children's bank accounts while they're in college. Within reason they should be ready to provide copies of bank statements and be generally accountable for their use of *your* money. Of course, you never want to give the impression that money is limitless. Work with your kids to develop a budget and monitor to make sure they stick to it. Depending on your financial situation and their course load, it makes sense to encourage part time and/or summer jobs.

As you can see, you have many tools available to you in your personal war on drugs, that is, preventing addiction in your own kids. I realize that some of these concepts and techniques seem somewhat draconian and "cloak and dagger." But the stakes are high and you are up against addiction, a most powerful foe. If used well and properly, these strategies and tools work, so be fearless as you go forward to raise a NAP (non-addicted person).

Points to Remember

• Strong forces that push your kids to experiment with addicting substances will usually lead them to show deceptive behavior—so expect it.

• When it comes to addicting substances, it is better to over-evaluate and over-test than under-evaluate or under-test.

• Detection methods are most effective when they are used to deter use.

• Curfews, along with time and location monitoring are just as important as detection, deterrence, and monitoring for drugs.

• Keep your kids' unsupervised time to a minimum.

• If your kids leave home to go to college or for other training, continue to hold them accountable for behavior and academic performance.

14

Diseases that often Occur With Drug Addiction

In an earlier chapter, I mentioned the concept of *co-morbidity* within the homes where addiction affects one or more family members. By that we mean that other diseases and/or addictions exist within the troubled family, such as mental illness, obesity, or family members with other addictions. This same concept also applies to individual addicts. This means that addicts may have co-occurring physical or psychological diseases, which usually complicate treatment and the patients' overall condition.

We face a dilemma when we consider the interaction between addiction and co-occurring diseases, which is summed up in the old question: "Which came first, the chicken or the egg?" This is what we ask when we treat addicts with multiple problems: Which came first, the addiction or the other conditions? And even more important, is there a cause and effect relationship between the two problems? Does addiction cause the other condition or vice versa? As you will see, many common co-occurring diseases or problems are seen with addiction.

Depression: A Common Disease
Depression, the most common disease in a larger class we

call mood disorders, can occur at any age. *Bipolar disorder*, the other main disease in this category, occurs in less than 5% of people with mood disorders. As much as 10% of our population undergoes a significant depression at some point in their lives. Paradoxically, however, not everyone with depression actually feels depressed.

To clarify, the disease of depression was discovered long ago before the era of modern medicine. Like many older diseases the diagnostic term for depression was based on its major symptom, feeling depressed, well before doctors developed a good understanding of the actual disease process. You see, in the early days of the diagnosis and treatment of depression, doctors didn't reach this diagnosis or treat the condition unless the patient suffered from *significant* complaints of depression. In fact, as recently as the 1980s a doctor rarely diagnosed depression in patients unless they complained about feeling "blue" to some degree.

Nowadays, we have a much better understanding of what causes depression, and we recognize many other physical symptoms and psychological problems as symptoms of depressive disease. We now know that feeling blue or depressed is just one of many symptoms of the disorder we call depression. The following is a list of common symptoms found in depressive disease:

- Anxiety, "stressed out" feelings, panic attacks
- Insomnia
- Quick temper, overreaction to stress
- Feelings of hopelessness, worthlessness, and guilt
- Chronic fatigue
- Chronic muscular pains (fibromyalgia), irritable bowel syndrome
- Chronic back pain and headaches
- Obsessive-Compulsive disorder

- Phobias
- Lack of concentration
- Crying spells, more emotional than usual
- Change in weight or appetite
- Eating disorders
- Depressed, feeling "blue"
- Suicidal feelings

It's no longer unusual to diagnose depression when a patient reports only insomnia or anxiety, for example, or fatigue alone, or one or two symptoms of this disorder. When we question patients further, they usually admit to experiencing several other symptoms on the list above. However, they don't mentally connect the relationship between their primary complaint and other symptoms. Doctors who fail to ask about these other complaints may miss the diagnosis, which means they treat only the reported symptoms, and that leads to poor results.

I discussed human brain chemistry in chapter 4, specifically the neurotransmitters important to brain function. As researchers studied antidepressant medication, they gained information that increased understanding of this valuable interaction between neurotransmitters and addicting substances. You may recall that addiction occurs in part by disrupting this form of brain communication.

Depression occurs when the levels of three main neurotransmitters drop too low. The first is *serotonin*, which is responsible for lifting our mood, helping us sleep, and calming our nerves. The second, *norepinephrine*, is responsible for our energy, and the third, *dopamine*, is the neurotransmitter responsible for "reward" or "pleasure" stimulation at the VTA (Ventral Tegmental Area). In day to day functioning, dopamine's purpose is to give us a general sense of well-being and to raise our threshold of pain, meaning that it decreases pain sensitivity.

When healthcare professionals and others use the term "chemical imbalance" to describe depression, what they're referring to is the imbalance of the neurotransmitters needed for normal brain function. More accurately, the imbalance is actually caused by a deficiency in the amounts of particular neurotransmitters produced. So, while we think of depression or other "chemical imbalance" disorders in terms of lack of serotonin levels in the brain, a deficiency of all three neurotransmitters usually occurs. Conversely, the medications we prescribe (antidepressant medications) will often elevate the low levels of all three neurotransmitters to one extent or another.

Diagnostic terms sometimes become antiquated. For example, tuberculosis was once known as consumption, and congestive heart failure was known as dropsy. Likewise, depression is really an antiquated term for the disease we treat by that name. I don't care for the term, "chemical imbalance" either, because it's neither accurate nor descriptive. When I've talked with patients, I've used both "serotonin deficiency" and "neurotransmitter deficiency," but the proper technical medical term is *primary affective disorder*, which is a mouthful and to those not medically trained it sounds vague. However, for reasons I've set forth, I hope we can come up with something better than just plain "depression."

How do Antidepressant Medications Work?

Since we know that addicting drugs can cause a major rise in certain neurotransmitters, especially dopamine, is it possible then, that antidepressants can cause addiction by raising the levels of neurotransmitters? Fortunately, the answer is no. Antidepressants can't cause addiction,

The reasons for this are threefold. First, antidepressants generally do not cause a direct rise in neurotransmitters; rather, they inhibit or block the enzymes that break down these important chemicals. This results in a gradual increase up to, but not higher than, normal levels. Second, as antidepressant medications are increased beyond routine doses, unpleasant side effects occur, thus patients do not develop tolerance to increasing doses. Third, unlike addicting drugs, antidepressant medications do not produce withdrawal symptoms when people stop using them.

Unlike addicting drugs, antidepressant medications do not produce a "high" or euphoria in the user, because neurotransmitter levels gradually rise over a matter of days, instead of minutes. In addition, patients do not experience relief from their depression for 5- 21 days after beginning therapy, which provides further testimony to the slow rise in neurotransmitters. Once the medication has been properly dosed and adjusted on follow up, patients should feel normal, that is, they feel "normally" well and functional in day-to-day life as they did prior to becoming sick. It's unrealistic and inappropriate for a patient to make feeling high or giddy a goal.

Not all Feelings of Depression are Caused by Disease

It's completely normal to feel depressed when you're in the midst of a depressing situation, and we call this *situational depression*. For example, let's say you're 50 years old and you just learned a 35-year old received the promotion you thought sure you were in line to get. In this situation, you will likely feel depressed, and probably angry or frustrated, too, and having this range of emotions for a relatively short period of time in no way means that you're ill.

Grief provides another example. Parents who lose a child through accident or illness will experience enormous grief and the symptoms are similar to depression. However, grief is not an illness. In both situations, those who do not have a chronic depressive illness will gradually and spontaneously begin to process their immediate feelings of depression or grief. At some point, and the time varies based on the situation and individual differences, they return to feeling normal without medication.

On the other hand, those with depressive disease may feel severely depressed or have other symptoms without any external explanation. In fact, when I discuss depression with newly diagnosed patients, they often protest: "I can't be depressed, because I have nothing to be depressed about."

This creates an interesting paradox, as an inverse relationship often exists between reasons to be depressed and the actual presence of the disease. In those for whom many external reasons exist for depression, the less likely it is that they have depressive disease (versus situational depression). On the other hand, those with few reasons to be depressed, but in whom depression is present, the more likely it is that they have depressive illness. This suggests a biological basis for depressive illness and mood disorders in general. So, if depressive disease is biological, how do you "catch" it?

Many studies verify that the tendency to develop depressive disease is inherited. One valuable study involved a retrospective genealogical analysis of the Amish. Though the members of this anachronistic culture don't allow themselves to be photographed, they keep detailed records of their ancestors. Through well chronicled histories of individuals within specific families, researchers found descriptions of multiple generations of Amish who suffered bipolar disorder (discussed below). In some cases, the evidence of inherited bipolar disorder went back hundreds of years.

Identical twin studies, the classic method to prove biological inheritance, also show a high correlation of depression in twins. In some of these studies, the twins were separated at birth and raised by two separate families, thus ruling out environmental influences.

Research also shows that while antidepressant medication can dramatically improve *biological* depression, *situational* depressions usually do not respond. In my clinical experience, the majority of patients I diagnose with a depressive illness have at least one close, biological relative who has a history of treatment for depression.

Psychology or Biology?

At one time, based on what I was taught and believed to be factual, I told my patients that a true depressive disorder occurs irrespective of their environment, situation, or stress level. I still believe that to be generally the case. However, after treating many patients for this problem, especially the milder forms, I believe that in some people, stress can definitely *trigger* a biologically-based depressive illness.

But if depressive disease is biologically based, how can environmental factors trigger the onset of symptoms? While we need more research into this area, I believe that in some individuals, psychological stress uses up neurotransmitters faster than normal. Individuals with a completely normal system of neurotransmitters may have an unlimited supply, no matter how much stress they encounter. On the other hand, those with mild, borderline, or otherwise asymptomatic depression may become symptomatically depressed when under stress. So, it's likely that millions of people—in this country alone—who ordinarily have no symptoms of depression are susceptible to depression while under stress.

I resisted the idea of stress as a trigger, but as antidepressants became more effective and safer, I became more liberal in prescribing them to people with less obvious depressive symptoms. But I also began to prescribe antidepressants to patients who appeared to have a situational depression, usually after a period of prolonged stress. To my surprise, many improved dramatically with antidepressant treatment. One could logically conclude that perhaps the stress and the depression were merely coincidental. However, most of these patients were able to stop taking medication once their stressful situation resolved.

In addition, PTSD (post-traumatic stress disorder) is a more recent example of this triggering effect. Though I have never treated a patient with this problem, the literature suggests that many doctors have used antidepressants to treat patients with PTSD, and have reported excellent results. And this makes sense, because PTSD provides a clear example of environmental stress triggering a latent depressive disease.

Depressive Disease and Addiction

The interaction of depression and addiction is very difficult to untangle. Those who feel bad because of depressive disease, especially when undiagnosed and untreated, will grasp for something to relieve them of these terrible symptoms—just look at the list of symptoms above! Sometimes this means turning to alcohol or drugs. Sometimes, however, people who have never had depression before becoming addicted to drugs will suffer from depression, especially during periods between drug uses. So, by the time those with both problems see a physician for depression, the diagnosis and treatment is exceedingly complicated.

I've never been happy with the results of treatment when addiction and depression occur together. Whenever I have prescribed an antidepressant to addicted individuals, they often return with complaints that they're still depressed. In most cases, I've recommended that patients enter a drug treatment facility where they can receive drug detoxification, counseling, and antidepressant therapy. However, addicts rarely take that advice, but instead they usually request addicting tranquilizers to feel more comfortable. These tranquilizers are themselves chemical depressants, and they give temporary relief while aggravating the underlying depression problem. To give depressed addicts tranquilizers or any other addicting drugs would only be enabling and worsening their addiction.

My frustration brings me back to the critical point that parents and doctors must diagnose depressive disease in kids *before* they choose alcohol or pot to relieve their symptoms— and that's a real danger. Kids can become quite depressed, and parents often don't notice what has happened. But according to some research, depression puts them at risk to experiment with alcohol and drugs just to relieve the pain of their depression or severe anxiety.

I believe that when kids use addicting substances to get relief from depressive symptoms, the transition period to full-blown addiction may be shortened. Once they are on their way to addiction, diagnosing and treating depression becomes very complicated and the results less satisfying. Obviously, kids at this kind of risk should not have access to addicting substances. (Likewise, adults with depressive disorders shouldn't use addicting drugs either.)

The correct approach involves detecting and diagnosing depressive illness in these kids early in the course of the disease. With appropriate antidepressant medication and counseling, if needed, their risk of addiction is lower.

Childhood Depression

We used to think that depression was exclusively an adult disease, but current studies leave little doubt that depressive diseases occur even in pre-adolescents. The disease carries many dangers in childhood, even apart from the risk that a depressed child may experiment aggressively with addicting substances. For example, childhood suicide, a symptom of depression, is one of the most common causes of death in children. Less severe problems of childhood depression include declining school grades, peer relationship difficulties, disruptions within the family, and antisocial behavior. Therefore, it's critical that parents be aware of the danger signs of childhood depression and absolutely *keep drugs and alcohol away from kids*, especially if they are depressed.

The symptoms for depressive disease are the same in children and adults. However, because teens typically display unexplainable and unpredictable behavior, it can be very challenging to distinguish true depressive illness from what is just "being a teenager." Still, it's important to look for both classic signs and some additional ones, including:

• Sudden and dramatic change in behavior
• Obsessive or delusional thoughts
• Preoccupation with a lost girlfriend or boyfriend
• Persistent violent thoughts or writings
• Persistent inability to have fun or enjoy life
• Suicidal or homicidal thoughts

Notice that I listed "*thoughts*." Far too often, kids have seriously disturbed thoughts, which are completely unknown to parents. In some cases, parents detect the thoughts or writings, usually in diaries, emails, letters, and so forth, but they don't take them seriously. However, it is crucial that you talk with your kids and find out what's going on in their minds. This represents another case that may merit monitoring their personal computers (as discussed in chapter 13). Finally, understand how critically important it is for these kids to avoid addicting substances, even beer and tobacco.

Bipolar Disorder (Manic-Depressive Illness)

Bipolar disorder is a psychiatric illness in which the patient's brain can't regulate mood. Individuals with this disorder may fluctuate from depressed (low) to manic (high), sometimes very rapidly. Symptoms of bipolar disorder usually begin in the late teens to early adulthood.

Note some important and unique characteristics of this disease:

• Highly inheritable
• Frequently, irresponsible behavior leads to experimentation and risk taking
• Sometimes poor compliance with medication
• Higher suicide rate than associated with conventional depression
• Sometimes psychosis occurs

If this disease runs in your family, watch for it in your kids. Respond quickly to any concerns by getting psychiatric help and protect your child from a very serious risk of drugs, sex, and other dangerous behaviors. Like depression, in those with bipolar disease, addiction seems to accelerate when they use addicting substances. As in all mood disorders, the outcome is usually excellent with proper and timely treatment.

Schizophrenia

Schizophrenia is more severe and disabling than the mood disorders, and those with it can become extremely ill, completely lose touch with reality, and never function normally again. Most permanently institutionalized psychiatric patients and a large percentage of today's homeless people are schizophrenics. Like bipolar disorder, the onset of schizophrenia usually occurs in late adolescence to young adulthood. Though it tends to run in families, no clear cut genetic link exists for this disease. Most experts believe that it results from a combination of inherited and environmental factors. Below are some symptoms and facts about the disease:

• It usually has a sudden, catastrophic onset with auditory hallucinations (hearing voices) and delusional thinking.

• Sometimes patients recover fully with aggressive, early treatment.

• The disease often takes a chronic course and patients become marginally functional (at best) and unemployable.

• Schizophrenics have poor insight into their illness.

• There's often poor compliance with medication.

Increasingly, we see reports of teens suffering acute schizophrenic attacks after using hallucinogenic drugs. Surveys in general show a higher incidence of drug use and addiction in teens that either have or will eventually develop schizophrenia.

As I've mentioned before, schizophrenia, a terrible disease, struck several members of my extended family, including my mother, though her disease was not related to drug use. I recommend doing everything possible to prevent the onset of this illness, and that includes protecting your kids from hallucinogenic and addicting drugs, plus intervening early if you suspect your teen is beginning to show symptoms.

Obsessive-Compulsive disorder (OCD)

In recent years, we've recognized that OCD is related, at least in part, to low neurotransmitter levels. It is characterized by either intense and frequent thoughts about usually mundane ideas (obsession) or equally mundane multiple repetitive behaviors (compulsion), or both. An obsessive thought might be leaving home, but then worrying endlessly about whether you locked the door, even though you checked the lock five times. Repetitive hand washing is a typical example of compulsive behavior; some people wash their hands as much as one hundred times daily, and continue even when skin rashes result.

Alcoholics, smokers, and drug addicts also may develop an OCD type of syndrome. For example, they typically obsess over the desire for their drug of choice and they tend to use it frequently. Again, the chicken and egg question comes up. Are these people becoming OCD-like in their behavior because of their addiction? Or, do they become addicts because they tend to be unable to stop the thoughts and behaviors that lead to compulsive drug use? At this point, no one really knows, and it's likely that this co-morbidity can occur in either sequence. However, this information certainly suggests that kids that demonstrate OCD-like behavior may be at higher risk for addiction if allowed to experiment with addicting substances.

Attention deficit disorder (ADD) and Attention Deficit Hyperactivity Disorder (ADHD)

You may recall a brief discussion about ADHD in chapter 4. Currently, myths abound when it comes to *attention deficit disorders*. In fact it has become "politically correct" to deny that this problem even exists. Because they consider the existence of these disorders questionable, many people, even some medical professionals, maintain that giving medications for this problem is being done to "drug" kids into submission and get them to behave in an acceptable manner. These "experts" claim that kids should simply be allowed to "be kids" instead, suggesting that hyperactivity is nothing more than benign and normal activity in children.

These attitudes show a complete lack of understanding of attention deficit disorders and their potential bad outcomes for children. They also show a lack of appreciation of how difficult the learning process becomes for these kids when they are not treated.

Many claim that sugar and certain dyes in foods cause the hyperactivity seen in some of these kids. Some kids have been put on extreme diets that limit sugar in order to control this problem. However, after much research, not even a smidgen of evidence exists to support this.

As previously explained, ADD is a problem caused by decreased activity of the part of the brain that controls attention span (concentration). ADHD is the same problem except these kids demonstrate the additional symptom of excessive energy and activity. This is probably because, like the attention-span center, the part of the brain that appropriately limits activity is under-active as well.

Other co-occurring conditions appear with ADD/ADHD. These kids often suffer from *dyslexia*, a visual perception problem in which children have trouble seeing letters properly oriented in words, though they have otherwise normal vision. They may also demonstrate *oppositional behavior,* whereby they behave in opposition to directions given by parents (strong willed); show easy distractibility, and exhibit forgetfulness and poor impulse control.

Because ADD/ADHD kids cannot maintain adequate concentration in learning, their school performance may suffer greatly. These kids fall progressively behind because school advancement requires a good, continuing foundation of learning. Frequently, ADD/ADHD kids develop low self-esteem due to their inability to concentrate and learn, and because they so often don't know why they have these difficulties. They believe they are dumb and will never be able to achieve academically or aspire to a good career and a well paying job. In truth, their intelligence level is the same as normal individuals. They simply have an obstacle to the learning process, an inability to concentrate on a task.

Anger, frustration, poor interpersonal relationships may emerge as the untreated ADD/ADHD child grows into adolescence. As you can see, dropping out of school, drug experimentation and crime are likely results if this condition goes untreated. This helps explain why learning disorders are frequently found among drug addicts and prison inmates.

I realize that suggesting an addicting drug (oral amphetamines) for kids who are at risk for addiction is self-contradictory. But that is exactly what I recommend. ADD/ADHD kids need to be recognized, diagnosed, and treated early so they do not fall behind in learning. Oral amphetamines "wake up" the flailing attention span center of the brain. Additionally, oral amphetamines are not highly addictive unless converted to inhaled or intravenous use. My personal experience is that of the many children I have treated for ADD/ADHD, I know of none who have become drug addicts or even abused this medication. Most of them, except for its benefits, would rather not take the medication because it reduces their appetite.

Conversely, I have concerns about parents of ADD/ADHD kids. Some parents of these children are drug addicts and may bring their kids for ADD/ADHD treatment only to divert the medication to sell or abuse. Secondly, it has become fashionable in recent years for adults to present themselves for ADD/ADHD treatment. While most truly have the condition, in some cases they are really addicts posing as ADD/ADHD patients seeking abusable medications. Most likely, addicted persons who divert prescriptions for this drug are not taking it orally, as it has little to offer them in that form. They are usually converting it to inhaled or intravenous use. Finally, Strattera, a new drug, is effective in the treatment for ADD/ADHD and it is not abusable.

Chronic Pain Syndromes

Chronic pain syndromes are extremely frustrating and controversial conditions that can co-occur with addiction. The pain can come from almost any source, but is most commonly due to back pain. These patients are usually on strong narcotic medications, have had multiple back surgeries, and are disabled and no longer can work.

On the face of it, these people should illicit sympathy, but when working with many, I find a cascade of perverse incentives in play. By this I mean that they have incentives to remain "ill." Once you look at a typical medical and social history, you find that the original injury, if any, was relatively minor. It led to some type of accident or worker's compensation litigation, multiple surgeries to relieve pain, stronger and stronger pain meds, then disability payments or insurance settlements. Over the course of many years, these adults become preoccupied with dealing with lawyers and doctors, mostly to obtain money and pain medications. Nothing offered in the way of rehabilitation seems to work for them.

On the other hand, I see patients who have had tremendous trauma from some type of accident, and that has lead to surgery and some use of pain medication. Many get off the medication quickly, spurn repeat surgeries to relieve pain, and work their rehabilitation program aggressively in order to get back to work and continue their pre-injury lives. They may continue to experience pain, but they seem intent on dealing with it without narcotics.

Healthcare workers vigorously disagree among themselves about how liberally we should prescribe pain medications for chronic pain. Some doctors believe that those who require indefinite, but long-term periods of narcotic treatment, are not truly addicted, but rather, simply have physiological tolerance to the drugs. This suggests that if the pain could be suddenly cured they would be able to wean off narcotics and never desire them again. I think that in many cases, this is naïve thinking. Based on my observation, many people with chronic pain that can never be relieved and has a questionable source usually demonstrate other addict-like behaviors. They often sell some of their drugs, shop doctors, fail to follow medical recommendations, manipulate and deceive doctors, and so forth.

In the late 1970s, I witnessed the same type of behavior among heroin addicts. At that time, I was a Navy doctor stationed in Guam, but I also worked part time as director of the alcohol and drug rehab program, which consisted mainly of prescribing methadone to heroin addicts. At first, all I knew about methadone was that it was a drug given to heroin addicts to help them detoxify from the drug. I went into this situation very naïve. I expected to see a group of unfortunate but well-meaning young adults who made a mistake in life by using heroin. I assumed they wanted to make it right by getting off the dope.

Instead, I found a group of unhealthy appearing people whose lives were dedicated to manipulation, deception, and often crime. Some would "lip" the methadone (save it in their mouths to be later sold); others would take a dose, and then go shoot-up heroin. Very few worked, except as prostitutes. They often requested other addicting drugs like Valium to "make them comfortable." In a short period of time my attitude shifted from one of optimism to cynicism.

In general, healthcare professionals don't seem to have a good handle on which chronic-pain patients have true chronic pain and must have narcotics to survive, and which are addicts who skillfully manipulate the system. That is, they manipulate the system for financial support in order to avoid work or to get drugs for their addiction, or both.

It is not my intention to show disrespect to men and women with serious diseases that cause intolerable pain. On the contrary, I have tremendous sympathy and respect for people who must cope with terrible diseases such as chronic shingles pain, amputations, war injuries, neuritis, and the many other causes of chronic pain. But increasingly, those who suffer are hurt by the problems addicts cause when they pose as chronic pain patients. State and federal drug agencies have progressively tightened the drug accountability standards for patients and doctors over the past few years. I'm concerned that more and more people with legitimate pain problems will suffer because of higher and higher barriers to needed medications.

Prevent Your Child from Becoming a Victim

If millions of healthcare workers can't solve the problem, then I don't expect you to either, but I maintain that many "chronic pain" patients are really addicts in disguise. I want you to understand that you can do a lot to avoid this situation in your child. Though this needs more research, I think many of these problem adult chronic pain patients were once kids who became addicted to drugs. So, by using the drug prevention techniques in this book, you have an excellent chance of preventing such a sad and unproductive adult life for your child.

Non-chemical Addictions

Over the past few years, comedians have made much of the explosion of recognized non-chemical addictions, many of which have led to the creation of a 12-step program. However, for victims of these non-chemical addictions, there is nothing funny about them. I learned about food addiction when it first received media attention in the 1970s. Overeaters Anonymous (OA), a 12-step program for food addicts now has chapters in every state, and uses the same steps of recovery as AA. After that, I heard about gambling addiction, which became well known about the same time (1980-90s) that lotteries and gambling casinos began to spread across the country. Gamblers Anonymous (GA) exists to help gambling addicts recover. Finally, we've also seen sex addiction discussed in the media, and a 12-step program exists for that problem, too.

I mention these non-chemical addictions in the context of diseases co-occurring with drug addiction for a couple of reasons. First, many drug addicts are also addicted to other behaviors. For example, in recent years several well-known celebrity actors have admitted to a combination of chemical and non-chemical addictions such as drugs, sex, and gambling. It is also important to discuss the dangers of non-chemical addictions and ways to prevent them in your children.

A Vast Range of Addictions

Virtually anything that provides pleasure can lead to addiction. In addition to food, gambling, and sex, we also see addiction to shopping, pornography (generally considered a form of sexual addiction), and the internet. There are probably some that I have never heard of.

You're probably wondering how to know if you're addicted to an activity, rather than simply drawn to it. Here is a list of characteristics of non-chemical addiction.

• Victims describe a feeling of euphoria (a rush) when they engage in this.

• They increase the frequency to excessive levels.

• Stimulation (such as lights and sounds in a casino) associated with the activity begins to cause pleasure.

• When away from the activity, they can only think about getting back to it.

• The activity begins to displace normal activities and relationships.

• Extreme discomfort and anxiety occurs when forced to stop the activity.

• Family and job problems or even failures can be linked to the activity.

• Financial problems and loss of family may result from continuing the activity.

These characteristics are eerily similar to those associated with chemical addiction, which is why psychiatrists currently recognize that non-chemical addictions are the same psychologically and physiologically as the chemical forms—except for lack of chemicals, of course.

Preventing Non-chemical Addiction

As you know, drugs affect the VTA (Ventral Tegmental Area) and cause addiction in the immature brain by spiking dopamine to very high levels. It is only logical to assume that activities that give us pleasure can cause similar dopamine spikes, although we need more studies to look at this issue more deeply.

However, as a parent, you need to be on the lookout for activities in your child's life that may trigger dopamine spikes, and thus, lead to addiction. To prevent non-chemical addictions, consider this list of suggestions in addition to those mentioned in previous chapters.

• Prevent drug addiction—as we know, one addiction can lead to another.

• Require kids to vary and rotate desired activities. A latent addiction to the internet can be interrupted by limiting use to an hour or so each day, especially for young children. Move them on to other activities.

• Just as you prevent smoking, drinking, and doping while the kids live in your home, prevent gambling and pornography viewing, too. If they choose to engage in these things when they leave home, then you hope their brains will be mature enough to handle experimentation.

• If you detect early signs of addiction to certain activities, intervene and get the child counseling. Don't wait until transition to full addiction has occurred.

And one more thing before leaving the topic of non-chemical addictions: what activities are you modeling for your kids? It's probably true that many adults consider gambling and pornography to be harmless fun. Maybe you are able to indulge in these activities without becoming addicted. But your kids want to be just like you. In their pursuit to have fun the way you have fun, are they learning behaviors that will later become an addiction?

My wife and I taught our kids that gambling is a foolish folly and a sin. If the purpose of gambling is to get rich, then I suggest buying a casino. Of course I mean this tongue in cheek. My point is that the only people really making money in gambling are the casino owners, not the customers. It is sad to see people with limited income spend their entire paycheck in a casino—or on lottery tickets.

My wife and I also condemned pornography. Apart from the fact that it's sinful behavior, we taught our kids another important lesson about porn. If you listen to interviews with porn-industry actors, they are very forthcoming about their motivations. Despite any remarks about wanting to be a model or an actor, they eventually reveal their real motivations— money. They're basically prostitutes because they perform sex for money. Well, if customers quit paying for porn, it would stop immediately and these poor souls would have a better chance to find traditional jobs.

This means that every time you purchase porn, you are supporting the industry and giving these actors a reason to continue this self destructive behavior. Like me, I am sure you have heard the arguments made by porn actors that they choose this form of employment by free will. That is a lie! Studies show overwhelmingly that most actors in the pornography industry were sexually abused as children and ran away from home. They fell into prostitution only to survive, and they considered participating in producing pornography a "promotion." Their careers are short and most end up with an addiction and some type of sexually transmitted disease, such as AIDS or Chronic Hepatitis B or C.

Additionally, only a peek at a pornographic movie will convince you that it provides to the uninitiated, our children, a distorted and unrealistic perspective of sexuality. Add to this the many odd fetish orientations of porn, and it is easy to see how a child or teenager could suffer serious negative psychological effects.

I have already mentioned one case of a woman who suffers from a penis phobia due to viewing porn. Many child molesters and violent sex offenders have pointed to porn as a catalyst in their criminal behaviors. So every time you or your children buy pornography, you are contributing to the downfall of fellow humans and possibly your children if they become addicted to watching it.

Points to Remember

- People may experiment with drugs to relieve the pain of depression.
- Untreated psychiatric diseases, especially depression, can lead to drug addiction.
- Some psychiatric diseases, especially schizophrenia, may be triggered by drugs.
- Left untreated, other disorders like OCD and ADD could lead to drug addiction.
- Non-chemical forms of addiction exist and probably can be prevented, too.
- Parents who show leadership by not indulging in certain activities may present a very strong role model to their kids to prevent addiction.

15

A Model Blueprint to Raise a Non-Addicted Person (NAP)

The computer age has been upon us so long now that I imagine that many of you have never seen an actual old-fashioned blueprint. But you probably know that a blueprint is a graphic representation of a structure and gets its name from the white lines etched out of a layer of blue ink printed on large sheets of paper. When architects conceptualize a future structure of a building, they must commit their concept to a plan, a blueprint, in order to construct the building. The word blueprint remains part of our language, even though these visual forms are displayed on other types of paper or computer screens. Some things don't change, though, and as any architect will tell you, the final form and function of a structure will never be achieved unless a good plan is laid out and fully executed.

As a parent or future parent, you are an architect, too. Of course, you may not have a lot to say about your children's physical structure, as God and your DNA have already developed that plan (though DNA engineering in the future may make this possible). But the type of individuals your children will become one day in the future is largely up to you.

My purpose here is to present a model "blueprint," created with the idea of preventing your child from becoming addicted to one or more substances. However, much of what you need to know about planning and "building" your children to become non-addicted persons (NAP) will help them—and you—in other ways. This model blueprint should function as a framework for you, because you have the responsibility for raising your kids, and it's your job to make the final decisions about their care and upbringing. So, use this model to create your own blueprint, using words instead of graphics, to raise your kids.

If you come up with a sound plan and execute it properly, then your child should not only be non-addicted, but he or she will likely grow up to be a good citizen with a loving spirit, a strong work ethic, and good moral character. Looking to the future, your adult children will have what it takes to be responsible parents themselves, not to mention good and faithful partners with their spouses, and a source of comfort, pride, and support to you during your retirement years.

As you consider this model blueprint, arranged by age, notice that just like all structures, you need a good foundation. You can't expect success if you skip or delay implementing the steps in your "child-building" process. Much of what appears below has been discussed in greater detail in other chapters. So, consider these elements for your blueprint as a checklist to refer to in your planning.

Before Birth

Children deserve to be planned, and we would hope that your blueprint includes a plan for marriage and an intended pregnancy. As previously mentioned, it's clear that children have a much better chance to succeed in this world, and especially when it comes to avoiding addiction, if two parents (whether biological or adoptive) want them.

Soon-to-be parents must also consider *lifestyle* issues, including the following facts about addicting substances:

• All addicting substances may be damaging to the fetus, including smoking cigarettes, which causes lower birth weights in infants. This also includes alcohol, because Fetal Alcohol Syndrome (FAS) is well known to cause a variety of birth defects and mental retardation.

• When used during pregnancy, the harder drugs, such as crack, heroin, and methamphetamines cause drug withdrawal in infants within hours of birth; these drugs also have other potentially damaging effects to their brains.

• Consider, too, that we see higher rates of addiction among kids who use drugs at younger ages. What are the implications for a fetus exposed to drugs? When a pregnant woman takes addicting drugs into her body, she bathes the unborn child's immature brain with drugs within minutes of intake. Does such premature exposure to addicting substances lead to a much higher risk of addiction for the child? While we need more research to explore that issue, I wouldn't risk using any addicting substances during pregnancy.

• Fathers have reasons for concern about their lifestyle choices, too, because children begin developing their personalities and attitudes at a very early age.

• Before a baby is on the way (or at the time a pregnancy becomes known), parents should take an honest inventory of what lifestyle choices need to be reconsidered. If either parent has an addiction, that's the time to do something about it. In other words, don't delay—get treatment!

Create family traditions: By this I mean, ask questions about the way you want to live. What do we want our family meals to be like? How will we practice our faith? How will we celebrate family holidays? These are only a sample of the kinds of lifestyle issues that a twosome should consider before they become a threesome.

Birth to Six Years

You'll probably not give much thought to the risk of addiction when your kids are in this age range, but please don't be naïve about things that occur at this time that may lead to problems later. Psychologists tell us that children's personalities are mostly formed by age six. So kids are the most malleable during these years.

By the time their kids are about six, parents' lifestyle habits are fairly well established, so evaluate your choices based on what their kids see. For example:

• Your small children see your behavior. They watch as you reach for orange juice, a sports drink, or a soda, instead of a beer.

• When your friends come to your house to spend the evening, you don't want your kids see you passing a joint—not to mention giggling about it and just generally acting weird. Instead, make sure they see you enjoying the company of your friends in appropriate ways, and acting like adults.

Building self esteem: In this age group it starts with affection.

• Kids love the physical affection involved in being held, hugged, and kissed.

• Begin telling them you love them and never stop as long as you live, always letting them know that your love is unconditional. That is, you love them and you will openly show it when they make a mistake or even if they exhibit bad behavior.

• Although you will discipline them, you'll show your love for them while doing it. This is an important point: you should always show love when you discipline. My wife and I make the case that we discipline them *because* we love them, not because we don't.

• Involve kids in activities that require some achievement.

Give them the opportunity to accomplish something, anything! Then praise them for their success. However, be careful that your child doesn't confuse praise and love—your praise may be dependent on accomplishment, but never your love.

• Kids can handle some responsibility such as picking up their things or feeding a pet. At this age, they enjoy pleasing their parents and showing pride for the things they do for you, themselves, and others.

Moral character: At ages five or six, kids can't—and needn't—understand the nuances of morality.

• Adults understand that "gray areas" exist between right and wrong, good and bad. In terms of attitude and behavior, young children simply need to be taught in a straightforward way what is right and what is wrong. They need to learn that when it comes to character, many absolutes exist.

• Children need help learning a degree of social sensitivity. For instance, you don't want your children insensitively pointing out another child with a social or physical defect or disability.

• Begin religious training in an organized setting, such as that offered by traditional churches. Kids love the programs that are geared to their age group and level of maturity.

• Bible study is usually focused on biblical characters and how God helped them overcome their struggles. As parents, we see our children not only begin their understanding of God and His Son, Jesus, but they learn a lot about discerning right from wrong and what it means to have good moral character.

• Attend church as a family. When parents attend church and Bible study, they strengthen the kind of behavior they want their kids to model.

• Reinforce at home the lessons they learn at church.

Indoctrination and education: This is your window of time to make a lasting impression against using addicting substances.

• Use imperatives: "tobacco is bad for you," or "alcohol is only for adults."

• With kids this young, it's unnecessary and ineffective to engage in elaborate explanations about the reasons these statements are true.

• No need at this age exists for descriptions of the bad outcomes of drug use. Through repetition you implant these anti-drug messages deep into their brains at this age; think of it as a kind of "thought immunization" against drugs.

Money: Preschoolers have no understanding of the concept of *money* as such, but you can teach the basic concept that collectively, these pieces of paper and metal form our medium of exchange, through which we buy and sell goods and services.

• Teach your kids to learn to count money.

• Discuss the benefit of saving.

• Begin a small allowance, based on chores and require correct and timely completion in order to earn it.

• It's not too early to begin teaching the concept of contributing money (and other items), thus introducing the concept of tithing.

Family traditions are likely well established, but evaluate them as you go along. Kids understand the emotional flavor of their home by these family habits and behavior.

• Do you pray before family meals?

• Have you taught your kids to pray alone and with you at bedtime?

• Do you talk with your children about God?

• Are you satisfied with your extended family holiday visits and traditions?

• Do you read to your children at bedtime?

• Do your kids see affection and hear loving expressions between you and your spouse, as well as with grandparents, other relatives, and close family friends?

• Are loving expressions part of daily life, often part of the rituals that signal greetings and partings?

Time and place accountability is extremely important at these young ages.

• Remember that children simply do not have the intelligence, experience, strength, or skill to discern predators from safe adults.

• Train your children about potential abusers, but know where they are and who they are with at all times—don't depend on your training alone to protect them.

• In general, young children should not be under the sole supervision of adolescent or adult males, with the exception of trusted members of the immediate family. Of course most boys and men of any age are caring individuals who would never inflict harm, but it's also true that predators endear themselves to parents and position themselves to supervise children in order to gain access to them. Male abusers outnumber female abusers many times over. The risk is too great and the stakes too high to allow adolescent or adult males to supervise your young children.

In addition, observe your kids' signs for possible ADD/ADHD and associated learning disorders. If you sense that your child's learning is inhibited in any way, have him or her evaluated. As long as it's done under the supervision of a well-qualified professional, you have no reason to fear treatment. However, stay away from quirky diets and unscientific therapies of questionable origin.

Ages 6-9 Years

In this age range kids begin to learn about life, lifestyles, and attitudes from neighbors, extended family, TV, and computers. They see others using tobacco and alcohol. You must discuss what your kids observe and explain addiction as best you can. In addition:

• Using plain, simple language, explain that tobacco is addicting and very dangerous, even though some good people use it.

• Explain that some adults experimented with tobacco when they were young, and now they can't stop.

• If you use alcohol, then except for religious rituals, as earlier discussed, drinking is best done in settings where the kids don't see you.

• Point out that drug-addicted individuals made bad decisions early in life and now they are addicted; some are unable to choose not to use drugs, and others have to work hard every day to stay away from them.

• If you are against drinking, even for adults, then explain that alcohol is a drug like other addicting drugs and neither kids nor adults should ever use it.

• If adult use of alcohol is acceptable to you, then simply explain that alcohol is designed for adults only and is unhealthy for children!

Your marriage: At this age, your kids are likely to notice marital happiness or unhappiness.

• If your kids in this middle age range see constant stress, they lack parental guidance, and experience issues around lost love in the family, they are likely to choose alcohol and drugs if opportunities present themselves.

• Parents owe it to themselves and their children to continue to love each other and work on their marriage, so seek counseling to help solve problems that seem intractable.

Self esteem: Most kids are involved in some kind of performance or competitive activities such as dance, music, or sports. In addition:

• Watch for the crude social hierarchies to develop. For example, overweight kids, those who wear glasses, are not athletically gifted, or have some other perceived limitation really have their egos stressed. Be sensitive to this because it is a real problem, and perhaps their primary source of stress.

• Anxiety over their position in the social hierarchy can make kids very susceptible to seeking anxiety relief from alcohol and drugs.

• Combat social tension by first and always first, showing them unconditional love, never contingent on performance or based on any system of measurement, including physical appearance. Your kids deserve *unconditional* love, which can show your empathy with their peer issues.

• Help the kids perform better by choosing different activities that suit their abilities. If your boy is overweight and perhaps can't play basketball well enough to compete, then he may perform well in football, or if that doesn't appeal, then he may excel in a checkers or chess club. If your girl isn't good at dance or cheerleading, she may be a competitive basketball or softball player.

• Be sympathetic with regard to perceived unattractive physical features. For example, if children are overweight, work with them to get regular exercise and eat healthfully. If they diet to stabilize their weight, they will slim down during the rapid growth period of adolescence. In extreme situations, such as a deformity, consult a cosmetic surgeon to see what treatment is possible or appropriate.

• Become active yourself and make fitness a family goal.

• Set your kids up for success and make accomplishments attainable. Once they become confident about their abilities, begin to provide more challenges to help them to develop more competencies and even better self-esteem.

Moral character development becomes even more important and kids need to understand self-discipline, consequences of bad behavior, honesty, and loyalty. Your earlier work that gave your kids clear concepts of right verses wrong will help as they develop their consciences.

• Deceptive behavior tends to emerge in this age group; address it quickly and vigorously. If you tolerate this behavior, it will only get worse and involve more serious problems later.

• In this age group, cheating at school takes place, or kids may steal some small item. When these incidents occur, ask key rhetorical questions. "Is throwing away your character worth the five dollars you stole?" Or, "Is an A worth discarding your character in order to cheat, when you could have worked harder and earned the high grade?" After constant reinforcement, they will begin to evaluate these decisions in the context of the character they are building in themselves and observing in others.

• Kids have a keen understanding of the concept of "practice what you preach." Be mindful of your own behavior: Are you teaching good moral character or hypocrisy?

• If your family is not established in a church community, do so now! We form our attitudes about God, religion, and life after death early in life. In this age group, the young impressionable brain searches for answers to these big questions. If you don't fill their minds with the correct information (at least correct in your view), they will begin to accept alternative answers to these questions.

Indoctrination and education: Kids need continued reinforcement of the non-use imperatives, the "don't do's" of tobacco, alcohol, and drugs. But because of their growing sophistication, kids in this age range must begin to understand the "why nots" as well.

• Provide real life examples of people your child knows who have had problems with addicting chemicals, including tobacco. You may have a relative with obvious health problems related to tobacco; perhaps this person needs continuous supplemental oxygen. Simply point out that smoking led to that problem.

• When your newspaper runs articles and photos of people arrested on drug charges, point out that these men and women were young kids once, too, but they experimented with alcohol and drugs, and eventually could not stop using, and that addiction led to an arrest and a jail sentence.

• Don't depend on anti-drug education and literature at school. At best, anti-drug education reinforces what you teach them at home, but these anti-drug programs may have no impact at all.

Money: By now, money is no longer an abstract concept and it's important that you monitor kids and their access to money.

• Avoid giving kids money for discretionary spending; instead, provide an allowance and assign the chores to earn it. Offer special projects to kids to earn additional money.

• Encourage kids to earn money by working for others, typically through babysitting and yard work.

• Encourage tithing and gift-giving. Kids can easily understand and compute the 10% of their income (their tithe) that goes to the church. This is a good time to teach the concept of giving to charity, too.

Family traditions: Continue to evaluate your family habits and behavior, including those involving prayer, church activities, holidays, affection, and giving and receiving gifts.

Time and place accountability: Recognize that this age group is at risk if parents relax their concern about where the kids are and who they're with. Too many kids tend to be home alone after school until the parents return home from work. This represents a tremendous risk when it comes to experimenting with tobacco and/or alcohol—and other things, too, including too many hours on the internet. Kids can find pornography sites or they can fall prey to email or instant messenger relationships with potential sexual predators. For these reasons:

• Provide supervision, or at least arrange for a responsible adult to check on them during after school hours.

• Don't assume that your child is supervised when visiting a friend's home. Carefully question your child or call the other child's home to determine the safety level of the situation.

• Establish a curfew, so in addition to knowing where your kids are, make sure they're home by dusk each day.

• Be careful with campouts and sleepovers. Get details about the supervising adults.

• If you and your child each have a phone, call him or her periodically during the time away, especially overnight. These situations often are very fluid and change rapidly, and your only hint that something doesn't seem quite right may come from a brief call to your child to check in.

Detection, deterrence, and monitoring (DDM) for addicting substances, sexual activity, and other dangerous behaviors should begin during this age period. This requires that you:

• Assess the existing threats, which typically include the availability of alcohol (and drugs in some situations), the internet, and potential dangers from older children and adults. Make sure you know about the potential threats in your home, your neighbors' and friends' homes, your children's schools, and other venues.

• Communicate—kids are usually too young to begin significant deceptive behaviors and not mature enough to pull it off anyway when it comes to addicting substances. So, talk with them about their activities *before* they leave home, and then again when they return. Ask them who was with them in the other home and what did they and their friends do. Pay particular attention to any computer/internet activities.

• If you keep alcohol in your home, lock it up; assume that alcohol isn't locked up in other homes, and sharpen your perception for any sign of alcohol experimentation.

Pre-addiction situations: *Learning disorders*, especially ADD/ADHD, and *depression* are two important pre-addiction situations that arise in this age group.

• Learning problems can lead to a lag in academic development, which then causes a "snowball effect" in which problems get worse and more complex.

• Depression can lead to all sorts of peer problems, emotional difficulties, and problems at home and school.

• If you suspect a problem, ask a trusted healthcare professional or guidance counselor for recommendation/referral and then have your child evaluated. Talking with friends, teachers, and your family doctor will usually lead to the right type of evaluation and treatment. Evaluations and treatments for learning disorders and depression are safe and relatively inexpensive.

• I'm often asked to evaluate children in this age group for ADD/ADHD based solely on behavioral problems, but understand no pill exists that can make your child behave. If you are not using good and consistent disciplinary methods, then diagnosing and treating your child for ADD/ADHD will be considerably more difficult.

Ages 10-12

Preteens are ready to be teens. When it comes to addictive substances, you better be ready, because they'll have opportunities to use.

Lifestyle: in this age group involves observing parents and friends and their families. This is the time that kids notice adult behavior at parties and holiday gatherings. Frankly, they know exactly who drinks too much or who started the big argument at the last family gathering—and they remember those events, too. So:

• If you're participating in poor lifestyle choices, then change your behavior if you can.

• If you can't stop smoking at this time, for example, do as my parents did: they explained that they were helpless to stop smoking.

• So, if you have an addiction and can't stop for them, use your addiction as an example of what *not* to do. Be frank and tell them of your health problems related to your chemical use.

• If your neighbors have an addictive lifestyle that you don't believe is a good model for your children, tell your kids what you think, and then minimize their exposure to this other lifestyle.

• Do whatever you can to reverse the negative role modeling that involves you and others adults.

Self-esteem: This issue continues. Your kids need your unconditional love first and foremost, and then they need to build on the successes and achievements already attained. By this age, kids have begun to differentiate according to their unique abilities and interests. So:

• Begin to focus on areas in which your kids have interest and ability. If your child enjoys taking piano lessons, works hard at it and shows progress, then continue to support this activity. On the other hand, if the child's interest has waned and the effort is forced, then consider doing something else.

• Kids want to identify their skills with who they are, which translates to wanting to be known as a good football player, good pianist, good speller, and so forth. Reinforce this and praise this identity, which can help kids feel equal to those who have other skills and abilities.

Moral character: Ego strength helps build moral character, and during these years, you can reinforce moral self-perceptions by reminding them that they are good children.

• Help make kids proud to be considered "good," remembering that among their peers, it may definitely not be "cool."

• Deceptive behavior, a reflection of bad character, is likely to emerge at this age, even from the best of kids. Kids don't want to disappoint their parents, but peer influence really intensifies in this age range. Therefore, look for this behavior because it is probably going to occur no matter how honest you think your kids are.

• Church life becomes critically important in order to withstand the immoral messages that come into your child's world, including the message that it's okay to use drugs.

• Church life also is critical because this is the age range that most kids surrender their lives to God (through His Son, Jesus) if it is going to happen.

• If kids pass this age without such surrender and move into adolescence, their innate sense of immortality, the "immortality syndrome" begins to "kick-in." No one really understands why almost all teenagers (especially boys) are willing to take incredible risks and feel so immune to injury and death. But it's a real obstacle to convincing teenagers or young adults that they are indeed mortal and need to think about what will happen to their souls after death, and perhaps an untimely death during youth.

• When it comes to avoiding drug experimentation, kids at this age need church more than ever.

Indoctrination and Education: Kids will begin to encounter social pressure to use addicting substances. They'll hear the message that "to be cool, you need to get high." They will also hear things that contradict what you've taught them, such as the myth that drugs won't hurt them and aren't really addicting anyway. This means that your kids need training about handling themselves in a variety of situations.

• Equip your kids with ways to graciously decline offers of drugs and alcohol.

• Train them to plan ahead when they're likely to encounter social situations where alcohol or drugs are likely to be used.

• Help your kids determine who among their social circle are the individuals likely to use or encourage others to use substances.

Money: Kids at this age should understand and value money and know what it takes to earn it. They also have at least a rudimentary understanding about what "keeping up with the Jones'" means.

• Kids are often very impressed by pretensions and trappings of wealth.

• Kids often model the pretentiousness of their parents, so be careful about the attitudes your kids pick up from you about the reasons you buy certain things.

• Be a model for the belief that morality, integrity, and people are more important than material things.

Family traditions: should remain intact, but other concerns may arise. Remember that young people in this age group continue to observe the way you treat other family members, which is part of your family value system.

• Do you treat members of your extended family, especially older ones, with respectful deference? Do your children model that behavior? In other words, how do your children treat their grandparents?

• Do the younger, healthy family members help others who are old or sick?

• The way you treat your parents teaches your children how to treat you; you can't assume that your kids will treat you well in your old age. You need to model helpful, supportive treatment of elderly parents.

• The positive way you treat your parents teaches kids to value people over money.

Time and place accountability: At this age, kids feel comfortable roaming the neighborhood. Their bikes allow them to travel beyond your immediate community.

• Kids should report where they are, when they leave, and where they are going at all times.

• Get details about plans and activities before they leave and when they come home.

Detection, deterrence and monitoring (DDM): depends on potential threats. Consider the following:

• Campouts, sleepovers, out-of-town trips with other adults, and other prolonged absences represent the biggest safety concerns.

• Use time and place accountability techniques, but if you suspect that your kids are using any addicting substances at all, question them and also speak with the responsible adults. If you are not satisfied with what you are told, test for drugs or alcohol, if practical.

• Be sure to use the simple but essential technique *every* time; that is, require a hug and kiss and nonchalantly do a quick physical examination of the eyes, breath, gait and speech of your youngster upon returning home. A good way to remember this is to remember this acronym:

> **B** for breath
> **E** for eyes
> **G** for gait (walk)
> **S** for speech

Learning disorders and depressive diseases: When they occur at this age, they can be difficult to distinguish from one another. I have seen several kids who came for ADD evaluation, because they appeared to be unable to concentrate. But in actuality, they suffered from depressive disease, which also can interfere with the ability to concentrate and stay on task. If you haven't fully evaluated any lag in learning or academic progress, then do so immediately.

Ages 13-17

The brain is rapidly maturing during this time (ages 13-17)

and literally, *every day that goes by that your teen has not used an addicting substance, the chance of future addiction drops a notch.* Remember that; imprint it in your own mind, because you will find constant challenges during this period. But don't give up because this day-to-day struggle will pay off very big someday for you and your child.

Family traditions and lifestyle: By this time you've done the best you could to model a healthy, non-drug lifestyle, and you hope this will carry over to your kids. Try the following ideas to reinforce what you've taught:

• Emphasize to your kids that healthy, drug-, alcohol-, and tobacco-free living will help them in sports and in later adult life, too.

• Point out the negative effects of addicting substances, including tobacco, on physical appearance. Research has shown that addicting substances advance the aging process internally and externally. As a physician I've seen adults in their forties, who look quite elderly because of their history of using addictive substances. And I've seen people in their nineties who never used drugs, tobacco or alcohol, who look like they're in their sixties.

Self-esteem: The sophisticated teenage social hierarchy can become extremely controlling. Typically, adolescents will do almost anything to be accepted into a group and develop a sense of identity and belonging. Watch for the following tendencies:

• Those teens at the "top of the heap" can be very cruel and abusive to those at the bottom. They, in turn can develop emotional problems, engage in risky behavior, and even develop suicidal tendencies.

• The lower-tier teens will organize into antisocial groups, which are where radical music, cultist ideas, body art, and drug experimentation may come in.

• The top tier group tends to be on the leading edge of adult-like social activities, which may mean heavy partying; they often make it clear that belonging to their group means using.

• The middle group of kids tends to follow the "highest" social group in which they can find acceptance, and they feel pressure to do whatever that group chooses as the standard of behavior.

Only a child with very good ego strength can resist these pressures. Therefore, continue to build on your kids' self-esteem by keeping them busy with activities that involve accomplishment and developing certain skills and the character traits that are strengthened in the process. Don't forget unconditional love.

Toward the end of this period kids with good self-esteem have begun to identify themselves with who they are or will be and less with their friends. For example, I made a decision to become a doctor at age 11, which meant that I identified with being a good student and being healthy. Reinforce this kind of positive self-image by talking about college and future careers.

Good moral character: All elements for good moral character should be in place by this stage of life. During adolescence, however, moral character is under constant attack. Kids observe and learn about morality in general, or perhaps amorality in our world. This worldly value system may include such realities as people who value self over others, freedom over responsibility, and who believe personal rights are more important than doing what is right. This value system teaches kids to get high, take what they want, and be accountable to no one. In that world, respect is demanded rather than earned, and the end always justifies the means.

• Your leadership is needed during this time, because teenagers will question everything you've taught them. And some healthy debate is okay.

• Let them know that a faulty value system can lead to possible destruction through immoral, unsafe behaviors, especially when it comes to sex and drugs.

• Don't live under the illusion that your kids are likely to find their friends among other kids with your value system.

• Teens may resist you when it comes to getting up on Sunday morning to attend Bible study and worship services. This may be normal, but hold your ground against their arguments ("I'm too tired," or, "I need to study.") Kids need to continue attending church in order to "hang out" with other Christian kids as well as to worship with the family.

• Resist the old argument that "you don't have to go to church to be a Christian." Christians want to fellowship among other Christians. If the habit of going to church is lost, it is hard to get back into the routine.

Indoctrination and Education: By now they know that tobacco and drugs are bad for them and alcohol is strictly for adults. But sometime during this period many kids will get a driver's license, which greatly enhances their mobility. This means parents have new challenges.

Spend time . . . and more time . . . reinforcing the need to wear seat belts, drive defensively and, most of all, not drive while impaired. Yes, it's problematic to say that the kids shouldn't drink and drive when they are not supposed to drink in the first place. Some parents are concerned that by teaching this they are implying that the kids shouldn't drink (wink-wink), but if they do, then they shouldn't drive.

We taught our kids that using addicting substances is unacceptable under any circumstance, period! However, it's possible that their friends may drink and drive, and if this happens while they're out with friends who are drinking, they are to either insist on being the sober driver or find another form of transportation home, including calling us. This has always seemed to work well because it drives both points home: don't drink and don't get into a vehicle with somebody who does.

Again, real life examples are important at this age. It's even more effective to use examples of problems their peers have had, and in smaller communities, this information is publicly discussed anyway. Small-town newspapers often print police reports that include arrests or injuries related to driving under the influence of drugs or alcohol. Reinforce that you appreciate not only your children's wise choices not to do these things, but also how disappointed you'll be if they choose this behavior. Make the point to tell your teens how much you love them and how badly you would feel if they came to any harm or harmed others while using addicting substances.

Money: Now more than ever kids need to learn that money is a finite entity and few people have as much as they want.

• They should continue earning money through an allowance in exchange for chores and additional part time and summer jobs. Earning money they save for college is a good idea, too.

• The way kids' earned money is used depends on family circumstances; some teenagers must rely on their earned money for many daily necessities, including those associated with school.

• In all circumstances, parents still need to hold the child accountable for money spent.

• Monitor attitudes, especially if cars or other material items such as jewelry or clothes become an outward show of wealth, status, or arrogance. We bought our teens a late model, reliable sedan or pick up—nothing flashy or expensive. They had to pay for special features, such as a custom sound system.

• As discussed earlier, too much money corrupts teens. But, if money is limited and has to be earned, it is much less likely to be spent on addicting substances (unless your teen is already addicted).

Family traditions: When given a choice, teens often choose to spend time with friends rather than family, especially extended family. Some develop an outright aversion to family! During their teen years, both of my sons went through a stage in which they literally didn't want to be seen with my wife and me in public! Kids also tend to avoid family during holidays, or they may insist on having friends with them at family events, which they see as easing the "burden" of interacting with their boring family members.

Fortunately, this odd teenage behavior is more or less universal and temporary. It's actually quite natural and part of the process of moving toward independence. You should insist that your teens remain involved with family functions, but bear with them. Once they reach 18-21, they again will look forward to family traditions and family gatherings.

Time and place accountability: This is challenging but extremely important. So:

• When kids go out for the evening, you need a detailed description about the where, when, and who of the evening. They need to report to you periodically (younger ones more frequently) and update you on any change of plans that may occur.

• Curfews are essential and upon returning home, kids should report to you so that you can evaluate them (part of DDM) and discuss the events of the evening. Teens will often consider this tiresome, all of mine who have reached adulthood have assured me that it was an effective deterrent against bad behavior and they got used to it anyway.

• Assume that campouts and sleepovers are opportunities to party (drink or use drugs), unless you know otherwise. Limit their frequency, and talk with supervising adults, learn the details, and talk with your teen about the event.

274

Detection, deterrence, and monitoring (DDM): I believe that by the end of this age period, a greater than 95% chance exists that your teen will experiment with alcohol, tobacco, or drugs, or a combination. So:

• Continue the tradition of hugs and kisses along with a **BEGS** evaluation when your teen returns from a night out.

• Be prepared to quickly ramp up to breathalyzer testing or even urine drug testing if you find any reason to be suspicious.

• If you detect any addicting substance including tobacco, punishment should be clearly invoked. At this age, the most effective punishment is grounding and loss of the internet.

• Privileges should be returned in stages depending on behavior and attitude. And I recommend implementing regular and random home breathalyzer testing and possibly urine drug testing, if appropriate, for the remainder of your teen's stay at home.

Learning disorders, depression, schizophrenia, and OCD: Learning disorders are unlikely to appear in this group, and any concerns likely will have been addressed already. However, depression and schizophrenia may appear at this time. Be especially on guard against schizophrenia if you discover your teen has been using a hallucinogen. In addition, watch for signs of severe anxiety, moodiness, and any other signs of emotional distress. Bizarre ideas, delusional thinking, or signs of auditory hallucinations (hearing voices) should be reasons to get help for your teen.

Look for *obsessive-compulsive* signs, which could suggest obsessive-compulsive disorder (OCD), a form of depressive disease. Or, the signs could suggest a non-chemical addiction, such as an addiction to food, porn, or gambling. Speak with your physician for guidance in this situation if you have concerns.

Finally, rebellious or radical behavior or an interest in groups that pursue body art, radical music, or strange spiritual ideas should arouse your concern, because a high risk for substance use is present among people who ascribe to these behaviors.

Ages 18-21

As I've said before, most of your addiction prevention work has been completed by the time your youngster has reached this age range. But don't relax—you still have opportunities to make a difference, and this is a good time to become a mentor.

I actually discovered this quite by accident. I naturally assumed that as my kids went off to college, what was done to raise them—was done! I couldn't have been more wrong. My wife and I get calls almost daily from our young adult kids who call mostly to give us an update on their lives. During these conversations we usually find ourselves giving important advice and guidance, not because we called them and insisted on dictating to them how to live their lives. On the contrary, they call us to tap into what they view is a wealth of knowledge and wisdom that they genuinely want to use to continue making the right choices in life.

However, not every parent is as fortunate as my wife and I have been during this stage. When reaching this stage, independent stage kids often arrogantly attempt to try to push their lifestyle decisions on their parents. One common example is a still-single son or daughter who brings home a sexual partner, fully expecting to sleep in the same bedroom. Chemically-oriented lifestyles, such as smoking, drinking, or even drug use may become a point of tension as well. You should feel no obligation to accept any of these behaviors if they conflict with your value system. By simply informing your adult child what is acceptable in your home, he or she will most likely conform to your wishes.

Self-esteem: Development in this area is largely complete by this age, but you can mentor them about college curricula and/or career choices based on interests and aptitudes. At this point in life, young adults often question their ability to be successful. Just a simple nudge, a reassuring word, or a commitment to be there if problems develop, should be enough to regain confidence. Again, nothing builds self esteem like success and the reassurance of your unconditional love.

Moral character: College students, new military recruits, and young people starting a new job will come up against new moral challenges in their new roles. Others, including students, professors, and co-workers will likely have varying moral values, which may create confusion and anxiety. So, be prepared to discuss these challenges, and confidently reinforce the value system and morality you have taught for years.

Money: If your young adult children are still in college and you're contributing to their support, then you have a duty to require:

• Accountability for money, including some explanation for the way money you provide is used. I always recommend caution about delivering a "blank check." As with younger kids, excess money can be dangerous, especially when it comes to the possible purchase of addicting substances.

• Performance for college students is measured by grades. Your kids should frequently disclose their grades, a step that reassures you that they're diligently working toward success. Too many kids party their way through entire semesters, only to flunk out or be put on academic probation. They then feed parents outlandish stories that blame the professors for their own failures.

• The burden of proof is on the kids, so don't call the college and demand answers (some parents have done this, only to learn their kid never showed up in class at all). Most college students can handle a bad break or two from unfair professors.

Family traditions: It may not be easy to maintain certain activities during this period because newly independent children live away from home. However, they're usually over their "aversion" period and enjoy coming home to be a part of traditional family birthday and holiday gatherings. At the same time, they have new friends, travel opportunities, and chances to participate in new and novel activities that end up competing for family time.

At this age, your kids become independent, which is good. But if your adult children are like ours, as soon as they become independent, they'll begin calling you every day and spending more time visiting with you than they have in years. That means that you've followed your blueprint and it has served its purpose!

Points to Remember

• Raising kids to become non-addicted adults requires a global approach pertaining to many aspects of your family's life.

• Raising kids to become non-addicted adults requires a good foundation at a young age and many methods that vary from one age group to another

• Methods that are successful in raising non-addicted person (NAPs) also serve to raise a good citizen who will be well prepared to raise other NAPs.

16

Outcomes of Addiction

Most people believe they understand the dangers of addiction, at least to an extent. However, when it comes to facing the potential problem in their own families, it may be more comfortable, at least psychologically, to attempt to minimize the seriousness of the issue. What if your child becomes addicted—would that really be the "end of the world"? The answer is complex, which is why I'm addressing it as separate issue.

It's critical that you understand the ways in which addiction influences every dimension of its victims' lives. As I mentioned before, addiction victimizes everyone involved with an addict; beyond that, it not only affects your family now, it reaches into future generations, too. Based on what we currently know, bad outcomes from addicting substances fall into two main areas, health and social functioning, which includes relationships, education, and careers.

Addiction and Overall Health

For those not involved in healthcare professions and who don't see addiction up close, its impact on health may be misunderstood, perhaps even minimized. For clarity's sake, I'll discuss the known health effects of individual substances.

Alcohol (alcoholism)

Since alcohol is the oldest known drug on our addicting

substance list, it doesn't take much imagination to conclude that there were alcoholics among the first humans who produced and used this chemical. Alcohol is the least addicting of all known addicting substances, but, with the exception of tobacco, it has the greatest number of people addicted to it. This is understandable because it's available, legal, and enjoys more social acceptance than any other mind-altering, addicting chemical.

In recent years, we've heard about the benefits of drinking small amounts of alcohol, defined for most as one to two drinks daily; valid studies show reduced heart attack rates among light to moderate drinkers. However, most doctors are hesitant to recommend alcohol for either prevention or treatment because of the obvious risk of uncorking (pardon the pun) a latent addiction problem. Unfortunately, most doctors have had experience with patients who think that if a little of something is good, a lot more must be even better. This attitude is not good when it comes to alcohol—or any other health matter—and no doctor cares to unwittingly lead a person into alcoholism.

Doctors also are concerned that if we unknowingly recommend moderate drinking to those who already have addiction issues, then they'll interpret what we say as a form of "professional approval" of their already harmful drinking habits. It's difficult to determine who has an early-stage addiction or is likely to develop one. In addition, alcohol offers no medical benefit that can't be achieved through other means. For instance, never using tobacco in any form and lowering cholesterol have far greater impact on preventing heart disease than moderate alcohol intake. For these reasons, most doctors steer clear of making recommendations to drink alcohol. The fear of doing more harm than good is ever-present in medical practice.

In reality, even moderate amounts of alcohol consumed over a significant period of time injures the cells in our organs, primarily, the brain, stomach, and liver. If you have drunk alcohol to intoxication, even once, you may have suffered some minor organ injury. For instance, if you drank enough to become nauseated or throw up, you injured the delicate lining of your stomach. Repeated use of alcohol can irritate the stomach lining and cause a stomach or duodenal (small intestine connecting to stomach) ulcer. The ulcer may go on to bleed or you may bleed from the direct injury and irritation of the lining of the stomach or esophagus. Some people with this condition actually bleed to death.

In the later stages of alcoholism, two factors cause the malnourishment we often see in alcoholics. First, the stomach remains so irritated that the alcoholics can barely drink alcohol, much less eat food. Second, what little appetite they have is satisfied by the calories from alcohol, which contains absolutely no nutrition.

Alcoholic *cirrhosis* is the end result of alcohol injury to the *liver*, and this means that the person has insufficient liver tissue left to sustain life. Most people have heard about this condition, but relatively few know how horrible it is to live (and die) with it. Of course, the liver is a remarkable organ that performs an endless number of functions related to metabolism and processing of waste. Even after great damage, it can regenerate itself, and we can survive with only a small part of it left intact.

Given how valiantly the liver will fight to do its job, it's easy to understand how much alcohol injury it takes to completely destroy the liver and the ramifications of allowing such a situation to occur. We are able to see and measure cirrhosis as it occurs through routine lab tests in which we can sometimes detect elevated levels of liver enzymes. These elevated enzymes occur as a result of active injury to liver tissue from alcohol and other causes. I may see these test results during routine physicals, but too often patients continue to drink after I sound the warning "bell," because they have not killed off enough liver tissue to have overt symptoms of cirrhosis.

However, once cirrhosis has become symptomatic, it's too late. These individuals can live for a while, but progressive symptoms appear that ultimately lead to death. Symptoms of cirrhosis include jaundice (yellowing of the skin caused by waste build up in the blood), extreme collection of fluid in the abdomen and feet, extreme weakness, and coma. During the last six months of life cirrhosis patients spend much of their time in the hospital with tubes in various openings and sometimes where there aren't any openings. The end usually comes from a dramatic bleed into the intestines from ruptured veins in the esophagus. Cirrhosis usually occurs after many years of drinking, but *I have seen teenagers die from this illness.*

The third organ, the *brain*, can show injury with the first use of alcohol. A blackout, which is a brief amnesia after an episode of binge drinking, is evidence of brain cell injury. Fortunately, the user quickly recovers. But in young people, studies show the potential for longer term memory problems with frequent or heavy use of alcohol. In the case of long term alcoholics, especially if they suffer poor nutrition, severe dementia (similar to Alzheimer's disease) can occur.

These negative health consequences are limited to alcoholics, but every year many innocent people die in traffic accidents caused by impaired drivers. These non-alcoholic individuals just happened to be on the same road as the impaired driver. Far too often, when we hear about these accidental deaths caused by impaired drivers, we learn of multiple previous convictions for DUI. Looking at the statistics, we see that for every episode in which a person is convicted of DUI, he or she probably drove impaired any number of times but wasn't caught. This suggests that a driver with a history of three or four DUIs may have driven impaired 30-40 times. Those numbers make it easy to conclude that people convicted of a single DUI are likely problem drinkers and that those with multiple convictions are certainly addicted. So, can you really say that a single DUI conviction for a teenager is *ever* a "benign" event?

Tobacco

While this drug doesn't cause erratic driving, it nonetheless is a "killer" drug. Virtually everyone knows that smoking causes lung cancer, which is the most common fatal cancer among smokers. Few people appreciate that mouth, throat, esophageal, stomach, and colon cancers are more common in tobacco users, and many greatly underestimate ways in which smoking kills people through other equally serious diseases.

Every day I see patients who have acute bronchitis caused by smoking. I may see those patients again on other occasions with the same complaint. Once again, I hear myself explaining that they're losing important lung tissue with each episode of bronchitis. After enough destruction occurs, too little lung tissue will be left to sustain life, which is what characterizes the disease of emphysema. I remind these patients of the frail, pale, old-looking people they see in public places sitting in wheelchairs and hooked to oxygen canisters. This is quite possibly a picture of my patients' future if they don't quit smoking. With their denial system in full swing, most smokers calculate that they'll quit smoking when they first get sick. But like cirrhosis, emphysema is not curable or reversible once enough tissue is lost and symptoms force recognition of the illness.

Pipe smokers, cigar smokers, and smokeless tobacco users

are not immune to disease either. Mouth cancer among snuff users is common and even occurs in teenagers. Pipe and cigar smoke are just as dangerous as cigarette smoke.

Finally, half of all adult deaths in this country are linked to heart and vascular disease, and smoking is a *leading cause* of these diseases. Imagine how dramatically the death rate would fall if tobacco users in the U.S. suddenly quit using.

Marijuana

I have nothing but bad news for pot smokers. Earlier, I dispelled the myth that marijuana is not addicting, and now I must report that evidence shows that marijuana smoke is as dangerous, if not more so, than cigarette smoke. What's worse, many pot smokers use tobacco, too, so this drug, once thought of as safe, has proven to be anything but.

Other Drugs (crack, methamphetamine, heroin)

The health problems with these drugs are just as serious, but less direct than those associated with alcohol, tobacco, and marijuana. First, drugs that require intravenous (IV) use put the user at great risk of diseases transmitted through the blood, namely HIV and viral hepatitis B and C.

Some argue that we should provide free needles and syringes to addicts to avoid this risk. From what I've seen, proponents of this argument are usually those who also recommend dispensing free condoms to prevent sexually transmitted disease. While logical in thought and noble in intent, studies show that drug addicts, prostitutes, and others who are sexually promiscuous have little regard for their health or the health of those with whom they associate. Therefore "dirty" needle sharing and sex without protection is still commonly practiced even when needles and condoms are available and free. It is easy to see why as many as 70% of IV drug users have hepatitis C, just to give one example.

HIV disease is discussed often and stories about it appear

in the news, but you may not be as familiar with Hepatitis B and C, two viruses transmitted mainly by blood contact that can lead to chronic, potentially fatal hepatitis. Coincidentally, this chronic hepatitis state eventually leads to cirrhosis, the disease that often kills alcoholics.

If drugs are ingested by inhalation, such as smoking crack, no direct risk of these blood-borne diseases exists. However, these users have the same lack of regard for their health and that of others. If given the opportunity, they will likely use drugs through the IV route.

Finally, all types of chemical addictions lead to high rates of suicides and overdoses. These sudden deaths among addicts represent a leading cause of death in young adults.

Addiction and "Life"

Tobacco may not cause negative behavioral problems, but it still has a negative social impact. First, when adults use tobacco in any form, they are negative role models for children, who want to grow up to be like parents, grandparents, coaches, and others who are important to them. It makes no sense to give kids a reason to experiment with tobacco, as in "my parents use it, so why shouldn't I?" I think most would agree that if we're unwilling to stop using tobacco for ourselves, we should do it for the health of our kids.

Second, tobacco divides families—it definitely divided mine. When I was seventeen, a conversation down the hall from my bedroom awakened me late one night. I heard my mother talking with a police officer standing in our kitchen. Instinctively, I knew something was wrong. I first thought he must have been letting us know that my grandmother had passed away. But from their mumbling, I also heard talk of "he" and "him." This is when my nightmare began. As it turned out, my father, age 43 and a heavy smoker, had died suddenly of a heart attack while away on business. Not only was I suddenly deprived of my father, whom I loved, but I was left with an awesome responsibility. As I mentioned earlier, schizophrenia had left my mother disabled, and I was about to leave for college. Since I had a 12-year old sister and a 5-year old brother, you can see that my whole life was suddenly turned upside down.

Despite difficult financial times, I went through college on loans and grants, but my siblings were raised by our mentally ill mother, a situation that ultimately led to further problems. Needless to say, my father's tobacco addiction not only killed him, but it hurt my family in numerous ways. My father, bless his heart, became addicted to tobacco before we were aware of its dangers. Today we know better.

In discussing the social impact of alcohol and other addicting drugs, it makes sense to discuss them together, because, when it comes to social-behavioral issues, the addiction syndrome differs little whether you are talking about alcohol, heroin, or crack.

Here is a list of typical behaviors seen in drug addiction syndromes:
- Deceptive behavior before or beginning with first use
- Dishonesty in relationships causes broken relationships
- Lack of character and conscience
- Unwillingness to take responsibility for actions
- Lack of responsibility
- Running away from problems instead of solving them
- Moodiness, irritability, inability to handle ordinary stress
- Low self-esteem and, ultimately, loss of self-respect
- Waning academic and sports performance while still in high school
- Destroyed dreams of achieving educational and career goals

• Loss of the ability for kids to achieve fill their potential in life
   • Severe family problems usually ending in divorce
   • Poor job performance with ultimate career loss
   • Loss of health
   • Legal problems and possible prison time

Deceptive behaviors kids employ that enable them to experiment with drugs, along with the lack of character and conscience development that allows them to continue using, become fixed when addiction occurs. When addiction develops, the immature behavior that a 12-14 year old would normally grow out of will persist into adulthood. In other words, addiction arrests emotional development

For example, if you've raised young teenagers, you know that you have to remind them about everything. You probably have to wake them up for school in the morning, and then you have to insist that they complete their homework before watching TV—and that's if they remembered to bring their books home. We usually expect this from a teenager, but we don't expect it from a 40-year old.

Addicts, with their arrested emotional development, are stuck in their teens, at least when it comes to developing good character, a conscience, trustworthiness, and a work ethic. In a family influenced by addiction, spouses and sometimes kids take on a parental role in relationship to the addict, and he or she becomes the child. As a rule, the worse the addiction, the more their behavior regresses. On the other hand, when an addict gets treatment and begins recovery, he or she begins to grow again.

As a parent of a young child, you need to assume that you are the parent of a potential addict. That being the case, picture what it would be like some day if your child actually does become addicted. In reality, you may have to continue to parent your child long after your job would normally be complete.

Over the years, I've known a number of families with addicted members. I've witnessed the pain experienced by parents, spouses, and children of addicts. Most parents in this situation find themselves continuing to provide financial support because the addict can't or won't hold a job. Sometimes parents spend their own retirement funds for this support.

Increasingly, I provide medical care to young children without ever meeting their parents. The father was only a DNA donor to begin with, and the mother provides little or no care for the child because she (and the father too) is an addict. This means that grandparents end up raising the child. So, instead of enjoying retirement in ways they dreamed of, the parents of adult addicts spend their hard-earned retirement years raising grandchildren. Too often, however, no close family members are willing or able to care for these kids, and so the young children of addicts end up in our notoriously inadequate foster care system.

If a family with one or more addicted parents manages to stay intact for a time, life is hell for everybody. Addicted adults become difficult to live with, and if the situation worsens, child or spousal abuse often results. And, when addicted adults leave home for whatever reason, the children are never sure what shape they'll be in when they come back. Kids often wonder if the adult will return at all, or instead, will be killed in an accident or just run away. Finally, as stronger drugs like methamphetamines, heroin, and crack become common drugs of choice, addicts may find themselves in prison.

Given how common addiction is today, you've probably

experienced or heard about the range of outcomes covered here. My purpose is to bring into focus the terrible problems of addiction—you must know what you're fighting against.

Turning to Treatment

Although this book is about prevention, and I wish it could address only that issue, today's realities lead me to address treatment. Information about prevention can't offer what you need once your child's chemical use has reached the level of addiction. You must move on to treatment options.

Briefly, the first legitimate addiction treatment began in the mid-1930s when two alcoholics, Bill Wilson and Dr. Bob Smith, began an organization called *Alcoholics Anonymous*, generally known to the world as AA. Based on its 12 steps of recovery, AA is now a worldwide private organization. Others have adapted it to treat virtually any form of addiction, the steps have remained unchanged over the years. AA and its "children" are free, open to anyone in need, and because it doesn't require disclosure of the addicts' names, it lives up to its promise of anonymity (a promise they take very seriously). Over the years, AA and other programs such as Narcotics Anonymous and Overeaters Anonymous have helped millions of people. Most hospital-based, paid private programs and non-pay programs are based on its basic concepts, although AA continues to maintain its independent status and runs its own affairs.

After "Dr. Bob" and "Bill W." started AA, virtually nothing else was available in addiction treatment for the next 50 years. However, during the 1980s this country underwent an explosion of sorts, in what became a new multi-billion dollar healthcare industry, that of drug and alcohol treatment. A number of private companies have large budgets and payrolls that essentially depend on a steady flow of addicts who are admitted for treatment, sometimes again and again.

Generally, government healthcare programs and private insurance pay for this treatment.

Though AA and its related groups have helped more addicted people than any other organization, it has its critics. Some attack it by claiming that it tries to push a religious point of view because of its deference to a "higher power" and admission that addicts no longer can control their lives. However, AA makes it clear that a person's higher power is an individual choice, not a requirement to believe in any god.

On the other hand, some religious groups criticize AA because it is not religious enough. They suggest that addiction could be cured by simply turning to God. Since addiction is a disease, this viewpoint makes no more sense than closing all the hospitals in America and praying for good health and cures for all diseases that exist. No religious person I know advocates that.

A number of alternative treatment programs have appeared over the years. These programs include behavioral training to make social drinkers out of alcoholics, herbal treatments, hypnosis, and other unproven therapies. I mention these only to alert you to the fact that as long as profit can be made by treating addiction, there will be an endless stream of treatment ideas in our capitalistic society. Some may promote these alternative programs in good faith and there may be good alternatives available in the future. But for now, AA and the other programs modeled on AA, are the most effective, according to the people who know best—recovering addicts.

Paradoxically, even as we spend so much money on addiction treatment, drug consumption continues to climb. Moreover, as I've pointed out, we incur ever-growing and already enormous indirect costs of addiction through our increasing prison population and direct family support through welfare, foster care, and growing Medicaid budgets.

I've been unable to find any *legitimate* claim about any program that can cure addiction. A number of programs claim "success," but success is usually not defined. Even when success rates are discussed in the literature, it appears that the definition is based on very low expectations, such as reduced drug use and fewer crime convictions.

I've called several well-known, reputable addiction treatment centers and disclosed that I sought information about success rates. However, my calls were either dodged or not returned at all, even though I had offered assurance that I was a physician conducting research. I made it clear that I sought general industry statistics, not figures for their centers specifically. It seems to me that we've seen the emergence of a strong financial incentive to keep the income stream steady by treating and re-treating addicted patients.

A newer development involves drug company research into chemical formulations designed to treat addiction by removing the craving for drugs. This is the basis upon which methadone was developed and used. However, as I've said earlier, I observed that methadone failed to control heroin addiction and did not help addicts move into normal life.

No "magic bullet" exists to treat, fix, or cure addiction. This is in essence the point of what I've been saying throughout this book: addiction results from *permanent* changes in the brain's circuitry, anatomy, and chemistry. Until we are able to reverse these changes, a cure or even reasonably effective treatments for addiction will not be forthcoming.

I don't mean to remove or discourage hope if you or a family member is addicted. As with everything in life, we have the option to make good and bad decisions daily. Your addicted family member can choose to get help and choose to stop using. With adequate motivation, it is possible to become clean and sober, and continue to live that way.

Family members can make important decisions, too, including becoming involved with Al-anon, the "premiere" support organization for family members of addicts. (Other groups may exist in your community, too, but Al-Anon, like AA, is well represented in the U.S. and elsewhere.) You must lovingly refuse to enable your addicted family member, remembering that anything you do to soften the blow of consequences from using drugs only facilitates continued using. A good support system can help you make good, but sometimes painful decisions about ways to stop enabling behaviors.

If your addicted loved one continues to choose drugs over sobriety, put yourself and your family first. Work on your lives and continue to get help with your grief over losing someone you love to addiction. Even when your family member or other loved one is in recovery, other problems and issues may emerge, such as depression or doing the work of cleaning up the messes made while using. Even with treatment and family support, recovering addicts must make their own way in their sober state. In fact, Al-Anon may be even more useful to family members after the addict is clean and sober because the recovery journey may be rocky, too.

Points to Remember
   • Alcohol, tobacco, and drugs are harmful to your health.
   • When addiction starts, emotional growth stops.
   • Children in addicted homes often bear the brunt of their addicted parents' problems.
   • Parents of addicts often never free themselves of the guilt and responsibility of "raising" their adult kids and their kids too.
   • Addiction is treatable but not curable.
   • Expectations of "success" of treatment must remain low to moderate.

• Stop enabling addicts in your family and seek support for yourself.

• If your addicted family member continues to use, keep up your support system to help you grieve and move on.

17

"The Beginning"

It's my hope that you have opened your mind to new ideas about addiction, and perhaps have had a few common myths dispelled. If you have experience with or specialized knowledge or training in addiction problems, then I expect that most of the material presented has reinforced what you already knew. In fact, what I've included in this book is based on the science of addictionology, as it is generally understood today. This book also supports the concept that addiction is incurable and individuals need 12-step programs for treatment. I also support the need for strict law enforcement to control distribution.

I also presented the most up-to-date information we have about the effects of addicting substances on the pleasure center of the brain, the VTA. However, most of us who have treated addiction know that this new information is not sufficient by itself, and large gaps in our understanding of this disease still exist, especially in the area of prevention. That's why I've attempted to fill these gaps by elaborating on recent research suggesting a window of vulnerability to addiction created by the young, developing brain.

I consider this new information a tool, which when used by parents who understand its implications, will "immunize" youngsters against addiction. The following ideas serve as a summary of key points for parents (and others):

• You must keep addicting substances out of the brains of young people *at all costs.*

• Speaking in developmental terms, young people are unable to apply what they learn about drug addiction prevention.

• Too many parents are unable to see signs of early drug experimentation and then to act decisively when they do see them—you can reverse that trend, however, by implementing the suggestions in this book.

• Parents need to see, understand, and overcome deceptive behavior that virtually all young people engage in.

• We need effective anti-alcohol, tobacco, and drug indoctrination in young people.

• Parents must recognize the need to effectively discipline young people and instill respect and accountability for money.

• Part of preventing addiction involves the need for children to have sound development of self-esteem, moral character, and conscience.

• An intact family also is an important factor in preventing addiction in young people.

• Parents must identify and prevent high risk behaviors and identify and treat co-occurring diseases in young people.

• Parents need to detect and monitor their children for the use or potential use of addicting substances.

• Parents must develop a "blueprint" to raise non-addicted people (NAPs).

Now that the information is out there, so to speak, where do we go from here? Most importantly, I hope this book has convinced you to hold the same concerns about the future of your kids as I have for mine. But beyond that, I hope you will become a part of a grassroots movement for change.

And if you doubt that such a movement could be effective, think again. Who among us would have imagined that a well-informed public would make the fundamental difference in addiction rates from cigarettes that we see today? Smoking rates today are half what they were in the 1960s. All this was accomplished simply by strongly limiting use of tobacco in children, limiting advertising to children, and getting the word out about tobacco's threat to health.

Why can't we achieve this when it comes to alcohol and drugs? The answer is we can! But to make this happen, we must recognize a few simple facts.

• The addiction process begins primarily in children, but is rarely diagnosed or even discovered until adulthood.

• The addiction process goes largely undetected by its victims and their parents.

• Addiction in children is not a fatalistic outcome based on genetic inheritance; it will occur or not occur depending on how children are raised and when they are exposed to addicting substances.

• Addiction is *preventable!*

To understand the message in this book, just remind yourself that *addiction is an adult disease with a childhood onset.* Of course, we can always cite exceptions—kids who drank and used drugs, but who appear never to have become addicted. And we can point to isolated cases in which adults appeared to become addicted only after reaching adulthood. Throughout all of nature, including humanity, exceptions to every scientific fact exist. But I didn't write this book to address the rare exception. I wrote it for the mission of families who fall into the group of 99% who are typical, like yours, like mine.

With you on board, we can all begin to spread the word, especially among other parents. Parents are in the prime position to make an impact on addiction through their preventive efforts, and their work can be augmented by coaches, teachers, ministers and many other adults in supporting roles.

Next, I hope to begin a not-for-profit organization whose purpose is to disseminate information to as many families as possible. I would also like to collaborate on more books, especially for kids, so that this message can be brought to them directly. If you would like to participate and be on the "ground floor" of something that will help change the world, I invite you to visit our website at *www.johncfleming.com*.

Resources and Selected Bibliography

To broaden your understanding of ways to prevent addiction, I have included the following list of websites, some of which include specific research reports and articles about the ways in which alcohol and other substances affect the developing brain. Many readers may find these articles and reports helpful in not only understanding this new science, but in reinforcing the critical importance of protecting their children from early first use. I found many of these articles when I was writing this book and researching additional evidence about the brain science. It is clear that this science is well established now and I am confident that further research will elaborate and expand on it, rather than refuting it. I recommend that you check these sites for notice of additional studies and reports. You simply cannot have too much information about this topic, especially when you're devising a strategy for effective parenting in this area. I also listed three articles and a book that outline and explain the pioneering work in brain science that helps us understand many diseases, including addiction, depression, and attention span disorders.

In other cases, the sites cover general topics about young people and addiction, including national organizations working to prevent drug and alcohol abuse in general, and in children in particular. Some address public policy and some are sponsored by government agencies whose mission includes substance abuse prevention. While we can debate the effectiveness of various publicly sponsored programs, much of the information collected is valuable to parents.

Websites:

www.al-anon.alateen.org

This is the website that explains the history and purpose of Al-Anon and Ala-Teen. It has a feature to help individuals locate a nearby meeting. Most telephone books also list AA, under Alcoholics Anonymous, and information about Al-Anon is usually available through AA.

www.drugfree.org

This is the website for The Partnership for a Drug-free America. It has features for parents and children, and posts articles about a variety of topics, from inhalants to steroid use among young people.

www.family.samhsa.gov

This website is sponsored by the U.S. Department of Health and Human Services, and links to SAMHSA (Substance Abuse and Mental Health Services Administration). It includes information about mental health issues and substance and the relationship between the two.

www.nationalfamilies.org

The website of National Families in Action, this site has articles, other resource lists, and provides links to other information. It's useful as an educational resource.

www.nida.nih.gov

This website of the National Institute of Drug Abuse tracks current research findings for doctors and the general population relative to chemical addiction.

Additional Online Resources

http://ajp.psychiatryonline.org/cgi/content/full/157/5/745

This article, "Age at first alcohol use: A risk factor for the development of alcohol disorders," David DeWit, Ph.D., et al, discusses the reduction of alcohol use as young people progress to adulthood and recreation gives way to family responsibilities.

http://www.acnp.org/g4/GN401000072/CH072.html

This site, sponsored by the American College of Neuropsychopharmacology, includes an article published in 2000, "Animal models of drug addiction," by George Koob. The article discusses the reinforcement power of brain stimulation with experiments on animals and covers electrical stimulation of the brain in rats as an addiction model, as discussed in the book. Other articles posted may be of interest as well.

http://www.duke.edu/~amwhite/Adolescence/adolescent2.html

This website includes articles by Duke University research, Aaron White, Ph.D, and includes a number of articles about alcohol use and abuse among young people. The particular article, "Alcohol and the adolescent brain," discusses the adult body/child brain mismatch leading to conflict and rebellion, and more time spent with peers and also points out the risk of teens drinking in their own homes.

http://www.ama-assn.org/ama/pub/category/9416.html

On a site sponsored by the American Medical Association, this article discusses brain damage and ultimate addiction from underage drinking. It is a site worth searching for information on many health-related topics.

http://drugfreeaz.org/drug/alcohol_stats.html

This article posted on a website sponsored by the state of Arizona quotes statistics supporting the contention that ultimately, smoking can lead to drug addiction and that alcohol and marijuana are gateway drugs.

http://www.theallengroup.com/members/Alcopatt.html

This site is sponsored by a company that has Employee Assistance Programs. This particular article focuses on the rise, since the 1960s, of early use of alcohol intake from age 18 downward. It also points out the relationship between smoking and drug use and that kids are changing from alcohol use to illicit drug use at an earlier age than ever.

Other Articles and Book

False Messengers, David P. Friedman and Sue Rusche, Taylor & Francis e-Library, 2005 edition.

This book is available to purchase online and as an e-book. It includes detailed information about the brain and neurotransmitters. Readers interested in learning more about the new brain science will find this book fascinating—and quite readable!

"Addicted: Why do people get hooked?" J. Madeleine Nash, *Time Magazine*, May 5, 1997.

Like the article below, this is one of the first published articles suggesting a relationship between addiction and neurotransmitters, especially dopamine. This article also mentions antidepressants and their known relationship to neurotransmitters as well, particularly serotonin.

"Addiction is a brain disease," Alan I. Leshner, *Science*, vol. 278, Oct. 3, 1997

One of the early articles about addiction and the brain written for a segment of the general public interested in scientific issues. The magazine has gone on to publish other pieces about the effects of various drugs on the brain.

"Age at drinking onset and alcohol dependence," Ralph W. Hingson, et al., *Pediatric Adolescent Medicine*, Vol. 160, July 2006

This report is a critical piece of information that provides family physicians and pediatricians with the hard facts about the dangers involved when young people drink alcohol at early ages. It is the foundation upon which we can build true prevention programs, designed and implemented by parents and supported by schools, churches, and communities.

Helpful Products

Today's technology can serve us as we prevent early use of addicting substances *at all costs*. I came across these products on my own. I want to make it clear that *I have no personal or financial interest in any of these companies. I cannot verify or warrant the accuracy or effectiveness of their products.* Do your own research to see if they might be useful to you.

Breathalyzers:

http://www.breathalcolyzer.com

http://uritoxmedicaltesting.com

http://www.breathalyzer.net

Home drug testing

http://medicaldisposables.us

http://professortestkit.com

https://www.homedrugtestingkit.com

Spy software

http://www.spectorsoft.com

Secret GPS tracking systems for autos

http://www.hiddengps.com

http://www.spytechs.com/gps

GPS tracking by cell phones (This is an emerging technology and more variety is likely to be available soon.)

http://www.accutracking.com

Order more copies of

Preventing Addiction

Call toll free: **1-800-747-0738**

Visit: www.crosshousepublishing.com
Email: crosshousepublishing@earthlink.net
FAX: 1-888-252-3022
Mail copy of form below to:
CrossHouse Publishing
P.O. Box 461592
Garland, Texas 75046
Number of copies desired _____
Multiply number of copies by $ 19.95
Sub-total _____

Please add $3 for postage and handling for first book and add
50-cents for each additional book in the order.

Shipping and handling$_____

Texas residents add 8.25% sales tax $_____

Total order $_____

Mark method of payment:
check enclosed _____
Credit card# _____
exp. date_____ (Visa, MasterCard, Discover, American Express accepted)

Name _____

Address _____

City State, Zip _____

Phone _____ FAX _____

Email _____

9 780929 292458